D1452462

To Elizabeth
& Buddy,

Blessings on your
journey in love!

The
LABYRINTH
of
LOVE

The Path to a
Soulful Relationship

Chelsea Wakefield, PhD, LCSW

 CHIRON PUBLICATIONS • ASHEVILLE, NORTH CAROLINA

www.ChironPublications.com

Cover design and interior art by Kevin Faulkner
Interior design by Danijela Mijailovic
Printed primarily in the United States of America.

ISBN 978-1-63051-952-0 paperback
ISBN 978-1-63051-953-7 hardcover
ISBN 978-1-63051-954-4 electronic
ISBN 978-1-63051-955-1 limited edition paperback

Library of Congress Cataloging-in-Publication Data
Names: Wakefield, Chelsea, author.
Title: The labyrinth of love : the path to a soulful relationship / Chelsea Wakefield, PhD, LCSW.
Description: Asheville, North Carolina : Chiron Publications, [2021] | Includes bibliographical references and index. | Summary: "The 21st Century holds tremendous potential for creating intimate relationships that remain vital and deeply meaningful across a lifetime, but our lofty expectations also put more pressure on our relationships than ever before. Here is a compelling and truly helpful work for navigating 21st Century relationships. Dr. Wakefield describes the twists and turns along the way that a modern couple will encounter as their relationship progresses. Achieving the kind of soulful love longed for by most seekers requires a commitment to the development of skills, capacities and consciousness and a willingness to enter into the alchemical processes of love's intensity. Dr. Wakefield offers an illuminated pathway, guiding disenchanted lovers thru the shadowlands of disillusionment and unresolvable conflicts. Beyond interlocking complexes and betrayal, she outlines the inner and outer work necessary to reach that land of meaningful and enduring love"— Provided by publisher.
Identifiers: LCCN 2021029793 (print) | LCCN 2021029794 (ebook) | ISBN 9781630519520 (paperback) | ISBN 9781630519537 (hardcover) | ISBN 9781630519544 (ebook)
Subjects: LCSH: Man-woman relationships. | Couples. | Interpersonal relationships. | Love. | Soul mates.
Classification: LCC HQ801 .W245 2021 (print) | LCC HQ801 (ebook) | DDC 306.7—dc23
LC record available at https://lccn.loc.gov/2021029793
LC ebook record available at https://lccn.loc.gov/2021029794

Praise for *The Labyrinth of Love*

"This wise, comprehensive, and well-written book will intrigue partners who are looking for a soulful, reparative, and life-long commitment to love. It will be helpful also to those individuals who are looking for love in all the wrong places. Chelsea Wakefield has done all of her homework and even more of her inner work. Her voice resonates with an awakened wisdom about what is possible in personal love in regard to individuation and the development of humanity in all of us. If you are interested in deepening your relationship or the topic of love itself, this extraordinary book is for you!"

-Polly Young-Eisendrath, Ph.D., Author of *Love Between Equals* and *Dialogue Therapy for Couples and Real Dialogue for Opposing Sides* (with Jean Pieniadz)

"We say we value relationships so much, but why are so many distressed, so many ending in bitterness and recrimination? Wakefield's *Labyrinth of Love* brings together the best thinking of many depth psychologists who address this dilemma, and adds her own personal and clinical experience to provide a rich source of information, insight, helpfulness, practical guidance, and finally, wisdom, for the reader. Any reader will leave this book more informed, more thoughtful, and more equipped for the adventure and accountability that relationship asks of us."

-James Hollis, Ph.D., Jungian Analyst and author of *Prisms: Reflections on this Journey We Call Life*

"Dr. Wakefield's Labyrinth of Love is a journey of soul and connection. While there are many good books about improving your marriage by solving problems, there are few that help you realize the full potential of why you got together. If you are a reader who wants to understand how to thrive amongst the challenges of intimacy, you will find your answers here. Get this book immediately and travel with Chelsea as she helps you build an inspired future of communication, deep connection and creation."

-Ellyn Bader, Ph.D. & Co-founder of The Couples Institute

"Dr. Wakefield shares her gems of wisdom and knowledge gained from an impressive and diverse career guiding couples through what they may often feel are dead ends to ultimately discover their relationship center. Readers will benefit from her savvy analysis and sound advice for their relationships, gleaned from a broad range of approaches in the couples therapy field. Importantly, Dr. Wakefield devotes significant portions of her book to sex and intimacy, an essential integration for couples derived from her expertise in both couples and sex therapy approaches. *The Labyrinth of Love* is the book couples need now to help guide them on their pathway toward a better relationship."

-Travis Atkinson, LCSW, Director of the Schema Therapy Training Center in New York, featured author in *Creative Methods in Schema Therapy*

"Dr. Wakefield's book *The Labyrinth of Love* is the book you need to study if you want a successful, fulfilling, long-term relationship. She draws from multiple theoretical traditions and combines her wide and deep understanding of these principles with extensive and profound clinical experience to develop an understandable guide through the labyrinth that many couples fail to complete. This highly readable book and the capacities she teaches will enrich the practice of clinicians specializing in couples therapy and support any couple seeking to develop a deeper understanding of what it takes to create a meaningful, enduring relationship."

-G. Richard Smith, M.D., Chair of the Department of Psychiatry, Director, UAMS Psychiatric Research Institute, University of Arkansas for Medical Sciences

"In my work at the Haden Institute I encounter individuals who have the desire and courage to do their inner, psycho-spiritual work to become their most authentic Self. The transformation that occurs, while deeply satisfying for the individual, can be disruptive for primary and other close relationships. *The Labyrinth of Love* is an elegant guidebook for restoring and deepening an intimate, soul-to-soul connection. For those seeking a Soulmate, this book offers guidance for avoiding the usual blind alleys that result in heart-break. In this single volume, Chelsea Wakefield brings decades of clinical experience as a Jungian-oriented couples counselor to create a practical, content-rich roadmap for satisfying, loving relation-ships."

-Allen Proctor, Director, The Haden Institute

"Chelsea Wakefield has engaged in a thorough contemplation about the transcendent nature of Eros, sexuality, marriage, and soul-fulness. In this labyrinth there are no dead ends, just turning points toward wholeness."

-Pittman McGehee, Episcopal Priest, Jungian Analyst, and author of *The Paradox of Love*

"Chelsea Wakefield knows from her own stellar marriage and shining relationships with others what deep relationship entails. This book is super charged with the wisdom of modern-day masters of couples therapy and as well as her own sensitive, spiritual, and surprising insights about commitment, courage, curiosity, communication, compassion, and creativity. Packed with everyday actions any couple can take, walk *The Labyrinth of Love* with her into depths and joys never imagined."

-Susan Sims Smith, M.Div., LCSW, Founder of the Arkansas House of Prayer

"Chelsea Wakefield has written an extraordinary book about couples and love. Throughout one feels the presence of her wisdom, compassion, and faith in the process of 'individuation in connection,' expressed through an astounding wealth of detail as to how this process actually works, or does not, and then how to work to support it. Chelsea cites many valuable resources for this demanding 'inner work,' but most impressive is her own capacity to hold the whole endeavor in a context that embraces all levels of our experience, from sexuality to soul. She is a master in this important work of nourishing and sustaining the art of human love in couples."

-Thomas Yeomans, Ph.D. Founder of the Concord Institute and author of *Holy Fire: the Process of Soul Awakening*

"Chelsea Wakefield has given the world a truly precious gift with this inspirational, and much-needed, book! In a lyrical, yet crystal clear fashion, she shows how to live life with another in an ever-evolving relationship that allows each person to grow as an individual. She uncovers the 'inner cast' that is determining their actions as they navigate the Labyrinth of Love. She shows how to untangle conflicts, separate from old patterns, and allow the relationship – and the challenges it inevitably brings – to open doors into new realms of consciousness, creativity and soulful connection."

-Sidra Stone, Ph.D. Author of *The Shadow King: The invisible force that holds women back,* Co-creator of 'Voice Dialogue and the Psychology of Selves'

For Tom,
Beloved husband and companion on the labyrinth path.

TABLE OF CONTENTS

PART THREE

Introduction

Life is a love story. Loving and being loved shapes us and defines the deepest dimensions of our experience. Human beings are relational creatures and those who experience "good love" thrive; those whose lives are bereft of love struggle and live a peripheral existence. However, intimate relationships are not easy, and the search to find someone with whom we can share a life is one of our greatest challenges.

My life has been devoted to companioning people through the mysteries and wonders of the human heart and walking with them in their suffering. I find myself sitting with couples who are stumbling and falling along the path, caught in love's quagmires. I see couples who committed their lives to each other, confident that this person would be the answer to their hopes and dreams, now living as disconnected strangers or defended combatants. They are bewildered and experiencing a loneliness greater than if they lived alone. The fulfillment of love transforms and heals people; the wounds of love can injure a person irreparably.

People long for love's elusive promise and are mystified by how a partner who once seemed so ideal has become so distant or so difficult. Is there such a thing as a Soul Mate? Is it possible to find a love that will last the test of time? Why does passion fade as time goes by? What does it mean to love, and what does love require of us? The labyrinthine path of love is not easy, but it is the promise of love that keeps us walking the path.

I often think about how little guidance we give people on how to navigate the winding path of love, particularly when we enter that difficult second stage of relationship, where we encounter disappointing dimensions of our partner's personality that were not so evident in the early stage of enchantment. In the midst of our disenchantment, it is easy to wonder if we have made a terrible mistake. Not knowing where to go from there, we begin to struggle and engage in all sorts of "misbegotten solutions" that only take us further into the forest of a dark fairy tale, where we can become truly lost.

If you are reading this book, you are a seeker, perhaps longing for love, perhaps struggling with questions about how the love you once thought would bring so much fulfillment has devolved into a relationship full of disappointment and frustration, even despair. The one thing I know for sure is that love requires us to grow. The promise of love only comes to those who engage in a process of personal inquiry and development and the deepening of the six capacities I outline in this book. This book offers a road map for seekers and sheds light on the darker passages that we will all encounter in the labyrinth of love.

In 1925, Carl Jung wrote a prophetic essay[1] about what was possible in a relationship where people encountered each other beyond the roles and scripts handed to them by society. He wrote about the kind of relationship that people are seeking today, a relationship in which we experience meaning and depth with another person, not just the living out of roles and obligations. Jung understood that we do not see people clearly at first. We see them as we wish them to be, need them to be, long for them to be. We project all of this outward onto idealized others and hope they will live into this ideal.

Loving deeply means that we must enter the world of that other person and come to understand them from the inside out in a soul-to-soul encounter. Relationship is about the creation of a co-world that two people will share together. We create that co-world from the raw material of who we are, and who we might become as we grow. A commitment to growth is the foundation of a love worth having. As we begin to taste the possibility of a soulful love, we are inspired to keep walking the path and clear away the baggage we all bring into relationship. When we commit to a person, as well as the process of co-creating a relationship, we begin to see beyond our projections and the interference of our childhood complexes. In doing our personal work, we begin to see this other person more clearly and love them more dearly. The process of moving beyond our initial idealization, our fears and demands into a soulful encounter is no small thing, but we can do it when we begin to develop love's capacities—commitment, courage, curiosity, communication, compassion, and creativity.

As you deepen these capacities, you will find yourself connecting to a storehouse of resources that spring from the deep Self. Problems that once plagued you will begin to dissipate. Conflicts that once ensnared you will untangle. If you are fortunate enough to have picked a partner who also wants to deepen and grow, you will begin to experience a love that stands the test of time. While I no longer believe in the romantic ideal of the "Soul Mate," I do believe in the possibility of *becoming* Soul Mates as we build a soulful relationship. However, even if you are with someone who is not drawn to a "growth journey," the changes that you make will begin to evoke changes in your intimate partner. You will become safer to relate to and this will relax your partner's defenses and draw that person in. As your communication becomes more skillful, your partner will feel safer to reveal themselves and you will begin to understand them more deeply. As you move beyond childhood wounding and rigid demands, doors of possibility will open.

To love deeply requires an open heart, but we build many defenses around that portal to protect ourselves from pain. It is through the door of the heart that we find an entry point into a soulful life and a soulful love. We long for love, but we also fear it, because love shakes us from our husks of self-protection. Love invites us to live ever more deeply into our truest potential— something Jung called *individuation*. While many people think of individuation as a solo process, when two people are walking that path together, it accelerates the process—something I call "Individuation in Connection."

Individuation is a process in which we peel away the impediments of our complexes, correct mistaken understandings of ourselves, others, and life, and lower the defenses we constructed when we had little power or voice. Individuation involves discovering the vast potential that springs from what Jung called the deep Self. People who align their lives with the guidance and resources of the deep Self enter a possibility sphere where paths open that were not previously seen or even possible.

In all of the stories in this book, I have protected identities by using alternative names and changing professions, ages, personality traits, histories, stages of relationship, issues, and creating composites. If you have ever worked with me, you are not a "case history" in this book. I honor our confidentiality too much for that.

For the reader, you will notice that many of the descriptors are capitalized. I do this in order to indicate that these are archetypes, systems of energy that people live into.

It is my hope that this book shifts the way you view love, and how you engage the process of relationship. If your heart has been broken, or you are lost in despair, I hope your heart begins to heal as you apply the concepts in this book. If you are searching for love, you will find guidance for what to look for in a partner, someone you can build a life with, who can go the distance and engage the depth. This means going beyond "box-checking," that list of requirements your ego thinks it wants and needs; it even means going beyond "compatibility." In looking for a life partner, look for someone who will commit not just to you, but to the path, all the twists and turns, and to the growth that love inevitably calls us to. If you are already in a loving relationship, I hope this book will open up conversations that will take the two of you into an even deeper level of understanding of each other, and what it means to love and be loved.

A soulful relationship is developed by two people individuating in connection, walking the labyrinth, deepening their capacities of commitment, courage, curiosity, communication, compassion and creativity. This is how we reach the promise of what love has to offer.

PART ONE

Chapter 1

ENCHANTMENT – THE START
OF THE JOURNEY

"At the touch of love, everyone becomes a poet."
Plato

There is nothing more compelling than the experience of falling in love. We don't recognize ourselves when we are in love. We are beside ourselves, head over heels, swept away by implausible feelings. We forget responsibilities that suddenly seem unimportant. We try to concentrate, but our minds keep wandering back to thoughts of this enchanting person, recent experiences, and anticipations of future delights. In love we become more generous, kind, accommodating, even sacrificial in a desire to please the object of our affection. People in love go to great lengths and expense just to spend moments of time together. People in love feel as if they have awakened and come to life for the first time. With senses heightened, the world seems filled with color and light, as if the previous world was lived in faded greyscale. In the early blush of love, our bodies need less sleep; sleep seems pointless when we could be talking into the night; or better yet, experiencing erotic rapture—lips meeting, hands clasping, wrapped in each other's arms, swept into the ultimate bliss of the body.

People in love do crazy things and take risks they would never take in an ordinary state of mind. Some completely upend their lives for this ecstasy. Once captured by love, it is hard to convince someone that they might be in an altered state. Well-meaning friends try to warn us, but to no avail. "Slow down, take your time," they warn; "Consider the consequences of the decisions you are making." People in love make decisions that will forever change the direction of their lives. They don't listen to reason. Under love's spell we are thoroughly enchanted. We feel as if we have entered a mythological realm and become partakers in one of the most significant stories of the human experience—the love story.

Is There Such a Thing as a Love Potion?

The mystery of love has been pondered by poets, philosophers, theologians, artists, and psychoanalysts. It impacts mind, body and soul and opens the heart in a way that nothing else can. But why is it that we become such fools for love? Modern neuroscientists have offered us some unromantic insights into this phenomenon. Love researcher, Helen Fisher[2] has discovered that under the "spell" of love, our brain's pleasure and reward pathways are lit up by a download of powerful neurochemicals. Our brains begin to push dopamine (the feel-good neurotransmitter) and adrenaline (why we need less food or sleep). Other neurotransmitters lead to a mild obsessive disorder which is why we cannot stop thinking about the object of our affection. It seems that the storytellers of old were onto something when they spoke of a "love potion." As we become obsessed, giddy, and expansive, we are under the sway of a powerful neurococktail, drunk on love.

Limerence

Psychologist Dorothy Tennov[3] coined a term for the elevated mood, obsessive thoughts, and reduced need for food or sleep that people experience when they "fall in love." She has termed it "limerence." This sparkly infatuation stage can also generate feelings of panic and desperation at the thought that one might lose this other person's affections. Limerence, and its intoxicating neuro-chemicals begin to wane as we move further along the path of love into the stability of a long-term relationship. This shift might occur after a brief period of time, driving "love addicts" to chase the high with a new partner, but more frequently limerence fades around the two-year mark, usually after two people have begun to weave their lives together. Now a different set of neurochemicals begin to replace the stimulating ones of that initial stage. Hormones like oxytocin take over, a neurochemical associated with bonding. Oxytocin soothes instead of stimulates and encourages proximity and attachment. If we think about prehistoric times, this would be nature's way of increasing survival for the species, drawing the biologically related close, with mother and baby being protected and looked after.

The Search is Archetypal

Archetypes are patterns of human experience that repeat in every time and place, and the progressive stages of love are archetypal. Archeological findings in every civilization show that we have always valued love stories, and the compelling experiences of seeking and finding, longing and fulfillment. The significance of love is found in our earliest recorded stories, and some of the greatest works of art, poetry, music, and literature have been inspired by the pain and ecstasies of love. Love poems describing enchantment and becoming spellbound date back as far as 2100 BC, with the Mesopotamian Epic of Gilgamesh. The stories of Romeo and Juliet, Antony and Cleopatra, and Lancelot and Guinevere, continue to captivate us. Modern poets, novelists, composers, and screenwriters keep us coming back for more tales of love's suffering and bliss.

Love as our Modern Religious Quest

Jungian analyst Robert Johnson suggests that in today's secular world, the search for love has become a sort of religious quest.[4] We find the same expressions of love's transcendent meaning in the great mystical religious poetry of the Middle Ages, as seekers expressed transcendent yearnings for the Great Beloved and described experiences of ecstatic joy in their passionate union with God. Some of the most sensuous poetry ever written, was written by the mystical poet Rumi. It is hard to discern whether his poems were written for a human beloved or in the yearning for God.

Being in love is sometimes described as a kind of divine madness.[5] It seems that human beings have an innate hunger for something to take us beyond the mundane aspects of life. We crave ecstasy and the ecstasy of love opens us to transcendence and takes us beyond ourselves. In love, we discover capacities that we never imagined before. People in love often speak of destiny, something that has been orchestrated by the Divine, of having found a "Soul Mate."

The Search for a Soul Mate

The search for a Soul Mate pervades history and has become an important archetypal theme in the human story. Jungian analyst James Hollis[6] tells us that we are actually in search of a Magical Other. We long for someone who will make us feel whole and provide us with a sense of going home—back to a blissful paradise, an Edenic experience where our needs were magically met, and nothing was required of us. This experience most closely resembles the experience of the womb, and there will always be a place in the psyche that longs to return to this ideal holding place.

At our core, we all long to feel safe, seen, known, and loved. We search for someone with whom we can experience the fulfillment of that longing. In the light of a lover's adoring eyes, we feel elevated, validated, even redeemed. It is as if we have finally been found.

You Complete Me

Even the great philosopher Plato pondered our longing for a Soul Mate. He told a story in which he explained this longing to find "our other half." According to Plato, human beings originally had four arms, four legs and a single head with two faces. These original humans were very strong and powerful and could cartwheel across the landscape. They became threatening to the pantheon of Greek Gods on Mt. Olympus, and Zeus, the king of the Gods, came up with an ingenious idea. He would split these original humans in half, reducing their power and doubling the number of worshippers. This was thought to be an excellent solution and the split was enacted with the strike of a lightning bolt. Unfortunately, what the Olympian Gods did not consider was that this original human housed only one soul, and when that soul was split, it went into mourning for its lost other half. Each half began to search for the other, and neither would rest until they had found that Soul Mate. When they found each other, the two halves joined together in a state of unparalleled bliss.

You Had Me at Hello

It is interesting to hear a couple's early love story—how they met, started dating, and what drew them together. There is a line from the romantic comedy *Jerry McGuire*[7] in which he tells the woman he can't live without, "You had me at 'hello.'" It is the perfect story about finding that Soul Mate and love at first sight. In the old song, *Some Enchanted Evening*, the lover sees a stranger "across a crowded room" and somehow knows that this is the one, experiencing that mysterious "click" that occurs when we encounter someone who matches our romantic ideal. It may happen in a close conversation, or across a crowded room, but when it happens, the love-struck person has the feeling that there is something destined about this relationship. The enchantment begins, and once smitten, we begin to weave love stories into the future—who you will be, who I will be, and how our stories will fit together. If the other person reciprocates, the two people will begin interweaving their stories. The "love potion" leads us to believe that love will lift us above the fray of life, and we will share in its bounty. We make many assumptions when we are drunk on love.

Our Love Grew Over Time

While some lovers feel as if they have been struck by lightning, others will tell you that their love developed slowly. They describe a sort of "waking up," suddenly realizing that one particular person, whom they often thought of as "just a friend," has suddenly become the most important person in the world.

Mark and Diane tell me that when they met in college, they enjoyed hanging out, studying together, and going on ski trips with their circle of friends. It was never romantic. After college, they moved to separate cities to pursue careers and occasionally tracked each other on social media. They dated other people, but never met anyone they wanted to seriously commit to. At a weekend reunion of their college friends, something clicked. It was as if they saw each other for the first time. Over that reunion weekend, they talked a lot and recognized that this other person had very special qualities they could not find elsewhere. Ten years into a happy marriage Mark tells me, "She was there all along, and I finally opened my eyes and saw her." That weekend, it dawned on both of them that this was the person they had been searching for all their adult lives. Diane says, "I always enjoyed being with him. He was a great guy— easy to talk to, intelligent, kind, secure, and confident. He even had a quirky sense of humor, similar to mine. I always felt safe with

Mark; my insides relaxed when he was around. In college neither of us was thinking about a serious relationship. We just wanted to get through school. When we met again, we wanted the same things out of life, and we were both ready to settle down. We found each other again, and that was it."

MODERN LOVE AND MARRIAGE

In Polly Young-Eisendrath's recent book, *Love Between Equals,*[8] she emphasizes that never in history have we had so much freedom to choose whom we love and how we love. We have the freedom, but we have not yet acquired the skills or capacities necessary for sustaining the kind of love we seek. We especially want someone to "get us," to be an "appreciative witness to our lives," something that was not expected in earlier generations.

Couples therapist and romantic philosopher Esther Perel tells us that we expect more from a relationship today than at any other time in history. We ask one person to be what an entire village used to provide – best friend, passionate lover, trusted confidant, and so on. In reference to marriage, she comments, "contained within the small circle of the wedding band are vastly contradictory ideals. We want our chosen one to offer stability, safety, predictability and dependability ... we then want that very same person to supply awe, mystery, adventure, and risk."[9]

Many young people are disillusioned by their inability to find someone who can do all of this for them. They don't want to settle for the tepid or unhappy relationships that their parents had. Their answer—forgo marriage, commit for as long as they are happy, or as long as the relationship suits them. Others are exploring alternative relationship forms in the search of a better solution.[10]

Dating on The Persona Level

The advent of online dating sites and "apps" has opened many more possibilities for meeting potential love mates, as well as increasing dating peril. The online world has created a whole new cottage industry, where consultants coach you on how to market yourself and draw the responses you want. You can craft a profile to put your best aspects forward, and the medium allows you to prescreen interested "applicants" and control the speed of the connection. For those with a small circle of contacts, or in small communities, it significantly expands the dating pool. The downside is that people have become increasingly clever at designing profiles that have little to do with who they are. This elevates the need to be wise and watchful for pretenders and bad actors.

An online profile will tell you little about a person's inner life or their capacity for a real relationship. We are living in an era of "persona dating." Online dating can also give the illusion that there are an endless number of possibilities out there. It is easy to reject someone based on an uninspiring profile or a bad picture, without ever being in their presence. Presence is of major importance in a relationship—it is part of the "click." Pictures and profiles will never capture the sparkle in a person's eyes, their delightful laughter, the rhythm of the conversation as it intermixes with yours, or the intricacies of a psyche that may capture your romantic longings.

FOMO

Researcher Barry Schwartz[11] talks about how our expanding realm of choices in life has served to escalate our anxiety and promote something called "FOMO"—the fear of missing out. It starts in the grocery store, where we have an overwhelming array of food choices, and moves into personal relationships, where we have difficulty committing because we fear that there might be someone better just around the corner. We become paralyzed by the fear that we might make the wrong choice.

There is nothing wrong with knowing what you want and having a standard, but keep in mind what therapist Esther Perel says—that we burden our modern relationships with impossible expectations when we want one person to provide us with what was once provided by a whole village.

What Sparks Chemistry?

Neuroscientists may be able to explain the neurococktail of early love, but they cannot explain the mystery of why chemistry sparks with some and not with others. Why are we inexorably drawn to certain people? Why do some people, who have the right "profile" lack the right chemistry? What exactly is chemistry? In my view, chemistry involves those mysterious elements that are largely beneath our conscious awareness. Each of us has a personal love story that resides in the depths of our psyches. *We fall in love with people who fit into our completion story.* The intertwining of two people's deeply held longings will determine if there is chemistry. However, it will be their capacity to make a life together that will determine if they will ever reach love's fulfillment.

Here is My Script, Please Read as Written

In the modern search for the "right person," many people treat romantic partners as if they were auditioning for a part, an actor on their stage. It is as if they were saying, "Here is my script, please read as written." Over time, if the other person does not play the part well, they are fired from the play and the seeker goes in search of another leading lady or man.

It is ironic that some of the people with the longest list of "what I'm looking for in a partner" have never made a list of what they offer in return. It is also dismaying to find that you may capture someone who checks all of your required boxes, only to find that you don't really like the life you are living with that person. People who don't know themselves create checklists that are designed according to the over-culture and their understanding of who they are—their Ego identity. This may be at odds with the deeper longings of the heart.

Over the years, I have seen any number of women who have "auditioned" for the part of romantic ideal in an eligible partner's life. Most women are raised to be accommodating and pleasing; however, if a woman has no taproot into the deep resources of her own soul, she will begin to wither. A woman living according to someone else's script will eventually become a persona with nothing behind it—smile pasted on, clothes looking great, but flat, empty eyes. Stuck in a relationship that is not really nourishing and a life that is about presentation, I see all too many women suffering from anxiety, depression, and a growing dependence on alcohol. I am not denigrating the woman who chooses a more traditional role, but that choice should be made consciously, felt as a calling, not because she has been relegated to a bit part in someone else's play.

I recall Sharon, who was offloaded for a younger, more adoring version of herself. When she came to work with me, she was devastated and bitter. Initially she sat weeping on my couch, and declared that she had given that SOB, "the best years of my life." Sharon started out feeling betrayed, but as she engaged in some inner work, she began to experience freedom, and an awakening that comes from getting one's taproot deep. She wrote herself an entirely new story, one significantly more fulfilling and in line with her "soulprint."

THE MIDLIFE MARRIAGE MALLAISE

The Story Completes and the Needs Change

People often mate based on finding someone who "meets their needs." The problem with this motivation is that needs change, and when they do, the couple may be in trouble. Mating based on a set of goals leads you into a particular story. The story may be the "settling down and having a family" story. Women who live into this story often find themselves adrift when the children are grown. With the kids launched, a house can get very still, and a couple can find themselves wondering what they are doing together. This very empty nest is part of what I call *The Midlife Marriage Malaise*.

Stephanie and Jack were such a couple. They had what their friends considered a perfect marriage, until the last child left for college. Over the course of their lives together, Jack worked long hours and focused on his career. He lived into the archetype of Responsible Father and Provider. She was the quintessential Nurturing Mother and Executive Homemaker. When the kids were grown, Stephanie and Jack had little in common and not much to say to each other. Stephanie was lonely, and with too much time on her hands, she was becoming a bit too familiar with a bottle of Chardonnay. A friend invited her to a conference where I was speaking. That weekend, she experienced an awakening of her inner life. It dawned on her that she could continue to grow as a person and live into a larger story. The deep conversations and sense of connection she felt with others during that weekend were compelling and she realized that this was the vital nutrient she needed for her life. When she returned home, she announced to Jack that she no longer wanted to remain in the life they had created together. It was just too empty. Jack was stunned. He had been perfectly happy with the arrangement, but Stephanie's discontent propelled them into couples therapy where they began to revitalize a stultified relationship.

Stephanie took a risk when she threatened to upset the apple cart, but Jack engaged and the two of them began to discover each other on a deeper level, beyond roles and responsibilities. Jack came to realize that there was a whole realm of existence that he would never have known, had it not been for Stephanie's discontent and the potential loss of the marriage. They will tell you that they were good role mates, but they have *become* Soul Mates, travelling together on the journey of individuation.

Midlife and Individuation

Midlife is a time when many people start to re-evaluate their lives. In today's world, we can consider "midlife" to be around the age of fifty. During this time, a common complaint arises among couples. It has to do with the loss of "spark" in their relationship. There has been a slow drift apart for years, and suddenly this comes into sharp focus. Midlife is a time when a general malaise about life may settle in. This often gets projected onto the relationship. "I'm not sure I want to be married any more. I'm just not happy," states Barry to his wife. He considers that perhaps there is someone else out there who would make him feel more alive. This enrages Sylvia, who has not been particularly happy for years, but has stayed the course.

In the midst of midlife restlessness, a deeper kind of growth becomes essential. Growth can be destabilizing, but it is precisely this kind of destabilization that is necessary to revitalize a life and a relationship. Unfortunately, when people don't have guidance about the natural push of the psyche in this passage time, they can upend their lives in the search to fill an aching emptiness. The "midlife crisis" is a real thing and can unravel a life when the search for inner meaning is projected onto one's outer life. People have affairs or leave marriages in midlife, thinking that the partner is the problem. While I do not believe that all marriages should be sustained, the wise course is to engage in a process of inner inquiry and development, before concluding that your partner is the problem. Growth revitalizes marriages, and can open up possibilities for two very bored, dissatisfied people as they discover new things about themselves and each other.

The Swiss psychoanalyst, Carl Jung, wrote a great deal about the "midlife passage." In subsequent writings, Jungian analyst, James Hollis,[12] continues this valuable exploration of how in midlife, the psyche begins to push for meaning and personal development and an alignment with what Jung called the Self, the inner compass, which guides from within, and sometimes orchestrates interesting coincidences in our outer lives called "synchronicities." The "big S" Self is to be differentiated from the "little s" self, which refers to our Ego identity. Most of us are defined by our Ego identities—what we usually think of as "who I am," but we are much more than our Ego identities. Our Ego identities are formed out of our early experiences, the demands of our culture, and continue to be shaped by the requirements of our adult lives. However, the Self carries the true blueprint of who we were born to be, and the process of individuation is about aligning the outer life with this deeper blueprint. People who begin to listen to this deeper call open doors within that lead to previously undiscovered treasure. The journey of individuation requires the courage to face oneself, shadow and light, to correct some of our deeply embedded distortions and heal the wounds of the past so that we can claim our intrinsic beauty and value. The process of that inner journey can be arduous at first, but as we walk it, the rewards become evident. Life becomes more meaningful, purposeful, and fulfilling as the path opens before us.

We really do continue to evolve across a lifetime, from birth to death, and midlife is an important time to do a life review and make sure that the remainder of one's life is headed in a direction worth pursuing. In midlife, big existential questions erupt, and we feel things emerging from our depths which require us to examine whether we are on our true path. When we begin to tune into the voice of the Self, we understand life differently and we interact in our relationships from a different place.

Journey versus Match

Regardless of how we define an ideal partner, there are elements of love that defy box-checking. People find partners who check all the boxes, only to discover that they still aren't happy. This is particularly likely when the boxes on a person's list are handed to them by others. People also find happiness in relationships where the loved one only checks a few of the boxes, but the connection occurs on a much deeper level. We all know couples who seem like highly unlikely love matches but must be suited for each other at a level we cannot see or comprehend. Other couples, who seem so perfect together, surprise us with unexpected splits. Keep in mind that couples have personas just like individuals. It is the face they show the world. We never really know what goes on in the heart, or behind closed doors.

There is research that shows that people who commit to the idea of a "relationship journey" instead of a "match," do much better over the course of a long-term marriage.[13] While very few of us would want to be in the obligatory marriages of old, many people give up on a relationship way too soon when the relationship becomes troubled. Our society provides very little helpful information on how to establish and sustain the loving relationships we so desire, and this is why so many "love matches" come to a dismal end. Couples that encounter the inevitable rough patches of relating and become willing to learn and grow will tell you that they are grateful they stayed the course. These relationships become increasingly valuable over time. When staying in a relationship is based on whether "you meet my needs," the relationship will eventually be found wanting. The metaphor of journey allows for evolution and discovery, and when we realize that a relationship is not an ultimate answer, but a catalyst for growth, the whole experience begins to shift.

INDIVIDUATION IN CONNECTION

When two people commit to a process of growth and discovery, they begin to walk a path I call Individuation in Connection. The relationship itself becomes an invitation into deeper self-under-standing and this shift of context takes the couple into a different kind of relationship—far beyond need meeting. Lovers on this journey begin to resemble two intertwining trees, each with a separate taproot. They are fed by an inner stream, which will nourish their individual lives as well as the life of the relationship. A relationship in which two people are individuating in connection will always be vital and will continue to evolve over the course of a lifetime. This is a love worth having and worth the inner work it takes to achieve it.

Chapter 2

DISENCHANTMENT

"You're Not What I Expected."
Polly Young-Eisendrath

How we long to remain in that glorified realm of early love, lofted upward into that exalted state, intoxicated by love's neurochemicals. For a time, we dwell in a mythological realm, living in a wondrous land of fulfillment. There is ease and magic in our interactions. In the light of a lover's adoring eyes, we feel elevated, inspired to be better people. We have a boundless feeling of desire and feel the thrill of being desirable.

It is one thing to fall in love, it is quite another to build a life with someone. Building a life requires us to consider practical matters, and as we begin to work all of this out, we descend from the mythological realm into ordinary life. From the lofty experience of being hopeful Soul Mates, now we must become Role Mates. In this unwelcomed descent, we sober up and start to notice areas where we are not exactly on the same page. In the enchantment phase of love, we believe we understand each other, and if we have differences, surely love will win out. Neither person is aware of how much the expectations of the future are based on assumptions and projections. We don't realize that we each carry a personal narrative of how love should go. In building a life with our chosen beloved, we must learn to navigate differences.

DIFFERENCES

Gloria has a particular way of folding everything so that it fits neatly in drawers. Greg has always just left things in a laundry basket. Stuffing things into drawers is new for him. He often leaves dishes around the apartment, clothes on the floor, and he loads the dishwasher in a completely random way. Gloria has dropped hints about all of this, but nothing is changing, and the frustration of her Inner Neatnik has been building. One evening she can't take it anymore. She explodes and begins to lecture Greg about how she cannot live like this. Was he born in a barn?! He's got to begin to get his act together and keep a proper house! Greg's eyes darken and he tells her that she is beginning to sound like his mother.

Darla and Dan seem to have two different biological clocks. She is a night owl, and he is a morning lark. Dan can barely keep his eyes open after 9:30 P.M. He would love for them to settle into bed together, but Darla is just getting her second wind at 9 P.M. Her most productive work time is between 9 P.M. and 12 midnight. Dan rises at 5 A.M., bright eyed and cheerful, and is out the door by 6 A.M. Daria sleeps till 8 A.M. and won't even talk to anyone until she has her morning coffee. They are hopelessly out of synch and beginning to wonder how they are ever going to connect for a conversation, let alone sex.

Shanice had dreams of how wonderful it would be to spend quiet weekends at home with her beloved Kara, but Kara's life is devoted to several worthy causes in the world and her weekends are filled with volunteer work and meetings. Shanice has always admired Kara's commitment to making the world a better place, but she begins to express feelings of dismay at how little time they spend together. Kara is torn inside. She feels guilty about being a "neglectful partner," but angry that being in a relationship is requiring her to adjust her priorities.

Brad and Gail seem to have quite different ideas about how to manage money. He grew up in a house where money was never a problem and when someone wanted something, they bought it. Gail grew up in a house where every penny was counted because there might not be enough money to keep food in the cupboards. She wants to save and then spend when the money is there. Brad wants to buy on credit so that they can have all the nice things they want today. This makes Gail intensely anxious and they have heated arguments about this.

Bob's mother drops by unannounced. She has always done this, but now that he is married to Marlene, this is not working very well. Marlene has a demanding full-time job and with both spouses working, the house is often a mess. When Bob's mother drops in, she makes sideways comments about Marlene's housekeeping deficiencies, which sends Marlene into an angry simmer. Marlene has her own internal conflicted feelings about how her career ambitions prevent her from being the archetypal Good Wife. She asks Bob to speak to his mother and request that she not drop by unannounced; that way Marlene has a chance to quickly pick up the house before his mother arrives. Marlene insists that they need better boundaries as a couple. It has not occurred to Bob that anything would change after marriage, and he doesn't entirely understand the dynamic between his mother and Marlene. A conflict-avoidant man, he delays the conversation with his mother, torn between concerns that he will hurt his mother's feelings and his sense of loyalty to Marlene.

Angie thought she and Alfred had a clear agreement about faithfulness. He assumed they were talking about sex outside the marriage. Angie assumed they were talking about emotional involvements as well. When she discovered that he had connected with an old girlfriend from high school via social media, and they were chatting and texting regularly, Angie hit the roof. Alfred doesn't consider this a breach. She does. With other conflicts in their relationship unresolved, Angie feels quite threatened by this old girlfriend. She fears that what Alfred claims is a harmless reconnection is becoming much more.

In most relationships, partners are shocked to discover areas of life where they thought they had an understanding, only to discover that they had entirely different definitions of what was agreed upon. There is a lot to work out when two people join their lives together. Standards of housekeeping, body clocks, balancing outside involvements and finding time together, saving and spending, boundaries with family, and what defines "fidelity." These are not just one-time conversations. In building a life together we encounter surprises, conflicts, and disappointments. With less time for oneself and with more responsibilities in life, people can begin to feel overwhelmed and depleted. Resentments may begin in response to partner needs and demands. Add children to the mix and a couple will become even more challenged by strained resources and differing ideas about how to raise children.

THE START OF THE REAL RELATIONSHIP

Fairy tales and romantic movies tell us that all we have to do is to find the "right person," and we will live happily ever after. However, *this second stage of relationship is the actual start of the real relationship.* This is a time of discovery, where we must draw upon or develop deeper capacities as we wind our way through love's labyrinth. The patterns established at this stage of relationship will set a trajectory for the course of the relationship. There is a fork in the road here. One path leads into growth, mutual caring, cooperation, and the co-creation of a relationship worth being in. The other path will lead into the toxic landscape of power struggles, avoidance, abdication, withdrawal, circular arguments, passive-aggressive acts, emotional manipulation, bullying, lying, and covert operations.

The Murky Stuff in the Space Between Us

In the early stages of a relationship, we send thousands of cues back and forth. We pick these up from each other and they evoke responses. Even without words, micro-expressions convey information; body language and the shifting of internal states is felt by the other and evokes defensive responses.

As the bond deepens, the two people involved begin to sense what can be described as an interpersonal "field"[14] that envelops them and flows between them. Into this field, a great deal of emotion and unconscious material flows. It becomes almost impossible to discern whose "stuff" each person is reacting to, but it is very visceral.

Each of us enters a relationship with an underlying love story that creates both hope and anxiety. This internal narrative informs us how love should go. It is an ideal formed from our early experiences—what we want to repeat, repair, or avoid, hoping to never encounter again. Our love narrative continues to form as we observe others, adopt norms from our family, the culture, TV shows, books, and movies. In recent years, our kids absorb an increasing amount of information from the Internet, including a lot of their sex education. Over time, we form decisions about what we want, what we don't want, as well as what we believe we deserve and can hope to find. On a less conscious level, we bring our unmet needs and longings into an intimate relationship in the hopes that finally they will be fulfilled.

We are drawn to people with whom we sense the possibility of living out that internal completion story. When we meet someone who fits the script, we fall in love, and cast them in the starring role. While some of this takes place consciously, a great deal of it is unconscious. We just sense that someone is a fit because they carry certain qualities, say the right words, or we feel a certain way around them.

Projection

A major function of the psyche is something called projection. In love relationships, our projections involve how we externalize inner ideals by sending them out onto our intimate partners, as if their faces were projection screens. Partners can pick up these projections and try to live into them (we loved to be idealized) or resist them and become entangled in them. Projections are part of our human survival system. They are automatic and we don't engage in this "on purpose," but the hopes and fears created by our projections cause a great deal of pain for lovers. In the early days of exalted love, we are unaware of how much we are living into each other's projections. The greater the distance between the Dream Lover[15] in our heads and the actual person we find ourselves living with, the greater the degree of relationship distress.

Undeveloped Aspects and Opposites[1]

Another aspect of our unconscious projections is that we look for qualities that are missing or undeveloped in ourselves.[16] When we find them in another person and we bond with that person, we feel more whole. Thus, the old adage "my spouse is my better half." In some couples, it is as if the two people have negotiated an agreement where each is carrying half of the archetypal spectrum. "You carry this quality, I'll carry that." "You be the one who plans for the future, I'll make sure we live for the moment." "You be the extrovert, who keeps our social calendar going, I'll be the cozy

---

[1] While Jung spoke of how every woman carries undeveloped masculine energies within (animus) and every man carries undeveloped feminine energies (anima) the division of opposites in the archetypal spectrum go beyond anima/animus into all dimensions of the possible personality. It is important to note that in a world where binary categories of gender are increasingly challenged, the concepts of anima and animus are being debated and redefined.

introvert, who makes sure we spend time alone together." This works well if each person values what the other brings; it can become a power struggle when two people become polarized and fight over whose way is the best way. When partners become polarized over their archetypal split, the very qualities that drew them in can become increasingly annoying. The Free Spirit is later experienced as an Irresponsible Flake, the Practical One becomes a Domineering Bore.

Difficulties can also emerge when one of the partners wants to live into something the other person has always carried. For example, when an accommodating, nurturing stay-at-home mom decides she wants to become more self-assured, go back to school, and pursue a professional career. I have heard many distressed men say, "If she no longer needs me, who will I be to her? How will I hold onto her?" There is great fear here that the man will become obsolete, as if his only value has been as Provider. The answer is to grow beyond one's previous limited role in the archetype of the Provider and explore the deeper dimensions of partnering.

THE CREATION OF THE "WE"

The Co-World in Which We Will Dwell

A relationship is a third entity, invisible, but felt by both people. Most people think of a relationship as something you find, but relationships are born. They are co-created by two people who birth a "we"—something greater than the "you" and "me." Relationships are created by a process of discovery, exchange, cooperation, and by the intermingling of the two partner's psyches. As Carl Jung was pondering relationships, he once described the process this way— *"the meeting of two personalities is like the meeting of two chemical substances; if there is a reaction, both are transformed."* In the containing field of a relationship, lovers are in an alchemical process, being influenced by mysterious forces created by the intermingling of their two psyches. Each person's history, expectations, projections, and underlying vulnerabilities begin to flow into the space between them, around them, and to awaken things inside of them.

There is a word in German for this creation of the "we." They call it the "mitwelt," which translates into "co-world." This co-world is a place the couple will inhabit. It can be a place of great refuge and strength or it can become a place of emptiness, insecurity, resentment, and struggle. Once created, the "we" must be nourished and sustained by the two individuals or it will suffer and may even die. You can tell when two people have created this third entity. There is a field around them. When I am working with a couple in trouble, who once had this, I hear things like, "What happened to us?" The two people are referring to the loss of that sense that they were once "in it together." Couples mourn the loss of that loving feeling, but they often don't understand how they lost it.

Relationship as A Path of Growth

A relationship may be viewed as a solution for many, but in truth, a relationship is a path of growth. One of the amazing things about a relationship is that it invites us to re-evaluate the worldviews we brought forward from childhood.

In recent years, couples researcher John Gottman[17] emphasizes the central importance of each partner being willing to be influenced by the other. This willingness is crucial in the establishment of a good, sustainable relationship, but it also requires a good deal of trust.

When one or both of the partners begin to resist the process of relational influence, power struggles begin. Power struggles can be overt or covert, but they always involve the insistence that one person's reality must rule. Carl Jung claimed that, "*Where love rules, there is no will to power; and where power predominates, there love is lacking. One is the shadow of the other.*" I see couples constantly where one person has insisted on dominating the terms of the relationship, but also wants to be with a Soul Mate. These two paradigms cannot co-exist because in order experience being Soul Mates, each must encounter the other, come to know and understand that person in their own right. When we come to know an intimate partner as a separate and cherished individual with whom we are sharing a life, we are ready for the journey of Individuation in Connection.

INTERLOCKING COMPLEXES

Something else happens when we begin to settle into a relationship. Our lovers start to feel like "family." As this happens, the ghosts of the past begin to awaken and the specter of early life parental figures hover over the face of these once idealized lovers. We begin to re-experience early life feelings and memories.

As we become attached to an important person in a love relationship, we become vulnerable. Our lives become interdependent and the choices and actions of one partner have an impact on the other. Much of the stuff that begins to flood the space between us is sourced in our early life experiences of being vulnerable and dependent. These feelings are confusing because they are often not awakened by relationships outside of this primary partner.

Complexes

Each of us has a set of complexes that are developed in our early years. A complex is a cluster of associations around a theme that has emotional significance. Complexes gather weight as the experiences of our lives seem to validate their subjective truth. When we are in a complex, it is as if we have put on a set of lenses and everything we see, and experience is filtered through that set of lenses. A complex is more than just a collection of thoughts or beliefs; complexes are felt strongly in the body and when a complex activates, it becomes a total reality. These experiential realities become so deeply woven into the formation of our personalities that we are unaware that they create a guiding narrative by which we interpret everything that happens to us. In today's medical context, we can think of a complex as a cluster of neurons that activate neurochemicals that download into the body and drive us to react in patterned ways. Complexes hijack us, and we become incapable of thinking or viewing a situation in any other way other than what the complex dictates. Jung described them as little sub-personalities, each having a life of its own.

Some complexes are positive, causing us to feel happy, even inflated. We typically enjoy these and sometimes overestimate our capacities while we are in them. Other complexes create a cascade of negative feelings. We defend against these or try to compensate for them. Sometimes we just succumb to their powerful influence. Complexes can be triggered by situations as well as by people who are important to us. Everyone has a set of personal complexes that haunt their life,[18] and these gather power as our life progresses and we collect evidence that they are "true."

Intuition or Activation of a Complex?

Complexes are so powerful that when we are caught in their hold, our body confirms that what we are experiencing is true. This is true for our positive complexes as well as our negative ones. When people insist that they should trust their gut instincts, I emphasize that we all need to assess whether our gut instincts are good indicators of truth, or an indication that we are in the grip of a complex.

Gordon has a raging mother complex, having been raised by a demanding mother who provided little warmth and was "impossible to please." He idealizes every attractive woman he dates, insisting that he has finally found "the one." This idealization continues until the woman he is dating makes a reasonable complaint about his behavior. Suddenly he is overtaken by feelings he felt growing up with his mother. The woman he is dating falls from her pedestal, is summarily dismissed, and he falls into despair, once again believing that women are "impossible to please."

"Shouldn't we trust our intuitions?" insists April. She is certain that her boyfriend is unfaithful, but she also has a lengthy history of abandonment and betrayal, beginning with her father. My answer is, "Sometimes yes, sometimes no." We always need to factor in the power of projection and how a complex becomes the lens through which we interpret everything that is happening around us. April may indeed be picking up on signals that indicate problems in her relationship, but this might also be coming from her insecure attachment history, which has been a problem in past relationships. When the man in her life becomes really important to her, inner voices begin to whisper, "Men lie to get what they want. They can't be trusted. They make promises they can't keep. No one has ever loved you and you will always wind up betrayed and abandoned." Until April sorts out her early attachment influences, it will be hard for her to differentiate between her attachment insecurities and her "intuitions." Currently, her insecurities lead her to become increasingly suspicious, controlling, and jealous in a way that drives good partners out the door.

Discovering Your Partner's Early Life Vulnerability

As any love relationship deepens, we will inevitably encounter our partner's vulnerability. We will begin to see the signs of their particular childhood wounding. We discover this in subtle changes in the space between us—a sudden bad mood, a withdrawal, an unwarranted accusation. We may complain about this or try to cajole the other back into a feeling of affinity. Some people try to ignore confusing feelings, or pretend that nothing is amiss, but a denial of this shift will lead into what I call a "no-fly zone"—things we avoid talking about because neither person understands what is happening or how to resolve it.

Relationship teachers Bader and Pearson call this denial the "dark side of the honeymoon."[19] It begins when a couple tries to maintain that early glow of the enchantment even in the face of subtle shifts in compatibility, even as differences begin to grate. When we ignore and deny the anxiety caused by disappointment and differences, it causes both people to back away. Conflict-avoidant couples develop a stiffness and formality and a slow deadening of feeling. Conflict-engaging couples begin to argue, and power struggles begin, each attempting to get the other person back in line.

The universal lover's cry in this stage of the relationship is, "You are not who I thought you were." The problem is that no one is ever who we think they are. Our perceptions of an idealized other are always riddled with projections and assumptions. Facing the human imperfections of an idealized partner can be downright terrifying, until we understand that this is part of the process of becoming a couple.

While I am a believer in "premarital" counseling, I also know that there will be unconscious content that will flow into the space between two people after the wedding. We cannot possibly know what will be awakened in us as we move more deeply into interdependence. Add children to the mix and it gets even more complicated. Even when we talk about how we will operate and who we will be to each other, these defining conversations must evolve because we discover things about ourselves that we can't possibly know in the earlier stages of a relationship.

This Only Happens with You

When our partner is idealizing us, we love it, and want to live into that projection. When their idealization flips to disappointment or judgment, we are hurt, and resist being cast in negative terms.

Sometimes we power struggle against how we are being characterized, and in the process, we inadvertently become drawn into acting out what the other is projecting.

One of the mysterious dynamics that begins to happen in a close relationship is how we evoke behaviors from each other, behaviors that do not occur in other settings. We respond to things in our partner's underlying script without even being aware that we are doing so.

Devin and Brenda are in my office. They have been together about five years and have become entrenched in self-protective dynamics which prevent them from feeling vulnerable. They think they are having trouble communicating, and they are, but their difficulties are sourced in how they keep triggering each other's underlying complexes and becoming entangled in power struggles. Each is drawn into extreme behaviors which are not evoked in any other adult setting. Devin has diagnosed Brenda as passive-aggressive and he's fed up with it. "She says yes to things just to shut me up, then she doesn't follow through. It is soooo aggravating!" Brenda tells me that Devin becomes loud, critical, and controlling—that he overwhelms her. She acknowledges that she sometimes agrees with him, "just to get him off my back!" He defends himself against her characterization. "I am not a critical, controlling person. It's just that she never does what she says! I don't have this problem with anyone but Brenda; my office colleagues will tell you that I'm cooperative and easygoing, but they bother to follow through on things!" Brenda retorts, "You bark orders like a Drill Sergeant. You badger me until I can't even think, let alone talk." Devin is trying to convince me that Brenda is the source of the problem; in turn, she points the finger at him.

As we begin to unpack their histories, Devin and Brenda begin to see how their difficulties are sourced in wounds of the past, echoing forward, and projected onto the partner in present time. Devin has begun to resemble Brenda's loud, intimidating father, who she called the Drill Sergeant growing up. He was a man who frightened the whole family when he became angry. When dad got mad, everybody jumped. What Brenda learned growing up, was to stay quiet, head down, and then go underground to do whatever she wanted. The frightened Inner Child and Sneaky Adolescent still live in her, and they are increasingly activated by Devin's anger. Devin grew up in a house with an older sister who was seriously ill for a while. His needs were easily overlooked because he was such an easygoing kid. As he talks about this, I see the sadness on his face, and he looks noticeably younger. "It's like I just don't matter to anyone," he says. Devin came into this relationship certain that he would be a priority in Brenda's life. Now she just dismisses him, and he feels the same feelings he felt growing up—overlooked and unimportant. Adult Devin insists that he deserves more, but it comes out in angry outbursts that frighten Brenda. He hadn't realized how much this triggers Brenda into her own early vulnerability. In stepping back and looking at how the angry Drill Sergeant and the Sneaky Adolescent get in trouble with each other, they begin to see each other's vulnerabilities and activate some compassion for the kids they once were. A couple of clear-thinking adults appear in the room and they begin to talk about how they can move forward without falling into the grip of these early life complexes.

The Pleaser and the Perfectionist

Jared has a strong Inner Pleaser that compensates for his underlying abandonment complex. One Saturday morning, he comes home from a ten-mile run. He is preparing for a half-marathon, but his wife, Karen, doesn't know this. She is overwhelmed by the demands of her corporate job and frustrated by the messy house. Karen has exceedingly high standards for herself and everyone around her. She is in the grips of a perfection complex. Her intense Inner Critic is on her case and she has a raging argument going on inside. It seems she is unable to be everything to everyone—a successful Career Woman, Enlightened Feminist, Loving Mother, and Perfect Wife. Her imperfectly kept house overwhelms her and causes her to feel like a failure. All of this inner turmoil has her really stirred up and when Jared returns from his run, she explodes. "Why can't you help more around the house?" she blurts out. "You seem to think you can go off running and leave me here with the kids and a mop in hand! I work too, you know. This is not fair!" This outburst unsettles Jared, who is committed to an equitable marriage. He suddenly feels insecure, ashamed, and afraid that he is failing with Karen. Jared's Inner Pleaser and Karen's Inner Perfectionist are about to get entangled in ways they don't even realize. Because Jared is also conflict-avoidant, instead of sitting down and talking this out, explaining about his running goal, and asking how he can be more helpful, he does none of this. He just gives up the running goal. This is a loss for him, but not mentioned at the time.

Later that year, Jared makes a sideways comment about how little he has been seeing Karen lately. He expects her to be fair, after all, he gave up his half-marathon. He suggests that she give up something—perhaps her book club. Karen doesn't realize that Jared gave anything up and states that her book club is important to her well-being. She keeps going, and Jared starts feeling resentful. He does a lot to support Karen. He knows she is working hard to achieve certain career goals, but he is often home alone with the kids. He doesn't discuss any of this with her, he just becomes more critical and irritable, which is upsetting to Karen, who was raised by a critical, irritable father. Her father complex begins to act up, and an Inner Rebel starts to operate. She begins to distance herself from Jared, unwilling to be dominated by his moods. He feels this cold space growing between them and becomes anxious. Karen works long hours, and he begins to wonder if she is having an affair.

Two years later, this couple comes in to work with me. They are caught in a downward spiral of disconnection and distrust. As we begin to explore their interlocking complexes, Jared comes to recognize that his underlying abandonment complex leads him into too much pleasing, conflict avoidance, and self-sacrifice. Karen begins to understand this about Jared and learns for the first time about the running goal that he gave up without comment. She comes to realize that she has been misinterpreting Jared's irritability and projecting the face of her difficult father onto him (her father complex). She also comes to understand that Jared has no desire to dominate her or undermine her career goals and Jared begins to learn how to express his desire for more time and closeness *directly*, instead of silently, sadly hoping that it will occur. As they become aware of each other's underlying vulnerabilities they begin to communicate from a place of gentleness and understand each other more deeply, untangling the negative spiral of assumptions and projections that led them into distance and despair. In deconstructing the progressive cycle of these tangled complexes, they began to relax their defenses, clear away the clutter of collected hurts and rediscover the love they once felt for each other.

INDIVIDUATION IN CONNECTION

When the spell of enchantment begins to fade, we stand at a fork in the path of love. This second stage of relationship is about learning who we are actually in relationship with, beyond our expectations, assumptions, and projections. This is where the real relationship is being forged.

We bring a lot of "stuff and baggage" into a relationship. As the baggage opens, it spills into the space between us, creating a lot of anxiety. This leads us into self-protective gambits, and we begin to close our hearts. The inner work we are invited into here will clear the path for a relationship worth having, but very few people realize that this stage of disenchantment is a normal stage along the path of love and not the end of the road. Deepening a connection with an important other activates early life complexes around how safe it is to need someone, rely on someone, and to trust in the safety of a deep attachment. When we become reactive and defensive, we end up entangled, fighting ghosts of the past. What we need is the courage to engage in the inner work that love invites us into. Only then can we co-create the kind of relationship that so many people long for, one that will nourish and support both people. As each person does their inner work, they will become more self-aware, and the two can then join together to transcend their underlying vulnerability and untangle the interlocking complexes that confound their relationship. Love promises much, but the path is like a labyrinth. It calls us to circle back and revisit some of the wounded places in our lives, places that have not been touched into since we were children. Love is the most powerful force in the universe. It draws us into relationship as a means of awakening us, so that we can become more whole.

CHAPTER 3

ATTACHMENT –
The Making and Breaking
of Affectional Bonds

"Love is a constant process of tuning in, connecting, missing and misreading cues, disconnecting, repairing, and finding deeper connection."
Susan Johnson

"Life is best organized as a series of daring ventures from a secure base."
John Bowlby

"We are hardwired for connection—it's what gives meaning and purpose to our lives."
Brené Brown

Human beings are born to bond, and how we were loved and cared for in our early years has a profound effect on our adult capacity for loving and being loved. Research in interpersonal neurobiology shows us how significantly early bonding experiences impact the developing nervous system and our capacity to regulate emotion. Some of these experiences are so early they are preverbal and simply felt in the body.[20]

Our intimate relationships stir up a wide range of intense emotions—longing, elation, vulnerability, anxiety, frustration, sadness, anger, and fear. Even our capacity for joy is determined by our nervous system's flexibility, our ability to get stirred up and then settle back down. Our experience with early attachment figures will determine how comfortable we are with closeness later on. Can we trust our heart to another person? How willing are we to be intimately known? Early experiences shape how secure or anxious we feel when we interweave our life with another person. Can we tolerate having another person draw close to us and depend on us, or does that level of closeness feel overwhelming? Our early experiences shape who we are drawn to in picking partners. While our neural networks signal us in our partner picks, we also pick partners who fit into our "completion story"—the sense that a certain person will finally give us the love we have always longed for. People whose neural networks were developed in a secure attachment are more regulated, and more likely to pick partners with whom they can create a healthy interdependency. Those with more difficult pasts will often pick a partner to "rework" something from their past. It feels familiar, perhaps even hopeful, but in many cases the person finds themselves in the disheartening experience of repeating old struggles.

Our Two Primal Fears

Human beings have two primal fears related to bonding—abandonment and engulfment. We are wired to seek connection and affiliation with a tribe, where we will find belonging and protection. On the other hand, the individuation process which Jung spoke so much about pushes us to develop our unique gifts and establish a separate identity apart from the collective. These two primal fears—abandonment and engulfment—pull at each other, and each of us must find the "Goldilocks zone" between our need for connection and belonging, and the freedom to develop into a unique self.

Every couple must find a balance between these divergent poles. In order to feel securely attached, we must learn to trust and support each other and share important aspects of our lives. We need a sense that the other person will be there for us in times of need. At the same time, it is important for each partner to self-define and be able to pursue important individual goals. In the interplay of these opposites, a healthy couple will experience a deepening trust that each can be themselves and still be loved. In his classic essay on love, Kahlil Gibran once wrote, "Let there be spaces in your togetherness, and let the winds of the heavens dance between you," … and let love be like "a moving sea between the shores of your souls."[21] We want the bond to be strong, but it is individual growth that will continue to vitalize the relationship.

The Origins of Attachment Theory

In recent years, we have seen a resurgence of interest in what is called "attachment theory." Attachment theory originated in the work of Dr. John Bowlby during WWII, when thousands of children were sent out of London to protect them from the bombs being dropped during German air raids.[22] Dr. Bowlby began observing how the children in his hospital fared as they experienced extended separation from their parents. Initially the children protested, calling out and searching for their parents. After a while they became despondent and sank into despair. Soon after that, they seemed to calm down, but Bowlby realized that this was not into a state of ease. The calm these children were exhibiting was born of detachment. It was as if they did not expect to see their parents again, had accepted the loss, and were moving on. After the war, these children had a difficult time reintegrating into their families and their difficulties with bonding continued over the course of their lives. Subsequent researchers continued Bowlby's work with attachment theory, and it became an important area of research in child development and child therapy.[23]

Romantic Love as an Attachment Process

In 1987, researchers Phil Shaver and Cindy Hazan[24] began to wonder how childhood attachment patterns impact our adult romantic relationships. Shaver and Hazan launched a whole new realm of research related to how we bond or fail to bond in adult relationships. At the time they began to study adult bonding and attachment, it was assumed that attachment patterns established in childhood continued throughout life. However, subsequent attachment theorists believe that our attachment orientations can change from insecure to secure as a result of positive, reparative experiences in adulthood.

Interpersonal Neurobiology

Psychiatrist Daniel Siegel,[25] is a leading attachment researcher. He tells us that what passes between us in an adult relationship activates pre-verbal sensations that are not stored as words or a story we might tell. Our attachment histories establish a "felt sense"[2] of whether it is safe to get close to and depend on the important people in our lives. A felt sense is not cognitive; it is felt in the body, originating from the embedded neural tracks of the brain. This embedded memory becomes the foundation for whether we trust people to be there when we need them.

We have learned that children who were securely attached in their little years, venture out into the world with more confidence

---

[2] The term "felt sense" has been integrated into many other kinds of work. Eugene Gendlin was the originator, and it can be found in the book *Focusing* (1978) New York: Bantam Books.

as they grow up. We see this in adults who have an innate sense of confidence in themselves. They trust more easily and enjoy close intimate bonds because their experiences in close relationships have been good. Securely attached people believe that people are basically good, and that relationship discord can be resolved. This has been their history. They don't escalate as quickly in the midst of misunderstandings. That in itself makes the misunderstanding easier to resolve. They make necessary sacrifices and have a sense that their loved ones will have their backs and support them in good times and in bad. People who have this foundation venture out into life with more ease and confidence and they take more well-considered risks. All of this adds up to a more successful and satisfying life.

Not everyone has this idyllic history. People who have never had this experience carry an underlying anxiety about bonding. When people with underlying attachment insecurities begin a romantic attachment in adulthood, it activates fears that may have gone underground for many years—fears of abandonment, of being overwhelmed, exploited, or betrayed. Because this is stored in the ancient recesses of a person's neural networks it is felt in the body and cannot be reasoned away by the thinking mind, regardless of how trustworthy the current partner may be. The body memorizes experiences of our critical early years, imprinting us with a felt sense of how safe it is to attach and whether we are deserving of love and care. Daniel Siegel calls these ancient memories *synaptic shadows* of the past.

The limbic system of our brains is more primitive than our thinking brain. It is also faster and more powerful than any "self-talk" a person may try to generate. If our experience with early attachment figures was insecure or threatening, any situation that reminds us of those early experiences will send our limbic systems into threat response. When we are in threat response, everything begins to look, sound, and feel more threatening. By the time our adult brain is trying to tell us that everything is fine, the limbic system has already downloaded adrenalin, moving us into fight, flight, or freeze mode. Most people are familiar with fight or flight, but if a situation feels life-threatening enough, some people freeze, unable to move, think, or speak.

In the context of my work, I think of attachment orientations as complexes, collections of memories around an archetypal theme.

Anxious/Preoccupied/Ambivalent Attachment— The Abandonment Complex

People with abandonment complexes harbor deep feelings of being unworthy, unlovable, or being defective in some way. They long for connection, but it is always paired with a fear of rejection. This complex may not even activate until someone becomes emotionally important, and this same person may be quite confident in other areas of their life. However, in love they will suddenly become hyper-focused on whether this desired partner is happy with them. "Do you still love me?" "Are we OK?" and "Are you mad at me?" are common questions asked by people with anxious attachment complexes. They need frequent reassurance and are often told they are "too clingy and overly needy." While they try not to be, they may develop ambivalent feelings about the partner, even feel angry about their "neediness," while continuing to seek reassurance in ways that make it more difficult for partners to extend it. Anxious, insecure types can become suspicious, jealous, possessive, and controlling. They manage their anxieties in maladaptive ways and end up evoking what they most fear—a partner who backs away. This only serves to reinforce a fear that they are fundamentally flawed, unlovable, and that eventually everyone will reject them.

People with anxious/preoccupied attachment complexes tend to collect hurts. They are overly sensitive and easily wounded. When they confront a partner, they often engage in a litany of complaints, where the partner can't figure out where to begin addressing issues.

If their repeated bids for connection and reassurance are not responded to, they can move into a despairing angry withdrawal. The partner may assume they have let things go, but this is a self-protective detachment. By the time this partner realizes that the other person has backed off, it may be too late to woo that person back out of their self-protective cocoon.

Avoidant Attachment—The Perpetually Cautious

If a person's history has been abusive, neglectful, or chaotic, they may carry a fundamental distrust of drawing close or becoming emotionally bonded. There is an underlying fear that eventually everyone takes advantage or betrays, and they feel easily overwhelmed by other people's needs and demands. When I ask people with an avoidant attachment orientation about who they turned to when they were little, in times of distress, they will often look at me blankly, and answer, "No one. I was sort of on my own." Early on, they learned to take care of themselves, not to make themselves vulnerable or rely on unreliable others. These children were sometimes treated as bothersome. Some of their caregivers were abusive or exploitive or had significant problems of their own. The child may have felt as if they were the ones taking care of the parent, instead of the other way around. Over time, these children acclimate to the feeling of relying on themselves, and this feels normal. For many it helped them be safe. In adulthood, when they need to settle and soothe themselves, instead of seeking connection, they will want space, and to withdraw into activities like video-games, screen time, reading, solitary hobbies, exercise, crafts, even things like meditation—something away from human interaction. They can also become over-giving caregivers, who think only of others, but cannot accept or take in the care offered by others. They can look very "adult," tend to be self-contained, seemingly strong and stoic, but have difficulty bonding in a healthy mutual way.

Virginia was one of my clients whose mother died of cancer when she was ten. Her father was so grief stricken that he shut down and did not allow anyone in the house to express emotion. Virginia had no one to turn to that would help her resolve her own grief and loss. Devoid of nurture and care, she carried an underlying sadness into her adult life, but became accustomed to presenting a pleasant persona. She avoided close emotional contact and it was hard for her to trust the love or support offered by friends or potential partners. People experienced her as cold, but she was really trapped in a shell of protective armor, unable to let people in, not wanting to re-suffer any pain of loss. This kept her chronically lonely, until she met Matthew. A quiet, gentle man, he slowly became an important person in her life. Like a timid deer, she slowly opened her heart to him, and his steady presence began to heal her early wounding. Slowly her fears of loving and being loved abated, and she experienced her first secure attachment.

Introversion and Extroversion

Some of what I'm talking about may sound like the difference between an extrovert and an introvert, but these are different constructs. There are people who are highly extroverted and enjoy interacting with a lot of people but aren't particularly close to anyone. They may not think much about their inner life or feel safe enough to reveal deep feelings to an intimate other, let alone turn to someone for emotional support. Two extroverted partners might enjoy a busy social life, going out on the town, meeting up with friends, or entertaining people in their home, but never share their inner lives with each other.

On the other hand, an introverted person might have a small circle of friends, dislike crowds or small talk, yet enjoy a close relationship with an intimate partner, who knows and understands their thoughts, feelings, and history very deeply. A romantic evening for two introverts might involve the two of them sitting by a fire reading their favorite book, content in each other's quiet company.

Emotional Regulation in Intimate Relationships

While many couples come in telling me that they are having difficulty communicating, I am aware that the real underlying problem is that they are struggling with *co-regulation*—the inability of their nervous systems to settle down with each other. This partner, who once felt so perfect and so safe, now feels dangerous as their underlying attachment systems activate. Defenses are up, and this makes communication and cooperation almost impossible.

Our early attachment experiences significantly impact our capacity for *emotional regulation*.[26] This refers to our ability to manage strong emotions, which is crucial to creating and sustaining a good relationship. When we are little, we rely on the big people around us to help us calm down,—to soothe us when we are distressed, and to come when we call out. This responsiveness imprints us deeply about whether life is safe or dangerous. Their ability to soothe and comfort us shapes the resilience of our developing nervous systems and this resilience carries into our adult lives, allowing us to move from distress back to calm more easily.

Because misunderstandings are an inevitable part of intimate relationships, how we respond is crucially important in building trust. When we respond in a meaningful way to a partner's distress, trust is built. When unintended hurts occur in the early part of a relationship, the sooner a reparative response is made, the more the trust deepens. People who have a secure attachment history do not become as distressed when misunderstandings occur, they are more forgiving and address upsets in the partner more readily. With more innate flexibility in their nervous systems, they return to a baseline of calm more quickly. For those with an insecure attachment history, an emotional upset, or a breach in the sense of security in an intimate relationship might keep them churned up inside for days, months, even years.

We need to be able to experience the full range of emotions in love—anxiety, fear, longing, frustration, boredom, confusion, anger, fulfillment, pleasure, compassion, and joy. A flexible nervous system means we don't get stuck in the difficult emotions and can open up our hearts and bodies to the positive ones.

Mirror Neurons

For a long time, therapists have been telling people that they don't have to be swept along by the negative emotions of another person, but we have learned something important about why another person's emotional state is so "contagious." In the 1990s, an Italian neuroscientist began to research something that we now call "mirror neurons."[27] It seems that as we watch a person's face, we catch subtle (and not so subtle) changes in their expressions. Emotions represent themselves similarly across cultures and when we recognize an emotion on the face of a partner, we register the emotion in our own neural networks, and a resonance occurs. This is why in a face-to-face exchange with a partner, their emotional state will impact us so significantly. It is our mirror neurons.

Our Innate Resilience

It was once believed that our early attachment experiences were set for life, but on a hopeful note, recent research has shown that our brains are quite resilient.[28] We are learning more and more about the brain's "plasticity" and how established neural tracks can be rewired into new formations.[29] Interpersonal neurobiology confirms that we possess an amazing potential for healing the past. This means that we can reconfigure the wiring of insecure attachment orientations and their accompanying complexes. We can expand our potential for loving and being loved.

Couples therapist Stan Tatkin[30] states that a good relationship will literally rewire the nervous system. We can "earn" a secure attachment orientation, and when we do, it is a kind of "brain upgrade." An adult relationship that provides the responsiveness, support, and consistency that was absent in the past heals our nervous systems. Reparative experience in a good relationship literally reshapes our neural pathways, switching neural connections away from old tracks and rewiring us into new pathways of love and fulfillment. This is how we rewrite old scripts and transcend the wounds of the past. Good love heals.

Rick Hanson is another author and psychologist who teaches us about the resilience we possess when we employ our inner resources. Humans are hardwired to be aware of threat. This aids our survival but also lead us into a "negativity bias." Our minds are more like Teflon for the good experiences of our lives, and Velcro for the bad. When we begin to cultivate a focus on "the good" and imprint these experiences with intentional practices, we begin to "hardwire happiness."[31] As we do this inner work, we become more resilient, less reactive, and navigate relationship challenges more effectively. As a result, we have more stable interactions and secure relational bonds.

The Difficult Pairing of Anxious and Avoidant Partners

Over the years, I have seen quite a few couples with opposite attachment pairings. This is always a difficult setup, because the needs for connection and reassurance in the anxious partner tend to activate the fears of engulfment in the avoidant partner. In an earlier time, this was called the Pursuer/Distancer dynamic and the negative feedback loop that can develop in these relationships becomes quite painful as the anxious partner becomes increasingly distressed about the distancing behavior of the other.

I recall how my client Serena struggled in her marriage to a successful, but self-absorbed and emotionally distant man. The two eventually divorced and she began to do a lot of inner work. After some time, she began to date a kind, open-hearted man who wanted a close relationship—a "secure attacher." They married and it was amazing to watch how her previously challenging behaviors began to fade as this man provided the engaged presence and responsive love she had always longed for. In this new marriage, her nervous system settled, and she became an entirely different person.

Annie and Andrew

Anxious Annie dragged Avoidant Andrew into couples therapy because she was convinced that there was something terribly wrong with their relationship. Annie explained in great detail how she had read many books on relationships and she knew that affection and communication were essential. In their early days of marriage, when Andrew came home, she would greet him at the door with a big hug and invite him to tell her all about his day. Andrew, however, was exhausted at the end of the day and he felt pounced on by Annie's exuberance. He needed some space to recover after all the relentless interaction at work. Annie was confused and hurt by this.

Annie grew up as an only child to a hard-working single mom. She would have liked to have played with other kids, but she was instructed to come home after school and remain safely inside until her mother arrived home later that evening. Annie was terribly lonely growing up and vowed that someday she would find someone to share her life with and never be lonely again. She imagined being married, and how she and her husband would talk together every night, sharing everything.

Andrew grew up in a chilly two-parent home with a mother who had no patience for needy, demanding children and an emotionally remote father, who retreated into the television when he was not at work. Andrew had no memory of anyone ever inquiring into his well-being. He did not recall ever being hugged or sitting in a parent's lap. When I ask him who his "go-to" person was as a child, he couldn't think of anyone. He does recall that his parents fought a lot and when they did, Andrew would retreat to his room to play online video games.

Andrew met bubbly, engaging Annie in a college class. She came up beside him one day as they were walking down the hall and began to talk about the class lecture with him. He was drawn to her sweet personality and they began to spend hours together, studying. This was perfect for someone who wanted company without having to talk much. Andrew had no idea how much talking would be expected of him until after they were married and moved in together. Annie had finally realized her dream of love, but Andrew was increasingly overwhelmed. She seemed to want to talk all the time, and he was expected to do half the talking.

When Annie and Andrew came to see me, they were trapped in the downward cycles of Annie seeking connection and Andrew getting more and more distant and shut down. She was overcome with fear and loneliness, and angry at the disappointment of her lifelong dream of companionship. She had come to believe that Andrew no longer loved or wanted her.

As we began to unpack their early histories, I explained how their histories led to two different wirings of their nervous systems. It was understandable that Anxious Annie would misinterpret Avoidant Andrew's need for space as rejection. It was understandable that Andrew would experience Annie's insistence on lots of conversation and emotional sharing, and more recently her escalating distress as unfamiliar and overwhelming.

In learning more about each other's attachment histories, they began to understand each other better, and interpret the other person's responses in a new way. As Annie began to understand Andrew's need for solitary settling, she stopped projecting rejection and abandonment onto him. She began to do some personal work of her own, comforting the lonely child that still lived in her, and integrating more resources that helped her stay more comfortably grounded in herself. She was able to calm down the need for constant reassurance that overwhelmed Andrew. Andrew engaged in some personal work that allowed him to experiment with opening up more and sharing more of his inner life. As Annie allowed Andrew some quiet time after work so that he could settle himself and regroup, she learned that he would engage later on. Andrew learned that sharing about his inner thoughts and feelings was not experienced as bothersome, but rather as a huge gift to Annie, who wanted to know him more deeply. This was inconceivable to him growing up in a home where no one engaged in "irrelevant" talk, and feelings were never mentioned. Over time, he learned to share more of himself, which reassured Annie that she was the special person in his life. As Andrew began to express more, he became more aware of his inner life, and began to discover more about the realm of emotion. He began to share some of his doubts and fears with Annie, and instead of dismissing him, as his mother would have done, Annie responded with warmth and caring. Andrew discovered that Annie was a kind and loving person who was safe to share his inner life with and Annie, feeling far more secure, relaxed about Andrew's need for downtime, no longer feeling rejected or wondering if he was hiding things from her. As their negative projections fell away, their nervous systems relaxed, and they found that mysterious "Goldilocks zone" between connection and independence.

CHAPTER 4

THE INNER CAST OF CHARACTERS

"Perhaps the depth of love can be calibrated by the number of different selves that are actively involved in a given relationship."

Carl Sagan

"We allow our lives to be run by our inner Rule Makers, Critics, Pushers, Perfectionists, Pleasers, Responsible Parents, and other selves. When we do, no real choices are available to us."

Hal and Sidra Stone

The Nesting Dolls

When I was a little girl, my godmother gave me a set of beautifully painted Russian nesting dolls. I was amazed as I opened them one by one. The outside doll was the grandmother, then came the mother, then a maiden, a girl, a smaller girl, and finally, when I thought the dolls could get no smaller, I opened the smallest girl to find a tiny baby. I still have those Russian nesting dolls and have collected others over time because they remind me of a truth about us—that nested within our psyches are the resonances of the past. Our bodies recall the felt sense of every age we have ever been.

The brain is an incredible organ, with its amazing array of neural networks that record every emotionally impactful experience we have ever had. The brain then organizes like with like and categorizes these experiences, clustering them together for quick association. As we travel the road of life, any situation that reminds us of a previous experience will call forward the feeling from that earlier time. The brain will open a neural network "file" from the scope of our emotional history and download neurochemicals into our nervous system. Some of those neurochemicals soothe us, some excite us, some create sadness and anxiety.

Life Scripts and Early Decisions

In our early years, we are particularly susceptible to the imprinting of significant emotional experiences. Based on our early experiences, we draw conclusions about who we are, who others are, and how life works for people like us. This includes our early experiences of being cared for and how safe we feel in attaching to important others. Out of these experiences we develop our complexes, our worldviews, and narratives that become the interpretative lens of our lives. All of this operates beneath our conscious awareness and we react in ways that open and close doors of possibility. Until we recognize that we are swimming in a worldview, like a fish in water, totally convinced that our constructed narrative is reality, we will never grasp that other narratives are possible. The complexes that drive our needs and defenses will continue to influence us for the rest of our lives until we become aware of them and begin to transform them. The past is not the past at all, so long as it is unconsciously influencing the present.

Our unexamined complexes gain validity over time because the interpretation of our life experiences seems to confirm them. People with abandonment complexes are on the lookout for indications that they are about to be abandoned. People who were treated like burdens in childhood become hesitant to ask for help and support in their adult lives, concerned that they may be bothering others. Those with histories of abuse carry more vigilance about future mistreatment. Those who were constantly torn down and criticized worry that they are unworthy of love. They may believe they are too stupid to reach for any form of success in their lives.

We each carry a set of individual complexes, but we also carry mother and father complexes. These can be positive or negative, and in an intimate relationship, we end up projecting them onto our partners. We don't mean to do this, it's just inevitable. As our early idealized projections flip from positive associations to negative ones, that same partner can begin to feel neglectful and selfish, possibly even dangerous. Complexes are more than mere thought-patterns. They activate emotions and strong body sensations.[32] They engulf us and become a total reality. When we are looking through the eyes of a complex, we don't see other possible interpretations for what we are experiencing.

Complexes descend on us suddenly and sometimes mysteriously. They hijack us without our being aware that we have been hijacked. One minute your partner is the sweet, love of your life; the next thing, he does something to remind you of your cold, judgmental father, whom you feared and could never seem to reach. The woman who was your Dream Girl gives you a withering look and suddenly becomes the Critical Mother of your youth. Now you are swimming upstream against a current of associations from the past where you could never win, where you had no voice or power, where loss or punishment pervaded the air. In that moment, you can't remember that this person is that beloved partner and someone you believed to be on your side. You enter a mysterious time warp, overwhelmed by feelings from long ago. You may find yourself fighting as if your very life was at stake. This reaction can be completely mystifying to a partner who has no idea what nerve they just touched or what they did to set this in motion. Your reaction can be just as confusing to you, until you begin to understand how your complexes get triggered. Complexes get in the way of relating because we overlay associations from the past onto the person we are relating with in the present.

THE INNER CAST OF CHARACTERS

In 1995, I began to work with the metaphor of having an "inner cast of characters." It became a way of personifying the different parts of me that were in conflict. As a new mother, I was enjoying a few months in the blissful cocoon of my home. I was nursing my infant son and advancing my culinary skills as I watched the Food Channel. My career ambitions were suspended in that lovely cocoon of time ... at least for a few months. Then they began to whisper to me from the background of my happy domestic life. I started to feel increasingly restless as the days ticked by. One day, I sat down and made a list of the "voices" that were chattering in my head. They seemed to be arguing with each other. Some came from roles I seemed unable to reconcile, some from simmering dreams and longings I had yet to realize. I also noticed that the feelings attached to these inner voices came from different ages and stages of my life and some were masculine in tone. I began to give each "voice" a name and to flesh them out as characters. Then I began a journaling process in which I gave each "inner character" a chance to express themselves, to describe their needs and agendas, and how they operated in my life. As I did this, I began to understand the warring sub-personalities that lived within me, and as I allowed them to express themselves by writing, the churning inside me began to calm down. Later on, I came to realize that I was engaged in a type of mindfulness practice, stepping back, observing my inner workings with curiosity, noting the thoughts, feelings, impulses, and longings without being overly identified with them. I began to find a quiet place inside that I started to refer to as my "calm core." I later learned that Arthur Deikman termed this the Observing Self.[33] In becoming familiar with my "inner cast of characters" I had lifted out of the fray. I was no longer compelled by the emotional pressure of one inner character or another and had a sense that I could make some choices about what aspects of self would be most beneficial in the varying aspects of my life. I could be intentional and "direct" the inner cast. As the quiet of my core deepened, I also began to recognize that there was some sort of guidance from within that came from a deeper place, beyond the pushing and pulling of all these inner selves and voices. In engaging in this process, my life became more centered and peaceful, and took on a whole new level of direction and meaning.

When I discovered Jungian psychology, and Jung's concept of "archetypal energies," his ideas gave me a framework to understand the process that I had been engaged in. I learned more about how our Ego identities develop, but that the Ego identity is not the totality of who we really are. Jung referred to the process of becoming more conscious and entering the process of self-exploration and inner growth, the journey of "individuation." Jung also gave me a name for that sense of inner guidance I was discovering as I dis-identified with all the interior pushes and pulls. He called this inner compass "the Self," something in us that is deeper than our Ego identity, something we can refer to and align with. As I did this, my life began to unfold in ways I never could have anticipated.

I wrote about this process in my book, *Negotiating the Inner Peace Treaty*.[34] In that book, I employ a theater metaphor because it helps us to understand our personal archetypal profile and "who" is on the stage of our lives at various times and situations. We also can discover who waits and watches from the wings, who is behind the curtain, and who is in the "shadow" of our lives. We have an Inner Cast of Characters, both public and private. They are various ages, carry different energies, and are up to all sorts of things. The more aware we are of what lives in our psyches, the more we can "direct" these energies, rather than merely reacting to the impulses they generate. Becoming conscious of what lives in us, and what (who) is activating our emotions in various situations is an ongoing process. The psyche is vast and there are things we have forgotten and disowned—they are relegated to the shadow lands of our lives. We also house potentials that we have not yet cultivated. These potentials lay like dormant seeds in the ground of our psyches, waiting to be awakened.

One of the processes I developed in working with an "inner cast" is what I call "Inner Round Table Work"™. Here, I gather various parts of self around an imaginary round table to dialogue, share differing perspectives, resolve conflicts, make decisions, and determine "who" should lead in a situation.

The journaling and dialogue work I engaged in led me into a lot of Inner Child work, the most important work of my life. Most people are familiar with the idea of having an Inner Child. What is less well understood, is that we house a group of Inner Children, at various ages, and in different modes of operation. I call this collection of children, "The Kids Behind the Curtain." Learning about these Inner Kids that reside in each of us, helps us to understand our life scripts and the influences that run so strongly in the under-stream of our lives. When we surface this material, we come to understand many of the choices we made that turned out so badly.[35]

We Slide Up and Down the Age Continuum

If you have never thought about having an Inner Cast of Characters, representing various ages and ways of operating, try tuning in to the chatter in your head, and ask yourself, "Who is talking right now?" As you are going about your day, notice how you slide up and down the age continuum as you interact with others. In one moment, you may feel like a capable adult. Then perhaps your boss, or a customer, or your spouse criticizes you. You may continue to present yourself on the outside like an adult, but inside you are stirred up and you may be sliding down the age track. If you really tuned into yourself, you might find that there is a part of you that feels hurt or scared, like a little kid. You might get defensive, or angry, or feel rebellious like you did as a teenager. Your body will tense, and whether you express this or not, whether you are consciously aware of this or not, an Inner Child is activated. Associative experiences of the past are cascading forward into the present moment. If you paused to explore this, you might find that this situation reminds you of a time in the past when you were blamed for something you didn't do or framed in a way that felt really unjust. You may become highly distrustful and wonder if this person is out to get you, or you might collapse into helplessness and unworthiness. It all depends on your history and your personal complexes.

We slide around the age continuum all the time in our interactions with a life partner. In an argument where you find yourself over-reacting, stop to consider why you were so reactive or defensive. What associations did this situation spark in your memory? What was the upset really about? If you track the sensations in your body rather than the thoughts in your head, you will most likely discover a memory of an earlier time that was painful. When you feel your nervous system rev up into some form of threat response, if you ask yourself, "How old do I feel in this moment?" you might discover that you feel fifteen, ten, five, or even younger. We will do more of this kind of exploratory work in Part Two of this book. For now, understand that what grabbed you and carried you away was a complex, a cluster of associations around a theme, with a history, a "lens" to view through, and a set of sensations in the body.

The Kids Behind the Curtain

Some of our Inner Children don't show up until we have entered an intimate relationship and become attached to someone who really starts to matter. This opens up those association "files" in the brain and they download into our nervous systems. We feel a level of vulnerability that was not previously present before we became attached and began to build a life with this person. Associations with an earlier time begin and younger selves come out from behind the curtain with memories of those early life experiences, sparking feelings we felt long ago. These "kids" come out from behind the curtain with all sorts of needs, ideas and concerns that begin to cloud the relational field between two people who were once basking in the wonder of enchantment. *Consider that in every relationship, there are two inner casts and encountering the Inner Kids in yourself and your partner is an inevitable part of an intimate relationship.* A major component of the work I do with couples is helping them to identify and understand these Inner Children and how central they are to our relationship problems. A couple that learns to be aware of and manage the needs of these Inner Kids, while keeping a Healthy Adult at the wheel of the relationship can work through almost anything.

The Scope of Our Inner Children

The emotional scope of our Inner Children is wide. They can be vulnerable, scared, needy, selfish, sensitive, insecure, impatient, impulsive, rambunctious, angry, anxious, lonely, sad, submissive, pleasing, compliant, and incredibly sweet. Our innocent, wonder-filled Inner Children also open the doorway into our intuitive and spiritual lives. This was something that Jesus understood well when he said, "Let the little children come to me, because theirs is the kingdom of heaven."

The Protector-Defenders

When we are young, we begin to develop inner Protector-Defenders, with strategies for getting needs met and protecting us from vulnerability. Much of the trouble adults get into in love relationships has to do with the strategies and defenses employed by our Inner Protector-Defenders. They are strategies we devised when we were kids, with little power, voice, or choice. However, these same strategies in an adult love relationship will disrupt the bond and keep us from the depth of love we long for.

Our inner Protector-Defenders have a range of styles. They can be overly cautious and suspicious, aggressive, cynical, controlling, manipulative, entitled, or demanding. They might silence you and encourage submission and compliance out of a deeply embedded belief that countering someone you need (love) results in retribution, denigration, or some other form of harm.

In relationships, our Inner Children and their Protector-Defenders are on the lookout for threats and danger. They are also on the lookout for the possible fulfillment of something they have always longed for. The hopes and dreams we project onto potential partners come from this place, and tremendous "chemistry" is created out of the possibility of fulfillment. When high chemistry is present, *it is our Inner Children who pick our partners, in the hope that this person will fit into our "completion" story.* When the hoped-for expectation of this fulfillment does not occur, our Inner Children can become extremely distressed, or feel betrayed and angry. As hope is lost, we experience a resurgence of the same pain we felt in the wounding experiences of our early lives.

As we grow into adulthood, we developed Adult Selves that can fulfill the roles and responsibilities of our lives. We have personas, the public face we show the world, and private selves that are only known to us, or a few trusted others. If we had parents and caring authority figures who provided guidance, reassurance, and helpful suggestions for living, we internalize their voices and hear them when we need comfort and encouragement. Unfortunately, we also internalize punishing, limiting, shaming voices from the past, and these voices can continue to haunt and torment us as Inner Judges and Critics. An inferiority complex can haunt a person for a lifetime, capping off what they reach for or ever expect to achieve in both work and love. An abandonment complex will whisper that love is only temporary, that everyone leaves or betrays eventually. Those who suffered early emotional deprivation may believe that their needs are not important and will never be met. People who do well in life have an inner resilience which is undergirded by Inner Comforters and Encouragers, and selves that can take a wide view of life. These inner resources help people to recover from loss, tolerate frustration and make their way through challenging situations.

When a person encounters "the rest of the cast" in their partner, it can frighten them. They may even feel deceived. "If I had known you were this needy, I never would have married you!" says Amy. Josh didn't know himself as needy until he began to experience terrified feelings every time Amy left for a business trip. "I just didn't realize you would never be home!" he replies. Amy is frustrated because she explained all of this before they got married. "Would you please stop exaggerating! I only travel a few days a month. You knew this from the day you met me!" she retorts. Adult Josh feels a lot of shame about how needy he feels. He is angry at himself and angry at Amy. He *did* know this, but it doesn't help him now. It's the child inside who feels like it is forever when Amy is gone. In therapy, we begin to unpack the history behind this. Josh's father died when he was eight and his mother had to take a job that required her to travel. When Josh's mother was gone, he was left in the care of her elderly aunt. The aunt fed Josh and got him to school but showed little empathy for his grief or the anxiety Josh felt about his mother's absence. As a young boy, Josh constantly wondered if his mother was OK. Perhaps she had forgotten about him? Would she ever return? When Amy travels, the eight-year-old still nested in Josh's psyche activates and he is filled with anxiety. We wear adult faces, but there are times when we are overcome by the needs of our Inner Children. As Amy began to understand this history, she felt less exasperated with Josh's "neediness." As Josh began to understand it, he learned ways to comfort and soothe the inner eight-year-old while Amy was gone.

IN EVERY RELATIONSHIP THERE
ARE TWO INNER CASTS

In the early stage of being in love, lovers spend time gazing into each other's eyes, kissing, caressing, making love, or just lying in each other's arms. They are in a time out of time, just being, with little concern for what they end up doing. It might be odd to think of it this way, but in the early part of a relationship our Inner Children are in a state of hopefulness and delight.

When two people get together, they are not thinking about how they have two "inner casts," and that the various selves will begin to interact. Some of those selves will do very well together, others will frighten and disappoint, and the couple will have to resolve these conflicts. Couples who are doing well together have Adult Selves that are in charge, planning and managing life. Their Inner Children are safe, cared for, and nestled inside. Couples who are not doing well, have Inner Children that are stirred up, and their Protector-Defenders are activated. While it is important to be aware of the needs of our Inner Children, we do not want them to be the dominant force in our relationships. The highly charged arguments we get into as adults are actually taking place between the two partners' Inner Children and their Protector-Defenders. We are dressed up in adult clothing, but our Inner Children are center stage at these moments. When our Inner Children and their Defenders begin to run the relationship, you can be certain there will be struggle and suffering, as partners try to manage the impossible demands of the other person's child ego states. We cannot manage the demands of an adult relationship from a child ego state. In an adult relationship, we need for our Healthy Adult selves to be in charge. As we learn to lead from our healthy adult states, we can address the needs and concerns of our nested children and attend to their vulnerability.[36]

When we become conscious of "who" is operating in us, the complexes we carry, and the strategies and defenses we go to, it gives us the opportunity to do some inner work before a troublesome inner self takes the wheel of the bus and drives the rest of the cast down an unhappy road. Anytime we experience a strong reaction in a relationship, it is an invitation to ask, "What is being stirred up in me?" When we feel strongly compelled to take an action, it is wise to ask, "Who is it in me that is compelling me to do this? Who is driving the bus?" When you can identify the physical sensations that accompany the activation of your Scared Little Girl or Rebel Boy, or the Demanding Three-Year-Old, you have the possibility of employing inner resources to soothe, contain, and redirect strong impulses. When we unconsciously discharge the energy of our riled up Inner Children, it always makes things worse. With self-awareness, and drawing from our inner resources, we can redirect troublesome "cast members" away from the driver's seat and invite our wiser, steadier, relational selves to take the lead. The research in interpersonal neurobiology confirms that the neural tracks that run through our brains can be remapped and we can develop new tracks that transform our darker impulses and the destructive reactivity in our relationships.

The Self is our inner compass, which is continually opening doors into inner resources, places in the psyche that will heal us. The Self is always inviting us to transcend the limiting definitions of our Egos and expand the life narratives that constrict who we are and what is possible. When we begin to pay attention to the invitations of the Self, and align our lives with this inner compass, we open doors of possibility that were not there before. These doors open into a vast storehouse of resource, wisdom, and archetypal potential, but we need to clear away the impediments to these resources. To revisit the definition of an archetype—archetypes are systems of energy (we can imagine them as brain states) organized around a role (Mother, Hero, Villain, and so on) or a theme (abandonment, the hero's journey, the fatal flaw, the redemption story, and so on). Archetypes are found across history in many cultures and are common manifestations of patterns embedded in the human psyche and the human experience. When we become conscious of the archetypal patterns that are running in us (unconsciously), we can begin to transform our ways of being and seeing. When we integrate archetypal energies and perspectives into our lives, we expand our potential for living.

Intimate relationships are powerful drivers in the journey of individuation. They stir up things from the past, and invite us to revisit, resolve, and rescript some of our early conclusions about life and others, and to revamp old strategies for getting needs met. This is why relationships can be such a powerful impetus for growth and evolution into the fullness of our potential.[3]

---

[3] Note to therapists: The historical evolution of what we are currently calling "parts psychology" can be traced through "Active Imagination" (Jung), "Two-chair Work" (Gestalt – Fritz Perls), "Inner Cast of Characters" Work (Wakefield), "Voice Dialogue" (Hal and Sidra Stone), and, more recently, "Internal Family Systems" (Schwartz).

CHAPTER 5

THE SWAMPLANDS OF LOVE

*"Love is a force of destiny whose power reaches
from heaven to hell."*

C.G. Jung

Michael and Marilyn

Michael is married to Marilyn, but he has a hard time believing that he has captured the heart of such a beautiful woman. While he is a successful thirty-eight-year-old man, the Teenage Boy inside him still carries a belief that beautiful women are always on the lookout for someone better and eventually they leave you. Michael's mother left the family when he was twelve and ran away with another man. The Nerdy High-Schooler in him still remembers being humiliated by the rejections of attractive girls, who opted for the popular jocks and never gave him a chance. Adult Michael elevated himself with brains instead of brawn. He is now the youngest partner in a big law firm, but the younger selves that still live in his psyche won't allow him to feel secure or worthy at home. He has become highly insecure about Marilyn.

When Marilyn met Michael, she was sick and tired of men pursuing her for her exterior beauty. She has brains of her own, in addition to her devoted heart, which is something that Michael recognized and valued. Michael recognized her intelligence, treated her with respect, and with Michael, Marilyn felt seen and loved for her inner beauty. Marilyn has early wounding of her own. Her father left the family for another woman when she was ten and disappeared from her life. Her bitter mother warned Marilyn repeatedly that men were just Players and Marilyn vowed that she would find a man who would be faithful and devoted to her. She wanted to marry a man who didn't chase skirts, someone secure and solid, and she believed that she had found this in Michael.

They had been married for about three years when those insecure younger selves living inside Michael began to whisper to him. He became jealous and suspicious, which bothered Marilyn greatly. It offended her sense of personal integrity and caused her to feel misunderstood and unappreciated. Then, at an office party, she overheard his coworkers joking about his steamy flirtation with the cute receptionist. She felt frightened and confused by this. The ten-year old girl nested in her psyche remembered her mother's words of warning. Michael was not serious about the flirtation, but it boosted his ego and reassured the insecure, Nerdy Teenager inside, who did not believe he could hang onto a beautiful woman like Marilyn. After hearing about the receptionist, Marilyn began to wonder about Michael's true character and his commitment to her. Maybe he was not who she thought he was. Maybe he was just a Player like her father. Perhaps she had been a fool. She felt self-protective and began to withdraw emotionally and sexually. This amplified the fears of abandonment and betrayal that had already gotten stirred up in Michael. He began to track her whereabouts. When she discovered this, she talked to her friends about it. They were alarmed and told her that Michael was far too controlling, that she should not put up with this. Marilyn became angry and threatened to leave him if he didn't stop his "crazy" behavior. This was the opposite of the reassurance that Michael needed, and he found himself continuing the seemingly "harmless" flirtation with the pretty receptionist. Michael and Marilyn were caught in a vicious cycle, projecting and reacting, each pulling up material from their difficult earlier lives.

If we think about this as a love story, it began with the archetypal Ideal Lovers. She was the Fair Princess, finally won. He was the Promising Suitor, faithful and true. They began a fairy tale life together, until their insecure attachment complexes got the better of them. Each fell off the pedestal of idealization and cast the other in their most feared role. He became the Untrustworthy Player and she the Opportunistic Seductress. These one-dimensional characters crowded the stage of their love story, and they could no longer find the security they once felt with each other. Their interlocking complexes evoked defensive gambits which made things worse, and they began to drown in dangerous waters, swirling with unconscious material.

When Michael and Marilyn came to see me, they were both convinced that the stories they had spun in their heads were true. Each was evoking defenses from the other that were escalating their sense of threat. Learning about his ego-reassuring flirtations escalated Marilyn's fears and protective withdrawal. Her withdrawal escalated Michael's insecurity and compelled his compensatory need to flirt. His accusations and controlling behaviors contributed to her angry protest, which increased his fears of abandonment.

Michael and Marilyn were so armored up that neither could reveal the deep vulnerability they felt at the potential loss of the other. They had no frame of reference for how two intelligent adults could become so entangled by the Abandoned Kids inside of them, who were driving their fears, projections, and defensive behaviors. Their early years together had been so sweet, and both were longing for the refuge they had once found in each other.

As they began to understand their inner cast of characters, they came to see how the Vulnerable Teenagers inside were struggling with ancient fears, they began to feel compassion for themselves and each other. With increased awareness, they were able to exit the protective mechanisms that kept them separated and insecure and rebuild their sense of trust. They stopped casting each other as characters in a sad tale and felt excited by the prospect of writing their own love story, a different story from the ones their parents had lived. As they did this, they became the devoted couple they longed to be.

We Are Story Making Creatures

Human beings are story making creatures. We spin stories to make sense of our world and those stories become the larger narratives of our lives. We cast ourselves and others in these narratives and anticipate how everyone will play out the parts. Our narratives become the lens through which we interpret life. Our worldview includes our underlying complexes and the maladaptive coping strategies we adopted as children, and we gather evidence for the truth of all of this as we move along the path of life. We make many decisions in our early lives about who we are and what we deserve. We also decide who others are and what we can expect from them. Once we become invested in a life narrative, we ignore evidence to the contrary.

As we become more conscious, we begin to separate out from the stories we constructed and how we were cast in those stories. We can recognize the rumbling of our "younger selves," and become better able to maintain an adult outlook and manage those feelings of vulnerability or demand. Our intimate relationships stir up a lot of memories from the past; feelings that have been slumbering for decades emerge. Once we understand this, it becomes an invitation to inner work rather than a signal to move into defense.

Expectations, Assumptions and Projections

Expectations and assumptions can be identified and voiced. Projections are more difficult. They operate outside of conscious awareness, products of the association mechanisms of the mind. All of us carry embedded fears, unmet needs, and deep longings. In romantic love, we meet our positive projections when we feel that "click" of fulfillment, the hope that this person will be the one we have always longed for. When people behave in certain ways, they "hook" our projections. Then we engage in confirmation bias—collecting evidence to validate the seeming truth we want to see. It's not that our projections aren't true; it's just that they are rarely as true as we make them. There is often a kernel of truth in a projection, but we amplify this kernel into a total reality, and it obscures other important information. This goes for both our positive and negative projections. Carl Jung once said that we don't "make" projections, we "meet" them. In many cases, we only become aware that we have projected when we bump into something that negates the projection.

One of the biggest problems with projections is that they often masquerade as intuitions, and while I support the validity of what we call intuition, the problem is that some of what we believe to be an "intuition" is actually an activated complex. Sometimes our intuitions, which may be strongly felt, can be the product of a wound, distorting our perception of what is really happening. We are definitely sensing something, but it may be an indication to do our own inner work. This is what was going on with Michael and Marilyn. Each of them was projecting that which they most feared from their difficult pasts. They believed that what they were experiencing was "true," unaware that they were responding to the deeply embedded fears of their Inner Teens. This was all happening outside of their awareness. Their interlocking complexes made it impossible to talk openly about their fears and longings or to re-establish a secure connection.

Our highly efficient brains are association machines. They tell us "this is like that." Projections are not pathological; in fact, they are simply inevitable. On the positive side, they aid in our survival. Falling in love involves meeting someone who captures our positive projections, someone who fulfills a deeply held "completion story," of which we may not be consciously aware. We don't realize that we are relating out of our romantic imaginations. Then as we move more deeply into the relationship, we bump into things that don't fit. In many cases, we may have already gotten married, and invested our lives and hearts with this other person. It is a scary thought that most people get married in the early stage of enchantment, awash with projections. Later, we meet "the rest of the cast" as they come out from behind the curtain of that person's adult persona or get activated by a deepening vulnerability.

You Are Not What I Expected[37]

Polly Young-Eisendrath writes eloquently about projections and how we grapple with the projections our partner sends our way. Some of these projections we love ("You are everything I've always longed for"), some we fight against (negative labels our partners give us about bothersome differences). "You are not who I thought you were," is one of the most painful realizations that lovers come to, and this is inevitable in any relationship, because no one is ever who we think they are. Our early love enchantments involve a significant exchange of positive projections. In those early days of love, everything we do and say carries special meaning. We interpret facial expressions, words, gestures, and nuances in the tone of voice, swept along in the archetypal story of longing and fulfillment. Later on, during experiences of disappointment or conflict, our projections begin to crumble. In shock, we can suddenly flip to a set of negative projections and find ourselves lost in the confusing forest of a dark fairy tale.

Robert and Sara

Robert and Sara got off to a beautiful start. They met in their final year of college. Robert was finishing up his accounting degree and Sara was studying to become a nurse. During the last semester of school, they were inseparable. As Robert began to consider life after college, he couldn't conceive of a life without her. The thought that he might lose her to someone else was painful. Sara was the ultimate woman, everything he had ever longed for—warm, loving, sexy, and smart. He had always been a bit shy around women, but Sara put him at ease. She seemed to accept him completely, just as he was, with no pressure to be anything more. Robert had grown up with a single mother, who worked two jobs and constantly pushed him to maximize his future prospects with his innate gift for math. There was no time for frivolities in his life; any divergence from school achievement was met with cold disapproval. This was how his mother showed her love, pushing him towards a better life that would lift him out of the financial insecurity she constantly lived with. When Robert met Sara, he was hungry for warmth and unconditional acceptance. She provided this and he began to picture a life with her. She was his Dream Girl, and he asked her if she would follow him to the dream job he had been offered in Atlanta. Would she marry him and love him forever? Her "yes" was the happiest moment of his life.

Sara fell head over heels in love with Robert the night he rescued her in the pouring rain, stuck by the side of the road with a flat tire. She called, and he came immediately and skillfully changed her tire. He got soaked in the process, but never said a word of complaint. That night he fulfilled a deep longing for someone to be there when she needed them. He soothed the fear that having needs made her a nuisance. This Rescuing Hero became her Knight in Shining Armor. Sara grew up in a stable, affluent, but emotionally chilly household. Her entire life, she sought to capture her father's attention, but he seemed to have little time for her, and she learned not to turn to him for help of any kind. Robert's adoration and responsiveness touched her deeply. She had always longed for someone she could truly depend on, who would be there when she needed him. Robert was that guy. Drawn to his attentiveness and devotion, she imagined the wonderful home they would make together. He would be a warm and loving father and they would have a home filled with connection and caring, so different from her own upbringing. Robert's career prospects were excellent and that would be the only thing her parents would care about. With great hope and optimism, they moved to Atlanta and were married in a fairy tale wedding the following spring. Here is a picture of the unconscious projections that were active in Robert and Sara's relationship.

After Robert and Sara moved to Atlanta, they both began their careers. Sara worked long shifts as a nurse and often came home too tired to talk or to respond to Robert's romantic overtures. This disappointed Robert, but he grew up setting his personal needs aside, so he did not complain. He told himself, "Be a grown-up and focus on your own career." So he set a new career goal, lived more deeply into the role of Provider for their upcoming family, and began to work longer hours. Over time he became more pre-occupied with his work and focused less on Sara. She noticed this, and it unsettled the Neglected Inner Child inside. She longed for the Attentive Lover that Robert had been in their college days. She told herself that Robert was not like her father, and that she should be grateful that he was such a good Provider.

Their first child was born, but Robert did not get up in the night to help with the baby the way Sara had anticipated. She complained about this, but Robert defended himself with an explanation that his work was incredibly stressful and required him to be well rested. Up in the night with a crying baby, she often felt angry and hurt, but she told herself, "He is working hard to make a life for our family. I shouldn't complain." One evening, Robert forgot to stop by the dry-cleaners and pick up the dress Sara was planning to wear to his office Christmas party. She didn't realize this until they were getting dressed for the party. Robert secretly felt guilty about this but defended himself by explaining how much he had on his mind these days. Sara repressed her anger and found a nice dress that made her feel quite ordinary, certainly not the stylish wife of a soon-to-be partner. During the evening, she noticed the slim, single, young women at the party, dressed in their slinky dresses, and she thought about how frumpy she looked in her dull dress, with all the baby weight she was struggling to lose. Her anxious feelings mounted, and on the drive home, Sara exploded. She accused Robert of humiliating her, of being self-absorbed and neglectful. Robert, not understanding why Sara was so upset, told her she was being superficial and ridiculous. Unable to make him understand, she fell into a stony silence, and thought about how Robert, who had once been so attentive was becoming more and more like her dismissive, work-absorbed father. Later that week, when she arrived home from a long nursing shift, she found him sitting down watching television at night, with laundry in the washer and dishes in the sink. Another argument ensued. When had he become so selfish and entitled? Didn't he realize that she worked too? Why was he treating her like a servant? Later that night, they lay on opposite sides of the bed and Robert began to think about how he never had a moment's rest. It seemed that he was never enough, always needing to do more at work and at home. Sara was starting to sound like his mother—critical, cold, impossible to please.

Their second child was born, and as her loneliness grew, Sara turned her attention away from Robert and invested her life energies in being a Nurturing Mother. Her children filled a lot of her needs for warmth and she looked to Robert less for that. A growing gulf was developing between them. Their easy sexual connection became difficult, and their memory of the passionate young people they had been began to fade. They were both tired and they rarely made love. They both loved their children and moved increasingly into the archetype of Devoted Mother and Responsible Father. Sara noticed that her friends complained about the same kind of issues in their marriages—feelings of emotional disconnection, of not being understood or appreciated. She thought of her parent's empty marriage and wondered if this was where she and Robert were headed. Was this all that could be expected of married life?

Robert quietly mourned the loss of the warm connection that he and Sara once had. He overheard the comments of other men in the office, complaining about how women lured you into marriage, but once the wedding ring went on, the sex ended. For Robert, it wasn't just about the sex. He missed the way Sara used to look at him, he used to be her Hero. He thought about how long it had been since he felt appreciated or wanted. He didn't initiate sex much these days. He had been turned down one too many times while the kids were young. The kids were older now and Sara was not as tired. Her interest in sex had returned, but Robert seemed indifferent now. She began to wonder if he was still attracted to her. They were unable to talk about these deeply sensitive feelings without arguing and one night, Robert commented that the young women in his office paid him more attention than Sara did. This inflamed Sara and she informed Robert that she regularly brushed off the come-ons of a certain attractive doctor at the hospital where she worked. They began to shout, trade insults and jealous accusations, fighting as if their very lives were at stake. Gripped by underlying fears and concerns, but unable to drop their defenses, neither could remember that this other person had once been the answer to their hopes, dreams, and deepest longings.

Suddenly their eight-year-old daughter walked into the room, looking frightened. "Mommy, Daddy, what's wrong? Why are you yelling at each other?" The two adults stopped in their tracks and glared at each other. Turning to their daughter, they tried to reassure her that everything was all right. Later, lying on separate sides of the bed, Robert dropped his wall and said, "I'm afraid for us. We need help." Sara turned towards him and replied, "I agree. It's like we lost each other along the way."

Our disappointed expectations in love can lead us into a desperate despair. The complexes that grip us in moments like this have a powerful undertow. When our early life fears and concerns invade our adult lives, our projections begin to flip to fearful ones, sourced from the important attachment relationships of our early lives. Sara was captured by a Negative Father Complex, with Robert becoming the cold, dismissive father of her youth, whose emotional disregard felt cruel. Robert was captured by a Negative Mother Complex in which Sara became the critical mother whom he could never please, the mother who demanded much of him but provided little warmth to sustain him. Both Sara and Robert were swimming upstream against a current of associations from the past, overtaken by the needs of their Inner Children, longing for the other to return to the warm, responsive, loving, affirming person they had known so many years ago.

Sitting in my office Robert and Sara begin to express their complaints about the other person and all the hurt they felt. Sara told me, "I thought he would be so different from my father. I thought he would be warm and involved, but he is self-absorbed, dismissive, and distant." Robert says, "I thought she would always be warm and understanding. When we were dating, she admired me. She was so appreciative of everything I did for her. I never dreamed she could be so critical and demanding. When I look in her eyes, all I see is disappointment."

I see Robert and Sara caught in the tangled forest of a dark fairy tale, with a lot of negative casting going on. Robert speaks of how hard he has worked to build a life for them and how lonely he is. Sara speaks of how much it means to be a mother to their children, but how much she misses their early years. I know the young lovers they once were are banked down somewhere within them, buried under resentment and hurt. I ask Sara about their early days and she begins to speak of a time when they had no money and all the time in world for each other. "We lost each other along the way," said Sara. Robert hangs his head, looking lonely and bereft. Then he looks up. "I remember those days too. I still love you. You are the most important person in my life. I don't know what to do but there has to be a way to find each other again." He has dropped the bitter tone and is speaking gently, from his heart. Sara looks up and meets his eyes. There is warmth there and she smiles tentatively. He holds out his hand and she takes it. The mending work has begun.

Entering the Dark Fairy Tale

When two lovers experience this flip of projections, they begin to write a grim story—a dark fairy tale. This is where our confirmation bias begins to work against us. Our lens has narrowed, and we are now gathering evidence for how this person is threatening, hurtful, unloving, and unlovable. Distressing pairings begin to evolve as we evoke reactions from each other. The Rescuing Hero becomes a Tyrannical Bully, the Girl of Your Dreams becomes an Ice Princess. Couch Potatoes are in the judgmental gaze of Critical Mothers, Judgmental Fathers stir up Scared Little Girls or Rebel Daughters, Scornful Queens evoke Whiny Wimps, and Misers, Martyrs, Untouchable Saints, Needy Boys, Cheaters, and Scorned Women all arrive to play their parts.

We Lost Each Other Along the Way

As we move more deeply into the responsibilities of adult life, we can easily lose touch with the Enchanted Lovers we once were— those two people who could linger in bed, touching, tender and filled with fascination about this wonderful Other. We lose the Playful Lovers inside who could wander through a lazy Sunday afternoon, where being together was all that mattered.

The negative projections we overlay in our relationship disillusionments are almost always parental—the dark sides of Mother and Father. As we move more deeply into relationship our ancient feelings and insecure attachment complexes fire up. The jarring disappointments we encounter as the projections crumble invite us to close our hearts and sometimes to armor up. We wonder how it is that someone who once felt so safe can now feel so dangerous. Because we get so little guidance on how to move through this stage of disillusionment, we move into defensive gambits that only make matters worse.

Chapter 6
MISBEGOTTEN SOLUTIONS

"Where love rules, there is no will to power,
and where power predominates, love is lacking.
The one is the shadow of the other."

C.G. Jung

We get very little guidance about how to get out of the swamplands once we find ourselves there. Because of this, people fall into "misbegotten solutions." This chapter is about the things we do to try to solve our relationship difficulties, solutions that only make things worse.

It's Not About the Dishwasher

Elliot and Max are arguing vehemently about the way Max loads the dishwasher. Max is appalled. He has just entertained six of their friends with his extraordinary skills as a chef and his natural ability to stir up lively conversation. He can't believe that all Elliot can think about at the end of such a wonderful evening is how he loads the dishwasher! Elliot is insisting on the "right" way to load a dishwasher, but what he is really upset about is how much money Max spent on the food and wine, and how introverted Elliot often feels like an outsider in those animated conversations at dinner. However, Elliot is not able to talk about what is really bothering him, so he begins to fuss over the dishwasher. Elliot has been calculating the cost of this evening since Max started to plan it. He was upset about the expenditure before the party even started and was in a sour mood most of the evening. Max noticed this but ignored him. He was not about to let Elliot spoil his own enjoyment. Max believes that Elliot is way too uptight about money. They both make good money, and entertaining friends in their lovely home is important to him. Max has the ability to pick up museum quality antiques at auctions and estate sales for pennies on the dollar, and he believes this demonstrates his appreciation for spending wisely. Max doesn't feel seen or valued for what he brings to the relationship—the fun, the food, the impressive design of their home, and the interesting friends he brought into the relationship. They are arguing about the dishwasher, but their argument is not really about the dishwasher; it is about all these other underlying issues. They can't seem to talk about them because the conversation escalates so quickly, and they polarize into their invested positions. Neither can listen deeply enough to understand the underlying anxieties, longings, and the history around these. Both feel unappreciated and misunderstood.

People are rarely arguing about what they are arguing about, which is why we find ourselves in heated arguments over "nothing." We also have arguments that seem unresolvable because we are not in touch with the underlying needs and vulnerabilities that are driving our intense reactions. When our partner's ways of operating are foreign to us or offend our deeply invested values, our nervous systems get activated. "Suggestions" are offered, and if not responded to, we resort to more insistent attempts at change. When one person does not understand why something is so important or upsetting to the other, requests for change can be easily dismissed.

Without insight and understanding, differences can become con-flicts and can develop into significant power struggles.

The Four Horseman of the Apocalypse

Couples researcher John Gottman has offered a name for the destructive gambits two people can move into when they are attempting to get an intimate partner to be who they want them to be. He calls them *The Four Horsemen of the Apocalypse: criticism, defensiveness, contempt, and stonewalling*.[38] They tend to pair with each other. Criticism elicits defensiveness or withdrawal, and when people withdraw, it escalates the other person's need to get through, which can lead to expressions of contempt. When the four horsemen are galloping through a relationship, it is headed for demise.

Other Negative Gambits

Criticism can also lead to counter complaining (a form of defensiveness), turning a complaint back on the other person. "I wouldn't do _____, if you would only _____." "I only did _____, because you did _____." When a partner's response to our distress is dismissive or inadequate, we feel hurt. In response to hurt, some people escalate their demands, others sulk, some will punish by withholding affection or attention. Blaming, shaming, even bullying can occur. Contempt can be demonstrated in snarky sideways comments, eye rolling, deep sighs, diagnosing, or ignoring the other as if they were not even worthy of engagement. Making a partner feel guilty can be an effective defense if the other person houses an insecure Inner Pleaser. Skillful manipulators will feign surprise or offense when confronted with being manipulative. Seduction can be used to gain power or to soothe ruffled feathers when there is a fear that perhaps one has gone too far with negative strategies.

Because partners live together and get to know each other so well, they know where the other person's "raw spots" are.[39] The low blows people can level, become particularly cruel when there is a feeling of desperation. What is so sad is that most of the time, each person is longing for the other to put their weapons down and respond in a way that says, "I care for you; I want to resolve things. Please, can we stop hurting each other? How can we get back to loving the way we used to?"

Conflict engaging couples have power struggles that are overt. They have repetitive arguments that go nowhere, becoming emotionally exhausted in the process. Conflict avoidant couples can become quite passive-aggressive. Passive aggression is one of the ways that people experience themselves as having power when they cannot communicate their distress directly. Adults who develop this strategy often act confused or innocent when confronted with hurtful actions. They "forget" important errands, don't follow through on agreements. They sulk or spend beyond the discussed budget. They may "accidentally" destroy something the other values or embarrass the partner in public with "innocent" comments, jokes, or careless behaviors.

The Creation of No-fly Zones

Some couples solve their struggle by avoiding any topic or activity that might raise the possibility of a disagreement. Disagreements create too much anxiety, so they make U-turns away from anything that might cause conflict. Couples get worn out from fighting and call a chilly truce. They are no longer at war, but nothing is resolved. They are in a cease-fire, with a clearly delineated "no-fly zone." A no-fly zone is a demilitarized buffer where warring factions agree not to enter. The no-fly zones that couples create are often unspoken, but clearly understood. No-fly zones tend to expand over time because avoiding conflict is rewarding in the short run. Unfortunately, relationship vitality and personal growth lie on the other side of the topics they cannot talk about. A couple operating like this will become more superficial. In being civil to one another, their conversations will be shallower, avoiding the realm of deep feeling. They may "get along," but the relationship won't deepen or grow, because growth would require them to enter the no-fly zone. If this same couple could learn to enter that scary zone, if they could also fly though it into the land of potential and possibility, their entire relationship would become revitalized, and they would discover deepening levels of intimacy and fulfillment.

Shadow-Boxing

In many of our intense conflicts we are "shadow-boxing," fighting against something we cannot name—something outside of our conscious awareness. Our partner touches a place of vulnerability, something with roots that go deeper than the incident at hand, but we aren't self-aware enough to understand what got activated. Anytime we are dealing with material that lies outside our conscious awareness, it is "shadow material." When we become really upset with a partner, they may well have done something objectionable, but we attach additional meaning and motivation to their actions; we project this onto them, and this amplifies our reaction. Our partner may not have intended any harm, but our reaction will set them off and invite defensiveness. The partner may feel confused or upset because they feel unjustly accused. Even when they have engaged in some breach of kindness or trust, our reaction, as understandable as it may be, will make things more difficult to resolve. It will evoke defense, withdrawal, perhaps counterattack, and round and round we will go, "shadow-boxing," our brains downloading stress neurochemicals that lead us more deeply into threat response. Our vulnerable Inner Children will be interacting, and their Protector Defenders will be in full force. While it may seem like we are arguing in present time, we will most assuredly be fighting ghosts of the past.[40]

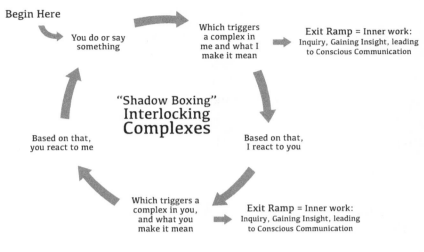

© Chelsea Wakefield 2019

While real violations of trust do occur in relationships, most of our conflict cycles are about those ghosts from the past. What we most need in those moments is comfort and reassurance. We need information that would help us settle back down into the belief that this partner cares for us and considers us and didn't mean to intentionally hurt or scare us. If these negative cycles happen too often, without any deeper understanding taking place, the partners can begin to feel hopeless about the relationship. It becomes easy to imagine an ongoing struggle with this impossible person. Catastrophic decisions are made, and a sad resignation descends, where a resolution would be possible with a deeper understanding. Many of these resignations are never spoken. We begin to "cast" our partners as a character in our developing narrative—with negative overtones. The ghosts of the past will lead to projections that will evoke corresponding responses in the partner—all of them archetypal. Critical Mothers will evoke Sulky, Resentful Sons; Judgmental, Controlling Fathers will meet Rebel Daughters or approval-seeking Good Girls; Domineering Bullies will stir up frightened Inner Children who act like turtles, pulling into their protective shells. As the love story of longing and fulfillment fades, the couple will enter their dark fairy tale, unaware that they are being carried along by powerful undercurrents.

The Drama Triangle

Years ago, Stephan Karpman identified an archetypal pattern that underlies unresolvable conflicts. He named it the Drama Triangle.[41] It involves three positions that people travel around when they are not self-aware, or willing to take responsibility and deal clearly and directly with each other. They will move around the triangle, switching from Victim, to Persecutor, to Rescuer.

When caught in this triangle, Victims will collapse in fear, unable to think clearly. They will lose their ability to speak up or set boundaries, abdicate what they need or want, believe they deserve nothing, begin to take more responsibility than the situation warrants, and apologize profusely in an effort to evoke mercy. I want to emphasize that there are true victims in life and in the world, who are legitimately wronged, but there are others who are centrally identified with this archetype and limit their lives by this identification. People who carry the archetypal energy of Victim magnetize Persecutors, Exploiters, and Abusers who seem to have special sensors for finding them.

Rescuers need someone to rescue and like the one-down nature of rescuing. It makes them feel strong and valuable (this can cover deeper feelings of being unlovable or defective). They may not like the change in the dynamic of a relationship where the person they rescued begins to gain ground, discover themselves, develop their own strengths, and may no longer need a Rescuer in life. Rescuers can become angry Persecutors if they don't receive the appreciation, loyalty, or reciprocal accommodation and sacrifices that they believe is deserved.

While some people are chronic Persecutors, others move into this archetype after they have been in the Victim archetype for too long, or when the Rescuer feels the anger that comes from no longer being needed or appreciated. People who feel deeply wronged, persecute. A Persecutor can also be someone who houses an Overly Entitled, Spoiled Inner Child who takes more than he or she will ever give, and expects everyone else to accommodate them and cater to their demands in life and in love. Persecutors always believe they are justified in punishing, retaliating, or demeaning the other person.

People travel around this triangle all the time or become over-identified with one of its positions. Anytime you are stuck, consider that you may be in one of these positions.

Ineffective Things Partners Do to Cope

Couples therapists and teachers Ellyn Bader and Peter Pearson[42] created a list of ineffective things that partners do to cope. We do these things out of our fear, frustration, and despair. If you've had no help in how to work through conflict and differences in a relationship, it is likely you will resort to some of the gambits on this list. Every one of them makes matters worse.

Blame and Shame	Interrupt
Always have to be right	Comply
Defend without addressing the issue	Lie by commission or omission
Pout or sulk	Get stubborn
Withdraw or Stonewall	Use contempt (Includes eye-rolling)
Give an extended silent treatment	Attempt to make the other guilty
Drink too much/Use drugs	Turn the tables
Deny	Counter-complain
Attack, Bully, Intimidate, Dominate	Interrupt
Lie or Keep secrets	Nag or Badger
Condescend, Belittle, Make fun of	Become condescending
Name-call or Diagnose	Compete for the most wounded
Escape into work	Bring up old issues
Become sarcastic	Micromanage
Yell and drown each other out	Cry to evoke a response
Judge, or become Self-Righteous	Close one's mind
Criticize the other person's family	Reject outright
Bring in the other person's family for leverage	Change the subject to deflect
	Distract
Bring in the Kids	Become dismissive
Walk out without a time out	Criticize, Become contemptuous
Tell the other what they think or feel	Manipulate
Lose Patience	

TURNING TOWARD, TURNING AWAY

Couples researcher, John Gottman, describes the significance of seemingly ordinary interactions in the life of a caring couple. He calls these "bids and turns."[43] They involve one partner tossing out a bid for connection and the other responds. These exchanges can be quite simple, but they speak volumes in terms of connection, caring, and attunement. His research showed that newlyweds who stayed happily married turn toward each other's bids for connection an average of 86% of the time, whereas those who only turned toward each other 33% of the time are headed for divorce. A really simple way to assess the health of your relationship is to ask yourself, "Do we turn to each other easily for both little things and big things? Who is the first person I want to call to share my joys and sorrows? How safe do I make my partner feel when they try to engage me?"

To illustrate this, consider Daria and Amir, who are eating breakfast together. Daria mentions a conversation she had with her best friend. Her friend is engaged in the bewildering process of college applications with her teenage son. "We will be dealing with that in a few years," Daria says. Amir does not respond; he continues to read his paper. Unknown to Daria, Amir is already stressed about their financial situation, and the thought of college tuitions escalates his anxiety further. Daria doesn't know this because Amir does not share his inner life with her. She has no idea how stressed he is. She is a potential source of support, but Amir does not reach out to her for support and Daria often feels shut out, sad, and lonely. She retreats into silence, at a loss about how to connect with Amir. This was yet another bid for connection, but he turns away. Amir ignores her because he believes that he is the one who should bear the financial burdens. He is upset about other things in their relationship, like their lack of sexual intimacy, but he can't seem to figure out how to talk about this, so he avoids all conversations that involve emotions. Amir is lonely too, but he cannot figure out how to bridge the gap.

At another breakfast table Rachel mentions that her sister and her husband are having trouble conceiving a child. Henry has been reading the morning paper, but he puts the paper down and looks up. "That must be very difficult for them," he responds. Rachel and Henry glance at their two young children and exchange a smile of gratitude, and tender understanding. As he butters his toast, she hands him the jam jar. Later they stack the dishes up together and carry them into the kitchen. There is a smooth flow in their coordinated movements. They are in synch, attuned to each other, engaged in simple gestures of easy connection which are so comforting to couples. This flow of bids and turns speaks of presence, togetherness, and being in synch.

The rhythms of ordinary life are incredibly important to the cohesion of a couple—how we wake up, rituals that start the day, helping each other out the door in the morning, how we greet each other at the end of the day, nighttime rituals as we turn in, cooking pancakes on a weekend morning, the familiar preparations for family celebrations and holidays. Couples who are doing well know each other's rhythms and coordinate their rhythms as part of the dance of "we." Simple considerations such as handing something the other needs in the immediacy of the moment indicate, "I'm paying attention. I care. I am here when you need me." Happy couples have insights into small personality quirks and extend empathic generosity about those quirks. They support each other's basic needs and rhythms as a way of showing that the other is known, understood, and cared for. In a couple that is doing well, "ordinary asks" are easy. For couples in trouble, ordinary asks become impossible. Consideration and coordination build the positive field around the two people and create a sense of security and trust.

Protest, Despair and Detachment

In Chapter Four, we talked about John Bowlby's observations of the WWII children at Tavistock Hospital. Over time he watched them move from *protest, to despair, to detachment*. This is the same progression that adults move through in the fraying of an attachment bond. When protests are not resolved in a meaningful way, partners gradually move into sad resignation and despair. They lose hope that a meaningful connection can be found or that ongoing conflicts can be resolved. Despair is painful, and people can only endure it for so long. Eventually, they will become tired of being angry, stop reaching for each other, and will move into detachment. When I see people who have become detached, they have little motivation to work toward repairing the relationship. They don't believe it is possible. Sometimes they are just checking a box before they head for the divorce attorney. Some will remain in this sad state because it is just too hard to break up a family, lose face in the community, or split up the assets. They will remain in place, but merely co-exist.

Partners in detachment ask less and less of each other. They will begin to invest more in activities outside the primary relationship—work, friends, hobbies. If they are raising younger children, the children will become a substitute for the emotional sustenance that the parents cannot find in each other. Sometimes people even use spiritual practices as a means of substituting for the emptiness and despair they feel about their relationship. Healthy couples have outside interests that vitalize them and they talk to each other about these pursuits. Healthy couples are artists, marathon runners, meditators, golfers, gardeners, and volunteer workers, and so on. Their activities enrich their lives but are not used as replacements for the missing meaning in a marriage.

Staying Married, but No Longer in the "We"

Some people will leave a relationship when it becomes too empty, others will remain in an empty marriage, but cease to engage in any form of intimacy or affection. The decision to stay together but apart may be based on concerns about the impact of a separation on children, or the disapproval that will be forthcoming from friends, family, and a religious community. Divorce is costly on many levels. As two people begin the huge project of dividing up a home and assets, each finds themselves poorer. Women will often end up with a reduced standard of living because they tend to make sacrificial choices based on what is best for their children. They leave professional tracks and lose ground in the professional arena. However, one of the major costs in a divorce is the loss of friendship ties and loyalties which will inevitably get divided up.

Divorced people are often shocked and dismayed when they are no longer invited to events held by old friends. We favor married people in this culture and many people find that including a single person to a couples event feels awkward. Custody arrangements can become profoundly complicated, especially when children are used to express lingering grudges. Even when children are grown, divorce has a big impact in light of future family gatherings—holidays, graduations, weddings, etc.

When faced with these possibilities, many people opt to co-exist in a marriage with little connection or meaning, continuing to share some outside activities and maintain a "couple persona" in a circle of friends. Many of them look around and see very few people doing any better. They will lead civil, tepid lives as role-mates, maintain their respectable positions in their communities, keep their homes, assets, and enjoy family gatherings with the children. Couples of this sort share little of their interior world except in the occasional eruption of bitter conflict that stems from the emptiness of their lives. As one man stated to me once, "All our friends are unhappily married. Isn't that the norm?" I acknowledged that this might be true for his circle of friends, but if more were possible, would he be interested in this possibility? His wife certainly hoped for more, and with some commitment, humility, and effort, they were able to re-engage and attain a significantly more satisfying connection. My work has shown me that disengagement, devitalization, and lack of meaning are not the inevitable destinations of long-term mates who once chose each other with such hopeful expectations.

I am saddened by how many people live in lonely marriages. Living in close proximity with another person who has absolutely no interest in you and never responds to bids for connection or intimacy is humiliating. A chilly, silent household is lonelier than a house filled with conflict. Sometimes couples start arguments just to evoke some form of connection. They fight to fill the silence. After years of unresolved conflict and failed attempts to connect in some meaningful way, "no-fly zones" grow, and complete silence can descend.

Loneliness and Over-bonding with Children

Adults living in empty marriages tend to over-bond with their children, who can become the primary source of emotional fulfillment in their lives. In working with adults who became pseudo-spouses for their unhappy parents I see the untold problems that this creates. When a child begins to sense that they must care for a parent's well-being, they forgo their own development. In the worst cases, the child puts their own needs aside in order to make sure that the parent is made happy and remains functional. They may even avoid the normal teenage development of a high-school romance or friendships. They often become adults who live in the archetype of the Caretaker, unaware of their own personal needs and continually giving to and accommodating others. On the other hand, daughters of fathers who shower their girls with special affection can find it hard to find a partner who will ever live up to the level of attention and adoration she received as a Daddy's Girl. Then there are the Mamma's Boys, who could do no wrong in their adoring mother's eyes. They can remain Entitled, Demanding Boys far into adulthood, waiting to be doted upon, unable to navigate a reciprocal relationship in which a partner might occasionally be displeased with them or have needs of their own.

Affairs

When the relationship landscape becomes desolate and dry, there are selves in us that will seek water wherever we can find it. While emotional and sexual disengagement are not the only reason why people have affairs, it is often stated as the reason an affair seemed allowable. An affair can seem like a good solution for remaining in an unfulfilling relationship, where leaving would disrupt too many aspects of that person's life. Becoming involved with someone outside an empty marriage becomes an easy alternative for lonely partners for whom there is no longer an "us." In a previous era (before technology made it so easy to discover a partner's errant activities), many people had affairs that may have been sensed by the partner, but not pursued. It was important to remain in the marriage, happy or not, and denial and looking the other way were often employed.

I see couples where the partners have been drifting along for years, detached, lonely, and unhappy, but suddenly devastated by the discovery that their lonely partner has found solace in the arms of another. In today's world, it is unrealistic to expect that someone will endure the misery of an empty marriage indefinitely and accept an involuntary celibacy without eventually seeking some form of consolation.

It is beyond the scope of this book to talk about the many reasons that people have affairs, but many of them begin with a meaningful emotional connection, which can evolve into an emotional affair. These are different from good friendships or positive working alliances. Friends and work colleagues can be significant sources of emotional satisfaction for a person, but they don't supplant the intimate partner. When an outside involvement becomes the main source of emotional nourishment, over-shadowing the primary relationship, that's when a limerence can begin, with a full-blown affair not far behind. An emotional affair is a wake-up call for a relationship that has deeper problems and these outside relationships can be just as threatening as any sexual affair. In an emotional affair, an enchantment has occurred. There is preoccupation and longing to be near this person, to talk to them, to spend time with them, to share meaningful dimensions of one's inner world. Positive projections are being exchanged and a flame is being kindled that can easily become the fire of irresistible desire drawing the person into a dreamy parallel reality where the life of home and family is forgotten.

Emily tells me that she had been hungering for connection and affection for years before she "fell" into Nick's arms. Nick is a married coworker, who seems to also be drifting along in an empty marriage. Nick and Emily began a work project, with an increasing investment of time. They began more personal conversations and their attraction "sparked." Each felt responded to and appreciated for the first time in years. Emily had been trying for years to tell Alex (her husband) how lonely she felt in the relationship—they never seemed to talk about anything of depth. Alex was dismissive of her complaints, telling her she complained too much. "Nick was warm and so easy to talk with. He listened intently to me and seemed interested in who I was at my core. With him I began to feel sensuous and desirable. With Alex I feel old and uninteresting. When Nick and I got involved, it was as if I had suddenly come alive again after so many years of being treated like a demanding bore." This feeling of suddenly coming back to life is common in affairs. Emily is still desperately in love with Nick, and the affair has yet to be discovered. She knows that their involvement threatens to destroy two families, but her need to be seen, appreciated, listened to, and lovingly touched are so great that it is hard to disentangle herself.

In another session, Ed explains his involvement with Diane. "Caroline (his wife) and I hadn't had sex in years. Anytime I approached her, she acted like I was offending her. I was so lonely, then Diane came along. She admired me. I felt desired and wanted. Caroline made me feel like I disgusted her. I never wanted to hurt Caroline. I didn't want to break the family apart. Having this affair made it possible for me to stay *in* the marriage! I didn't think Caroline would mind that much because she obviously didn't want to have sex with me." The couple is now sitting in my office in the wake of Caroline's discovery of texts and hotel bills. It unfolds that there were other reasons that Caroline had retreated sexually, reasons that had little to do with sex and more to do with unresolved hurts, accumulated over the years. Ed is now aware that Caroline cared a great deal more than he knew about their relationship and when he gave his passion, devotion, and attention to someone else it devastated her.

I Am Not the Judge or Jury

When couples come in to see me, in the wake of a betrayal, they are often looking to me to condemn the betraying partner and name the bad guy or gal. The betrayed partner may be in a state of righteous indignation, but I know enough about the interlocking complexes and the unconscious to know that there is no such thing as a one-sided debacle in a relationship. I also know that many couples have had no help in how to exit the toxic dynamics they have been stuck in. Those that betray will tell me of the years of suffering they have endured through contempt or neglect. The betrayed partner will counter with an outraged explanation of how their protective retreat was spurred on by the other person's insensitivity or unwillingness to listen. Projections will be rampant, and the vulnerability, defensiveness, and devastation will be overwhelming when discovery has taken place.

I am often cast in the role of judge and jury, enforcer, advocate, or protective mother. In the discovery phase of an affair, crisis work is called for, because the marriage that the two people once had is over. A new marriage can be negotiated, but only if the couple decides that they want to grow beyond the people they have been— to themselves and to each other. In the initial discovery phase, neither is ready to see how their interlocking complexes and defense mechanisms led them into this debacle. What I know is that sometimes these seemingly catastrophic experiences open up possibilities that could only happen when old patterns and paradigms were broken up and the two people began to create something new. If this couple has the courage to engage each other more deeply, much can be accomplished.

THE PATH TO A SOULFUL RELATIONSHIP

What are couples to do when they are so miserable and stuck? Carl Jung said, "When you are up against a wall, put down roots like a tree, until clarity comes from deeper sources to see over that wall and grow."

The path into a meaningful relationship involves a commitment to personal growth. In the next section of this book, I will outline the pathway out of the swamplands of love and into the land of love's potential. There are crucial capacities that partners need to develop in order to deepen the love and create a relationship worth having. These are dimensions of commitment, courage, curiosity, communication, compassion, and creativity that most people don't consider when they enter into a relationship based on "box-checking" or "need meeting." The requirement that another person live into our picture of an Ideal Lover always leads us into a dark fairy tale. I instead offer a path of Individuation in Connection—the path into a soulful relationship.

PART TWO

CHAPTER 7

THE LABYRINTH

*"All journeys have secret destinations
of which the traveler is unaware."*
Martin Buber

*"When I fall into the arms of my lover, ready for anything ...
I am preparing to risk all for the sake of realizing my inner
world. The lover offers the bait, is the instrument of the
incentive, but it is something personal, something within me,
that bites the hook."*
Aldo Carotenuto

One of the most beautiful cathedrals in Europe stands in the center of the city of Chartres, France. It is a magnificent, soaring Gothic structure and embedded in the cathedral's floor is a beautiful stone labyrinth measuring over forty feet in diameter. It is important to note how different a labyrinth is from a maze. A maze will take you into dead ends, while a labyrinth will inevitably lead you to a center. You just need to stay on the path and keep walking. As you can see in the opening figure, the labyrinth winds back and forth through four quadrants, and eventually opens into a six-petaled center.[44] Carl Jung believed that quaternities represent wholeness. The four quadrants of the labyrinth could be considered realms of heart, mind, body, and spirit, and the integration of these four dimensions of living will lead to an experience of wholeness.[45]

Labyrinths are still found all over the world and walking one is a form of meditation, even of prayer. People walk the winding path of these labyrinths in search of insight into some life question, seeking a healing, wanting to let go of a burden they have been carrying, open to an illumination that might free them from something that has limited them. In the center of the Chartres labyrinth are six petals that originally represented a sacred rose. As one stands in the center, quieting the mind, open to illumination, something will shift. It is as if the guiding Self is speaking, and whatever the message, it will carry the seeker beyond where they have been before. The walk back outward is a time for reflecting on whatever one received in the center. The labyrinth offers a symbolic experience of pilgrimage, of voyage and return, of entering a liminal space where we suspend our preconceived understandings of life and returning in a different state of being. When you first walk a labyrinth, there are moments when you are certain you are heading straight into the center, and then suddenly the path turns and takes you back to the path on the extreme outside of the circle. You are far away from where you are seeking to go. This can create a feeling of dismay—so close, but so far away. Walking a labyrinth is stirring in ways that are hard to describe without the experience—the movement around, the winding back and forth, the arrival at the center, the pause for reflection, and the walk back out all have an impact on the psyche. I encourage you to walk a labyrinth if the opportunity presents itself, following this internal process of voyage and return.

There is a teaching in the winding path of the labyrinth. It mirrors the path of intimate relationship. Relationships do not provide straight paths to fulfillment. They are filled with unexpected twists and turns. Intimate relationships stir things up in our psyches that have been resting undisturbed for a long time. We often need to circle back and revisit formative experiences that have created narratives and worldviews, insecurities and defenses that will only present themselves when an intimate "other" starts to really matter.

Even when you have done the initial work of establishing a good relationship, there will be times when something shifts, and once again you will have things to work out. If you fall back into those old strategies of self-protection, you will find yourself in the swamplands of love once again, mired in interlocking complexes, triggering each other's sensitivities. In a long-term relationship, periodic cycles of mis-attunement are inevitable. Our needs change over time, and when these misalignments occur, it is an invitation to do another cycle of inner and interpersonal work. Love is calling us to deepen our understanding of who we are, who this other person is, who we are together.

The teaching of the labyrinth is that the path unfolds as we walk it. We gain courage and confidence as we experience the loosening of longstanding complexes. Sudden breakthroughs take us into a much deeper security—beyond the demands of our Inner Children—beyond the idea that our partner "meets our needs." When we invest in a process of inner work, we discover a bounty of resources that exist in the guiding Self, a storehouse of riches that begins to fill up the empty places of deprivation we once experienced. In engaging the journey of Individuation in Connection, we learn that we have a deep capacity for loving and being loved. The relationship itself becomes a solid vessel on a changing sea and we find our balance on the deck of that ship. We are carried forward by our commitment to this person, to the process of a deepening relationship, and to remaining engaged and present. Love opens us to new understandings of life and evokes things from us that we never knew existed. In this section, we will visit the center of the labyrinth, where a soulful relationship is truly attainable, and delve into the six petals that represent six capacities of love—commitment, courage, curiosity, communication, compassion, and creativity.

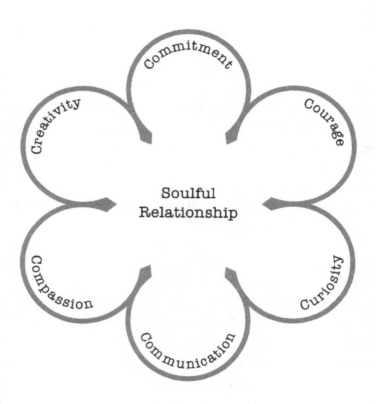

Chapter 8

COMMITMENT –
To a Person, a Process and to Presence

"Until one is committed, there is hesitancy, the chance to draw back, always ineffectiveness. Concerning all acts of initiative and creation there is one elementary truth … the moment one definitely commits oneself, then Providence moves too. All sorts of things occur to help one that would never otherwise have occurred."

W. H. Murray – Scottish Himalayan Explorer

"It is only with the heart that one can see rightly … what is essential is invisible to the eye."

The Little Prince – Saint Exupery

Half-hearted lovers do not make good life partners. There are just too many challenges to overcome along the path of love. In order to build a life that will sustain and grow, we cannot be half-in, half-out. The necessity of commitment is obvious ... but committed to what?

The Challenges of Commitment in the 21st Century

In the modern world, we live in a society that is constantly upgrading. When something breaks, we don't repair it, we discard it and buy something new. We seem to have transferred this mentality into our intimate relationships. When they "aren't working," instead of considering the part we ourselves are playing in creating the difficulty, or how we need to grow, many people just discard the relationship and go in search of an upgrade. Then we wonder why the same problems repeat.

Commitment always involves a decided choice. "I choose you." These are the words spoken in many modern vows as people lawfully wed. While marriage is often considered the ultimate commitment, in today's world it has become easy to "un-choose" a partner if things don't work out as anticipated. There are an increasing number of young adults disillusioned with the model of marriage they grew up with. They are opting out, considering alternative forms of relationship, or cohabitating with a conditional commitment like, "as long as we meet each other's needs," or more likely, "as long as this works for me."

The Way We Were?

I recall a conversation I had with a man who became quite upset with me for disrupting his idealization of marriages in the distant past. I was pointing out that his view was not historically accurate. When we look back to earlier times in history, romance, happiness, and fulfillment were not priorities in a couple's life— survival was. Stephanie Coontz is one of our leading scholars on the history of marriage, and she provides us with a more accurate account in her book, *The Way We Never Were*.[46] Our current nostalgia for the *Leave It to Beaver* family of the fifties leaves many people with the haunting feeling that family life today is second-rate. Coontz reminds us that *Leave It to Beaver* was not a documentary.

Today, many people are seeking "Soul Mates." If we look at the longer history of marriage, beyond one-hundred years, the institution was not based on romance or compatibility, but on what was good for others. Marriage has long been considered a foundation for the raising of a family and the creation of a stable society. Marriages of long ago were often arranged by parents or elders to fit into the needs of a community or establish societal and economic alliances between families. The fleeting nature of feelings (a "love-match") would never have been trusted for something so important. In royal families, marriages were sometimes arranged with the goal of creating a political alliance between two countries. The feelings of the young people were not of great importance, and the young people involved didn't expect the marriage to be based on feelings. Compatibility between partners was a bonus if it occurred, but the suitability to fulfill roles was the major concern. In small rural communities, where choices were few, marriage partners settled for what was available. In earlier eras, when more women died in childbirth, it was not unusual for a younger woman to enter into a marriage with a widowed man and take on the raising of his children in addition to her own. Marriage ceremonies involved vows before God that held people in place for a lifetime, happy or not. I still see the strong influence of parental approval in certain countries and communities where there is strong emphasis on an alignment of religious and cultural traditions, acceptable social standing, and the compatibility of two families.[47]

The Origins of Modern Romantic Love

Our current interest in romantic love began with the troubadours of France in the high Middle Ages, with their focus on courtship and romance. The concept of being "in love" as an important motivator for getting married began only about 100 years ago. Today, if the feelings are there, if the person fits our romantic ideal and we anticipate that our needs will be met, we are willing to stand at the altar and commit. Ironically, the love matches of today are less enduring and often less happy than marriages arranged by wise elders who knew the families and matched two young people whom they had watched growing up. Spouses of that time had fewer expectations and an understanding that they would need to learn to care for each other and build a life together over time.

In 1970, no-fault divorce was introduced. The upside of this was that it became easier for people to get out of truly miserable or abusive marriages. However, we now live in a world where people can readily "un-choose" their previously ideal love partner based on "irreconcilable differences." Midlife is a time when many people re-evaluate their lives, and feeling disillusioned and unfulfilled, they can easily project their current unhappiness onto a partner. They have climbed to the top of the midlife hill, and from there, they can see that they no longer have an unlimited number of years in which to find that elusive happiness. "I'm just not happy," is currently a reason that many people in midlife leave their marriages. What many people in midlife don't realize, is that this general feeling of malaise and dissatisfaction is more about a lack of meaning in their own inner lives than it is about the partner.

The kind of relationship that people want to remain in today requires significantly more sophisticated relationship skills than before, and we have very few teachers or role models to show us the way. Relationship philosopher, Esther Perel, states that we want more from our intimate partners than what a whole village used to provide—be my best friend, my confidant, my passionate lover, a great parent, and more.

We want it all, and we want it to be maintained over the course of a lifetime. Meanwhile, people are living almost 30 years beyond the life expectancy of the 1900s. Modern couples in our isolated nuclear families shoulder the responsibilities of dual careers, paying bills, raising children, and possibly caring for aging parents, who may live in another city. They also attempt to exercise, engage in enjoyable hobbies, spend time with friends, and devote some time to religious or civic activities. It's no wonder we feel in chronic need of a vacation where we can decompress. Unfortunately, most family vacations are more a source of stress than an experience of joyful reconnection. Our attempts to do it all, and have it all, places tremendous stress on our relationships. The essential element of meaningful connection—the capacity to "be" with each other—becomes harder to attain as we race around, trying to keep up with everything. Happiness is elusive where stress pervades, and we are living in a world where it becomes easy to leave someone just because you are unhappy.

The Marriage Equality Act

For all the challenges we encounter in marriage, it also offers many rewards, and continues to be our most significant symbol of an abiding commitment. Gay and lesbian couples have fought long and hard for the right to marry and gain the privileges that marriage confers. The fight for marriage equality centered on the right to enter into this important institution because it confers certain rights and privileges, but marriage also has deeply symbolic meaning for those who want to commit their lives to each other. When the marriage equality act was signed into law, Supreme Court Justice Anthony Kennedy stated that, *"No union is more profound than marriage, for it embodies the highest ideals of love, fidelity, devotion, sacrifice and family. In forming a marital union, two people become something greater than once they were."*[48]

COMMITMENT ... BUT TO WHAT?

Commitment is crucial, but what exactly are we committing to? I would like to offer that a commitment in an enduring intimate relationship must involve three important dimensions—a *commitment to a person, a process, and presence.* We make a choice about a person to whom we will commit our heart and our life—to joining with this beloved one for an ongoing journey. We are also committing to a process of ongoing development, personal and interpersonal growth, and to the co-creation of a relationship worth having. The most powerful and difficult aspect of that commitment involves remaining engaged and present over the wide arch of time, encountering all of life's changing circumstances. These three dimensions—person, process, and presence—form a deep commitment.

The Paradox of Choice

In Barry Schwartz's book, *The Paradox of Choice,*[49] he outlines how in Western society, the amazing number of choices we are offered has only served to escalate our anxiety about making any choice at all. After we make a choice, it becomes easy to imagine how we could have made a different choice ... a better choice. Instead of being happy with what we have chosen, we begin to doubt and rethink our decisions. When there are lots of alternatives, we imagine the attractive features of what we passed up. We suffer from an escalation of expectations—the more options we have, the greater our expectations. Subsequently, we have less satisfaction, and we are almost never pleasantly surprised. What enables this vast array of choices is our material affluence and advances in technology. These are the peculiar problems of modern Western society, where our overabundance of choices makes us less happy.

This applies to dating in the 21st century, where technology gives us the illusion that there are "plenty of fish in the sea." The more choices we have, the more likely we are to be sure that we could have made a better choice. This proliferation of choice has not made our lives better—it has made us significantly more anxious. Schwartz emphasizes that too much choice has produced paralysis instead of liberation.

An aspect of the difficulty in committing to a particular person is that people begin to search for "the right person." The illusion of many choices promotes the idea that we might be able to find someone even better, someone who checks all our boxes! *The idea of becoming a quality relational person or building a relationship over time does not occur to most people.* The central premise of this book is that many people do not look beyond checking their "requirement boxes." They forget the box that asks if this other person possesses the deeper *love capacities* that are necessary for creating a lasting relationship. In the flurry of emotion, most people don't think about these capacities and they often neglect to evaluate the depth of their own.

Ambivalence

Most people don't understand that ambivalence is archetypal. It is a universal truth that anytime we commit to one thing, we close the door on another and wonder about that other path. Commitment is the choice of one path to be taken, and it instantly evokes its opposite, the longing for freedom. In our modern world, where we are told we can have it all, it is difficult to consider taking one path and closing the door to another. What is interesting about people who are particularly ambivalent about committing to anything is that their character does not deepen, and subsequently, their lives have less meaning. People who are willing to commit understand the magic of what happens when you invest in a choice. People with love capacities understand that when two people commit to deepening their relationship, and developing their inner resources, they create a relationship worth being in.

Love Between Equals

Jungian analyst, and relationship teacher, Polly Young-Eisendrath, has written much about what it takes to sustain a love relationship in the 21st century.[50] In her book *Love Between Equals,* she explains that the kind of mutuality many people seek in a relationship creates far more complications than the patriarchal framework, where the man is considered the "head of the house," making decisions for others, and where others are expected to fall in line and follow his lead. While this traditional family system sometimes resulted in negative consequences for all, it also required minimal relationship or communication skills, and eliminated the need for negotiation.

In our modern approach to love, we develop a picture of an idealized partner, and the greater the distance between that ideal and the actual person we live with, the more disillusioned we become. Polly refers to this idealized partner as the Dream Lover. Couples enter relationships with a lot of projections, but they need to move into a series of deepening dialogues if they are ever to move past the idealization stage into "true love."

Where Real Relationship Begins

The gap between our ideal partner and the person we are with can dismay the best of us, especially when we begin to meet the rest of that partner's "inner cast of characters." This is where the real relationship begins. Now we are in the discovery phase, and the depth of commitment in each partner will become evident. People who think you can just "find" a perfect partner or "get" a relationship, will be greatly dismayed at this point. They don't understand that a relationship is something two people build together—they birth it. A relationship is a living entity involving ongoing co-creation by the two people involved. It must be created and nurtured and sometimes re-created as the two partners travel across time.

We cannot understand the essence of another person or establish true intimacy until the projection lenses drop from our eyes and we can begin to see more clearly who we are living with. When "the rest of the cast" begins to emerge from behind the curtain of the enchantment stage, many people get scared. The most surprising "selves" are often the ones we meet that come from that person's early life—the "kids behind the curtain." As the bond deepens, our attachment histories will activate and the vulnerable Inner Children and their Protectors in each partner will begin to meet each other. Strong reactions can result as we encounter this set of inner selves. The enemy of love at this point is not hate—it is fear.

Life is full of path choosing, which means that when we go through one door, we don't go through another. We choose a career path, a life philosophy, one house over another, this pair of shoes over those, where to vacation, and who we will spend our leisure time with. If we have children, we (hopefully) give up time, money, and other priorities to invest in their nurture and care. Mature adults know that life has limits, but in the modern world, many people house inner selves that want to live without constraint. Limits can create a channel into which we can focus our energies. When we grow in place, we can get our taproot deeper and develop inner resources. We can use the situations we find ourselves in to develop character.

The most significant experience of personal freedom and expansiveness will come from the inner work we do. Those who talk endlessly about not wanting to "settle," are looking for the "perfect person." They don't understand that finding a person who checks their expectation boxes is not a guaranteed ticket to happiness. Beyond the romantic ecstasies, finding someone who will commit to growing together is the real ticket. There are rewards in the depth of commitment that cannot be known until one is committed—to a person, a process, and to presence. This is long-game thinking, and this is how we sustain love worth having over the arch of a lifetime.

COMMITMENT TO A PROCESS

"The meeting of two personalities is like the contact of two chemical substances: if there is any reaction, both are transformed."

Carl Jung

Love will feel constraining for two people who are not willing to enter the process of becoming a couple, birthing that third entity that is greater than the sum of the two individuals. I call it the "we." Serial monogamists miss the riches of an enduring connection, which can only be known by remaining in place, growing ourselves, and seeking a deeper understanding of ourselves in our connection with this chosen Other. It requires a future orientation, including a sense that this investment of self will pay off over time. People with insecure attachment histories have more difficulty with that inner sense of trust. When partners are "all in," they begin to understand the value of having a trusted life partner, someone who has your back, and who is committed to your well-being as much as they are committed to their own. These relationships develop huge emotional "bank accounts" over time, from which partners can draw to sustain them when they are facing the vagaries of life.

Two Inner Casts

Beyond establishing a household and a way of life, an intimate relationship is shaped from the interplay of two psyches—two "inner casts of characters." These two inner-self systems will mix and match, and the pairings of their inner characters will evoke responses. Our histories, underlying life schemas, reactive complexes, and differences in personality and temperament will be like the mixing of two chemical substances in a beaker. There will be reactions, some of which may be explosive, some involving the boiling off of old stuff that needs to go if we are ever to form a meaningful bond. If we are truly "in" the relationship, we will be influenced and transformed.

Understanding your partner's "inner cast" will be helpful in solving your relationship problems. If you know that you will be interacting with the Grouch when your husband doesn't eat for an extended period of time, you will likely attend to the gap between feeding times. If your partner descends into a Silent Supplicant during every holiday visit to her parent's house, you can prepare for that and develop ways of supporting her. When partners become aware of each other's vulnerabilities, the mutual support offered is part of a secure attachment.

Some of the pairings in two people's "inner casts" will do well together, others will struggle and become grist for the mill of growth. Some of this will be impossible to know in advance, even if you have gone through "premarital" counseling. Keep in mind that developing the capacity to "shift states" and relate from a different stance (a different inner self) will change any interaction you are in. Becoming more self-aware of times when your Inner Kids are activated and getting a Healthy Adult on board will take you out of the shadow realm of unconscious reactivity. Continue to wonder about "who" (in you) is interacting with "who" (in your partner's inner cast).

COMMITMENT TO PRESENCE

"Love is touching souls."
Joni Mitchell

Martin Buber's "I-Thou" Encounter

Martin Buber was a philosopher of the early twentieth century, who wrote a book in 1923 entitled *I and Thou*.[51] His writing influenced countless thinkers, theologians, and writers, including this author. Buber described an experience that only happens when we move beyond our projections and personal agendas and begin to relate to another person at their essence. He emphasized that most people relate to others in the context of transactions, where we keep score and measure things like, "Am I giving more than I'm getting?" or "Are my needs being met?" Buber referred to these transactional relationships as *I-It* relationships. While reciprocity is an important component of a good relationship, Buber suggested that the deepest joy of relationship comes when we can "meet" the other person in an encounter with their core essence, when we become deeply interested in what animates them, brings them to life, what matters most. When we are having this kind of encounter, we are honoring the soul of the other, in an *I-Thou relationship.*

Jung and Buber were contemporaries and I believe that they were opening up the same theme. Carl Jung was writing about the possibility of a deep, meaningful marriage—beyond the traditional idea of being role-mates. Martin Buber was writing about *I-Thou* relationships—our capacity to have soul-to-soul encounters beyond roles and projections. While the word "soul" is sometimes used to describe something which lives on after death, these men were using the term to refer to a person's essence in this life—that which animates us and makes us uniquely special. Things that are soulful inspire and enliven us, move us, and connect us to something deeper.

Being present to another person, open to seeing and understanding them, soul-to-soul, is one of the most meaningful things we can do in a relationship. In moments like these, our personal agendas drop away, and we can enter that other person's world without all of our baggage. Couples therapist Hedy Schleifer refers to this as "crossing the bridge."[52] Moments of true meeting have a timeless, sacred quality. When we develop our capacity for this kind of presence, we will see our beloved more clearly, and love them more dearly.

People's souls are inherently beautiful, and soul-to-soul contact elicits love, but the soul will only show itself with someone who has a capacity for presence. Hal and Sidra Stone used to talk about how the soul sits close to our vulnerable Inner Children, to our core innocence—the soul, to show itself, must feel safe. Those who knew Martin Buber, spoke about his quality of presence. Buber once wrote, "all of life is meeting," meaning that these I-Thou encounters are the sweetest moments of our existence, where we come to understand and appreciate the beauty of another person's soul.

Sometimes when I am working with a couple, I can see that their relationship has been based on transactions—role negotiations and script fulfillment. I recall Martin Buber's words and I will say to them, "You two have never met." They have never entered each other at a deeper level, never visited their partner's inner world. In my work, I am looking for this level of encounter and it can only happen after a couple lays down their weapons of defense, relinquishes their projective demands, and forgives the intended and unintended wounds they have inflicted on each other. Then they can truly "meet" each other. Their soul children can emerge, and a gentle openness will settle into the room as they connect at a heart level. In these moments, a special light will shine from their eyes, and they will experience a wondrous experience of healing and soul encounter.

Mindfulness and Presence

We live in a highly distracting world. Our capacity to settle in and be present to one another is impaired, and down-shifting into this state is extremely difficult for most people. Our motors are continually running! This is why mindfulness practices have become so important in our modern world—we must rehabilitate our capacity to just "be." We need to learn that the chatter in our heads is often just foolishness, sourced out of our underlying complexes. The story-weaver within us crafts stories based on these complexes and distortions, creating reasons for why we are upset or dissatisfied. When we are ruled by our reactive complexes, we are often misguided.

Presence with another requires us to settle down and attune. In this space we can begin to see beyond our projections and expectations and to listen deeply. It is the foundation of a soulful relationship. When we establish this, something shifts in the space between us and love grows.

CHAPTER 9

THE COURAGE TO LOVE

"It takes courage to love, but pain through love is the purifying fire which those who love generously know. We all know people who are so afraid of pain that they shut themselves up like clams in a shell and, giving out nothing, receive nothing, and therefore shrink until life is a mere living death."
Eleanor Roosevelt

"Our willingness to own and engage with our vulnerability determines the depth of our courage and the clarity of our purpose."
Brené Brown

It takes courage to love, to open one's heart and entrust it to another. It takes courage to stay the course and grapple with what we will face as we walk the path of love. The challenges of love will show us what we are truly made of. We need courage when we find ourselves in the swamplands of love and encounter things about our beloved that were not evident at the start. When we hit experiences of disenchantment, and our expectations are not met, when our projections begin to crumble, it is easy to become alarmed. At this point, courage is defined by standing strong in the face of perceived danger.

Gaining Courage

How does a person gain the courage to love another human being? We develop it. We begin to face small challenges and we lean in. We seek wise counsel and learn. We start to face ourselves and identify our own shadow characteristics, some of which will be pointed out by our partners, whose close interaction with us will cause them to see our blind spots. This can cause us to feel terribly exposed and we must fight the dragons of shame, draw upon the healing balm of self-compassion, and engage in some serious inner work. When we face our own wounds and shadows, we are inevitably humbled. That humility allows for the compassion we need to embrace our own human imperfection and the imperfection of the beloved Other we have chosen to share our life with.

"You are not who I thought you were," is the lover's cry everywhere when we encounter aspects of our partner's inner self system that contradict our romantic ideal. Of course, no one is ever exactly who we think they are. That initial stage of "falling in love" involves so much romantic imagination. Once we begin to know this chosen one, we realize that they are neither Hero nor Goddess. Likewise, they are not the Frightening Monsters that our Inner Children would sometimes have us believe. Relationships are built by two grounded adults who co-create them out of the raw material of their lives. A relationship is birthed out of the intermingling of two psyches and is unique to the two people who live in that co-world. The co-world they create will range from heaven to hell—largely dependent on their courage and the willingness to deepen their love capacities.

The greatest enemy of love is fear, and the two most primal fears in close relationships will be the fear of abandonment (catastrophic loss) and engulfment (being overwhelmed and overpowered). These are the fundamentals of our attachment system and the tension between these two poles will be a continuing part of the dance of love.

When I was a young woman, I pulled down a book from my mother's library. It was her copy of Kahlil Gibran's *The Prophet*.[53] In this work, people seek the advice of this wise man, who speaks on a variety of themes. I was deeply moved by Gibran's words on love and they became a part of my love template. The Prophet states that "*love is for your growth, but also for your pruning.*" He goes on to say that love will thresh you naked, sift and free you from your husks, and that "*if in your fear you would seek only love's peace and love's pleasure, then it is better for you that you cover your nakedness and pass out of love's threshing-floor, into the seasonless world where you shall laugh, but not all of your laughter, and weep, but not all of your tears.*"

There can be no deep love without vulnerability and the courage we find to open our hearts is part of the mystery. Our capacity to manage that vulnerability will depend on the inner work we have done and how deeply we set our taproot. Those who are in relationship with the deep Self, will find the courage to love deeply, because the Self will supply them with sufficient resources to endure the process of love's threshing floor, by which we will be loosed from our "husks"—the protective defenses around us that prevent us from experiencing the deeper dimensions of love.

Courage is forged in the fires of falling down and getting up and seeking the wise counsel of those who have walked this path successfully. As I think back over my life, I am thinking of the couples who have been my teachers, couples that I watched and admired for how they loved each other and worked to build a life that supported each of them individually, while continuing to walk the path together.

You Can Bond Without Giving Yourself Away

People can avoid vulnerability by refusing to be "all in." They can simply not bring their full selves to the relationship. Others will abdicate who they are in an attempt to be who their partner wants them to be, but in doing so bring less life into the relationship. A vital relationship requires the interplay of two alive, self-defined human beings, not a dominant actor with a bit player on the side. Another important aspect of a vital relationship is that two people must continue to grow, but growth always brings an element of destabilization. This is one reason couples avoid growth. The paradox is that while growth destabilizes old patterns, it continues to re-vitalize that love over time. Couples who learn to navigate these passages continue to re-story their relationship as it continues to develop. They find their sea legs on the deck of a moving ship— the relationship.

There are couples who are so afraid of anxiety and destabilization that they avoid all conflict. They don't bring up topics that would ruffle feathers, and they end up not talking about things that really matter. They do this to keep the peace, but it devitalizes the connection. Pleasing a partner can be very satisfying, but in a healthy relationship one should not need to give up who you are to keep the other person calm or avoid making them feel insecure. Secure attachments are not formed by avoiding conflict or making oneself small.

Anytime one or both partners become so invested in getting along that they no longer voice thoughts, feelings or anything that might upset the balance of their pseudo-harmony, they will be in trouble. These couples have entered into what Hal and Sidra Stone call a "Positive Bonding Pattern."[54] While this kind of bond may sound lovely, the harmony is fragile and superficial. Two people in this kind of relationship can never know each other very deeply, because to do so would be to discover areas of difference. The unspoken contract is that both will fulfill the script they originally agreed to. Once established, no big changes are allowed, no dissenting opinions are to be voiced. Over time, no fresh air enters the relationship, and while they may appear to get along, both may feel suffocated, even trapped. A sluggish stability pervades, with a resigned sense of boredom in the background. The key indicator that a couple is caught in a positive bonding pattern is the mechanical feel of the relationship, accompanied by a lack of joy and tepid sexual interest. We see this kind of relationship in many couples of a previous generation, who stayed together as role-mates, with not much to talk about. They never sought to know each other deeply, perhaps sensing that they might uncover things that were truly disconcerting. Feeling suffocated and unable to be one's true self is one reason that people have affairs. Their spirits begin to feel too confined, and if they meet someone who opens the door to freedom, allowing them to express or explore aspects of self that have been suppressed, this person is a candidate for an extramarital involvement.

Ellyn Bader and Peter Pearson of the Couples Institute refer to this pattern of superficial harmony as the "Dark Side of the Honeymoon."[55] It begins when a happy couple begins to feel small degrees of discord, disappointment, or frustration. Both are invested in their early sense of compatibility and they don't want to lose these early lofty feelings, so they sweep things under the rug. Unfortunately, in denying negative feelings they begin to dull the positive feelings as well. The two will begin to behave more cautiously with each other, and there will be less spontaneity and less ease in the relationship. They are trying to be "good partners," but their avoidance of conflict will lead them into more superficial ways of relating. Hopefully, this will be a temporary stop in the development of their relationship. What will be required of them is the courage of self-definition, and to encounter each other more deeply, as unique individuals who will need to work out a life that allows for grappling with difference, while maintaining a connection.

Real Intimacy

The experience of knowing and being known are the core of intimacy and we can't be intimate if we don't reveal who we are to our partner and if our partner cannot reveal who they are to us. Revealing oneself requires that we know ourselves, shadow and light, and this cannot occur unless we have the courage to look in and face what we find. It also takes courage to face what we find as we come to know our partner more deeply, come to understand their vulnerabilities and particularly as we encounter each other's shadow dimensions, which we are always blind to in ourselves. As we walk this path of relationship, we are both going to learn things about each other that were not part of our early understanding. Intimacy is impossible without courage and mutual self-revealing is the only path to intimacy. For some, the fear of being seen and then rejected or shamed leads to avoiding closeness.

Courage, Vulnerability and Whole-Hearted Living

We need the courage to fail in life and love, and then engage in a learning process. We need the resilience to fall down and get up again. We need courage to let go of old stories that limit us and to embrace a larger story that provides the space for who we are becoming. I am grateful for the clear and accessible voice of Brené Brown[56]—academic researcher turned "storyteller"—whose TED Talks and books have launched international conversations about the necessity of vulnerability as an important foundation for a fulfilling, purposeful life. Brené emphasizes that embracing vulnerability is the necessary first step in whole-hearted living. Vulnerability and courage are bedfellows, and we cannot find the courage to dare greatly or love deeply if we are avoiding vulnerability.

Brené also speaks of how we are impacted by a culture that promotes "unrelenting standards."[4] We live in a culture of com-

---

[4] Unrelenting standards is one of the maladaptive schemas listed in Jeffrey Young's Schema Therapy.

petition where what we have, what we accomplish, and what we are is "never enough." Our current culture is shame-based, and shame leads us to hide ourselves, something that will prevent us from ever being truly intimate with another. Shame tells us that we are not worthy of love and belonging. Growing our capacity for self-compassion will help us to cultivate shame-resilience, so that we can fall down and get up again, learn some more, and return to love more deeply. Cultivating the courage to show ourselves, to be present to another and to just "be" is crucial. Two people who dare to engage this process together will truly know a deepening love.

Facing Shadow Characters

Even healthy partners have "shadow characters" who will come out over time. That is to be expected and most of us can meet this challenge by drawing on courage. The most difficult of these are Rogue Characters. These are aspects of self that live in our shadow-land, not really "in" the relationship. They can emerge like Grendel (from the ancient tale of Beowulf) who crawls from the murky deep to destroy the trust in a relationship. In some relationships, the partner houses an emotional or physical Abuser who emerges in moments when you are no longer a Pleaser. The discovery of this can be terrifying. Your husband may house an Inner Frenchman who never had any intention of being confined to one partner—in fact, the Frenchman didn't even attend the wedding. You may meet an Alcoholic who only emerges when the stress level gets high, or a Spendthrift who comes out when the two of you get stuck in a power struggle. Whether or not you can resolve the difficulties that emerge when you meet these Shadow Selves will require courage and an evaluation of the level of commitment to *the person and the process* of creating a relationship that is sustainable. Sometimes the greatest act of courage is to walk away, but much discernment is required before we give up on love.

Love and trust can only deepen and grow in the fertile soil of the six love capacities. In my system of working, we always need to be aware of our Inner Children, to care for them, but not allow them to "drive the bus." Courage is ultimately sourced from having our taproot in the resources of the deep Self. Courage is a spiritual capacity and allows us to be "all in," even as we face the dangers we will encounter in the fray.

CHAPTER 10

CURIOSITY –
Inner Work and Interpersonal Inquiry

"Asking the proper questions is the central action of transformation. Questions are the key that causes the secret doors of the psyche to swing open."
Clarissa Pinkola Estes

"Faced with the irrefutable otherness of our partners, we can respond with fear or curiosity."
Ether Perel

"To ask the right question is already half the solution of a problem."
C.G. Jung

While many people come into couples therapy saying that communication is their problem, the real problem stems from a lack of sincere curiosity. Both people are trying to be heard, understood, and responded to; neither is listening very deeply. People who aren't getting along listen to prepare their own defensive responses. They are not interested in gaining understanding, and lacking the capacity of sincere curiosity, they will never get at the root of their problems.

Relationship as an Anthropology Study

I often tell people that relationship is an anthropology study. We look across at this other person from our world and don't fully understand what their behaviors and customs mean. If we ever want to truly understand this other person, we are going to have to move out of our own point of reference and visit that other person's world. Loving another person is not just about treating them well; it's about understanding them deeply, and grasping what really matters and why. We also need to understand what couples therapist and researcher Sue Johnson calls a partner's "raw spots,"[57] those places in the psyche that are tender and likely to be inadvertently wounded. When a partner has a set of "raw spots" that differ from ours, their reactions may not make sense to us, but if we want to be truly intimate, we have to enter their world and look out of their eyes of experience. We need to understand that person's history and formation, what matters to them, and why. We must learn how life works *over there*.

We tend to love people the way we would like to be loved, without wondering what would be most meaningful for the other person. We tend to assume that an intimate partner will enjoy what we enjoy, see things the way we do. This is the source of many misunderstandings. People feel most loved when we know them and give to them in their primary love language. Ultimately, an act of love is defined by the recipient.

When partners insist that they have the "right way" to do things or view things, they are not relating. When one person asserts that they have the one true reality to rule them all, they may wind up with compliant "subjects," but never open-hearted lovers. Domination leads to abdication, withdrawal, or the misery of perpetual (sometimes passive-aggressive) power struggles.

The "What Happened" Argument

This is a place where a lot of people get stuck. The discovery that your partner remembers an experience differently from you can be a source of bewilderment and dismay. You were there, after all! You may be convinced that you have an excellent memory and believe that you remember *exactly* what happened, or what was said, or agreed upon. An argument may ensue, each person asserting that their memory is correct. These arguments pull the two people away from whatever they were trying to solve in the first place, and they are pointless. Research demonstrates that our memories are notoriously unreliable. We focus on and remember what we each deem important and our memories grow increasingly less accurate when there are high levels of stress. When we retrieve things from memory, if there are gaps, our minds fill them in with something that makes sense to us. We are not being intentionally dishonest here; we are engaging in something called "confabulation." Add projection to the mix—how every person's memory records, processes, and assigns meaning differently—and we are in an even bigger muddle. When we consider all these factors, it becomes easier to let go of our "what happened" arguments. A better idea is to move into curiosity, wondering what memory reveals about each person, and getting back to what you were trying to resolve in the first place.

Shadow-Boxing

In previous chapters, I have explained how we get entangled in "interlocking complexes," triggering each other, and projecting meanings and motives that may or may not be there, one partner's reactions evoking the defenses (and projections) of the other. In highly invested arguments, we are never arguing about what we are arguing about. We would need to look deeper to discover what the real issues are. When the argument gets heated, you can be sure that you are wrestling with ghosts of the past—shadow-boxing, captured by complexes, with Inner Children and their Protector-Defenders running riot.

When our early life complexes get activated, we begin to look through the eyes of those complexes. We project the historical themes of the past onto our partner and begin to interpret everything that is happening through that lens. If the complex is about how others use and abuse, we may begin to look for clues that we are being taken advantage of, interpreting innocent actions as signals that the partner is about to betray us. If the complex is about unworthiness or abandonment, we may become convinced that our partner is looking for someone younger, sexier, more interesting, or easier to live with. People who believe what their complexes are telling them, can collapse into hopeless dejection, or protective withdrawal. Some become highly suspicious and defensive. Our protective mechanisms can set into motion the very things we are most afraid of—alienation, retaliation, rejection, abandonment.

Troubling situations that seem to mysteriously repeat themselves originate in the shadow recesses of the psyche. I'm not talking about individuals who live in environments where resources and role models are so limited that making their way out is almost impossible. I'm talking about people who continually gravitate towards situations that will fail and people who will undermine their lives. There is personal work to be done here.

There are people who seem to have chronic bad luck. They can't seem to keep any money in the bank because some catastrophe is always befalling them and cleaning them out. Others repeatedly wind up with "terrible bosses," and can't seem to hold a job. If you meet someone who tells you that their last three relationships were with "crazy people," be careful. You are likely to be the next on the list.

When people become willing to do their personal inner work, their lives change. Some of the best people I know are in 12-step recovery programs. They have had the courage to look inward, face their inner darkness, rework some of their distorted ideas about life, heal early wounding, make amends to those they have hurt, and commit fiercely to consciousness and truth.

If you repeatedly find yourself with dysfunctional partners, this is not an accident. Get curious about the subtle signals you send that attract certain partners. Are you a Rescuer? Do you like "renovation projects" with people who have a lot of potential, but in your view have never had the love they needed to reach it? Do you expect their gratitude or loyalty because you were their benefactor? Do you house a young and naïve inner self that tends to trust and idealize before looking behind the curtain of a person's dating persona? Do you house an Unworthy Self that tells you that no one would ever love or stay with a person like you, settling for the crumbs you can get? Are you trying to "undo" something from your past by repeating it in the present and attempting to get a different outcome?

The Overstory and the Understory

Underneath our terrible relationship tangles is an understory, where we will find the answers to the perplexing dynamics that plague our relationships. Our adult story is an over-story, formed out of the protective strategies that we adopted to succeed in the world. It is cobbled together over time and the over-story helps us present a face of invulnerability to the world, an adult "persona" that hides the fact that we all have vulnerable children inside.

Your overstory may be shaped by internalizing the ways in which *others* have defined you. Many people live into the expectations held by important others without evaluating if those expectations fit who they really are. When we live out scripts handed to us by others, that run counter to our true gifts, we dim the brightness of our inner light. The world also loses out on those gifts. There are people who are chronically depressed because they are living a life that has been handed to them by others, instead of the life within them. Many of them are on antidepressants that don't budge their distress until they begin to align their outer and inner lives. This is the journey of individuation.

Some people try to overcome a painful understory by ambitiously building a reputation or resume. The hope is that achievement and power will lift them above the underlying feeling of unworthiness, rejection, anxiety, or fear. Some people deal with a painful understory of helplessness, hurt, or alienation by inhabiting the archetype of Rebel—rejecting anything that might stir up vulnerable feelings—living an anti-script, which cuts them off from aspects of self that are genuine and worthwhile. Being a Rebel, a Warrior, or an Armored Amazon may protect you, but it will also cut you off from some of the most precious experiences of life and love. They require vulnerability and an open heart.

History and Formation

Anytime we have strong present-day feelings, we can be sure that there are tendrils into the past. Our underground needs are the foundation of our completion story and what draws us inexorably to certain partners in the first place. When we feel safe and happy in a relationship, something is being fulfilled, and that fulfilment soothes and delights us. When we feel empty, angry, or scared, we are tapping into a place where we didn't get important needs met. We might feel compelled to fight, flee, or just give up, which means we have descended into a much younger ego state. When people's crucial early needs are not met, they do not go away; they go underground, where they wait for a future opportunity. This creates the scaffolding of our inner completion story—and is a major factor in choosing the partners we do. We are always seeking to fill in the missing pieces that we sense will make us whole.

Becoming intimate with one's beloved involves understanding their history and formation, their tender places, and the defensive complexes that are likely to activate in them. When we picture a partner as the child they once were, we begin to understand what it was like for them long ago. Hopefully, a sense of compassion will emerge as we grasp the reasons behind certain defenses and reactions. When compassion is evoked, and a person feels "gotten," a healing occurs. This is one of life's most wonderful experiences, and people long to receive this gift from an intimate partner. The loving accommodations we make for the tender places in a partner's world are quite different from the capitulations we engage in to avoid reactions, punishment, or a feeling of guilt. It all begins with curiosity—the sincere desire to understand the other person, to visit their world, and imagine their experience.

People Are Not Projections

One of the most unloving things people do to each other is to cast the other person in a certain light and refuse to let them out of that box—to paint them with a broad brush and not see that they are multifaceted beings, as we all are. We need to be careful that we are not becoming angry that a partner won't be our Dream Lover, that we are not handing someone a script and insisting they read it as written. Loving is not about casting someone as bit-player in our play. People exist in their own right, and we cannot begin to love them until we learn who they actually are.

Think about the archetypal shifts that occur in your partner and the impact that these shifts have on you. What do you do when the Girl of Your Dreams occasionally acts like an archetypal Witch? Does your Poet Lover ever feel insecure and shift into a Demanding Bully? When the Hero meets the Ice Princess, does he begin to sulk like a Teenage Boy; does the Free Spirit who can forget some responsibilities evoke a Self-Righteous Judge? What archetypal story do you move into when your partner is not who you want them to be? Archetypal energies evoke corresponding matches. Positive or negative, our projections pull a partner into a narrow band of possibility. When you step back, out of the drama, what do you see? When either of you gets activated, do you both enter a dark fairy tale, or do you move to curiosity and inquiry?

You cannot love a story in your head, you can only love a human being, and to genuinely love someone—beyond who you hope them to be or what they can do for you, you have to move beyond your ego demands and reactive defenses and seek to understand them. This takes a lot of personal maturity. To get there you've got to do some inner work.

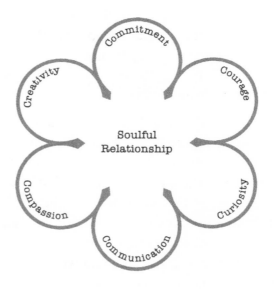

BEGIN WITHIN

Activation is Invitation

There is no such thing as a relationship without misunderstanding or conflict, and people deal with conflict in different ways—some are conflict-engaging, some are conflict-avoidant. This will be based in your temperament and experiences along the way.

When you find yourself annoyed or hurt by something your partner has said or done, pause and begin to wonder, "What is this situation stirring up in me? Why does it matter so much?" Before you protest, strike back, or retreat, listen to the voice in your head. Ask yourself, "Whose voice is it? How old do you feel in this moment?" Think about the "inner cast of characters." *In an upset, I have always found it most useful to ask, "Who's upset?" versus "What's wrong?"*

Beginning within doesn't mean you can't ask for change in your partner's attitude or behavior but do your personal inquiry first. When we dump our reactivity and projections into the inter-personal space, it makes it harder for a partner to hear what we are saying or respond in a meaningful way. Our hurt or aggravation evokes defensiveness. You will be more successful when you sort out your own reactions first—get clear, then communicate. What is this situation touching into in your history and inner world? Activation is an invitation to inner work.

Why Are You So Upset?

"Why the big reaction?" When you ask it of yourself, it becomes inner work. When a partner asks this of you, it often feels, dismissive, critical, possibly even shaming. Likewise, when a partner becomes upset about something you did or said and this makes no sense to you, it means that you touched a nerve and activated a complex. Curious partners committed to knowing their partner more deeply will turn to curiosity and ask some sincere questions. What we do or say may have no negative significance to us, but each of us has a different history and a different set of sensitivities. Telling the other person that they are being unreasonable or ridiculous will only get you into more trouble. When any partner is confused by the other's reaction to something, it is time to get into a learning conversation.

It helps to separate intention from impact.[58] Especially when you have good intentions that land poorly in another person's world. Anytime we are hurt, angry, or scared, there is always an Inner Child involved. These "Kids Behind the Curtain," can become painfully activated and our partners may have an immediate protective response—moving into defensiveness, taking offense, retreating, or counter-complaining.

If you are the hurt one, take a pause, and do some inner work before you conclude that the other person is being insensitive or "intentionally" trying to hurt you. If you are with a caring person, it is more likely that they don't understand you deeply enough yet. Keep in mind that this can be true even if you've lived together for many years. I am always amazed at what long-term couples really don't understand about each other. The only way of untangling these confusions is to activate curiosity and get into a learning conversation.

Who is Interacting with Who?[5]

In any relationship there are two casts of inner characters and we need to notice how our pairings work. Who (in your inner cast) is interacting with who (in your partner's inner cast)? Notice which selves work well together and which ones get you into trouble. When you think about your relationship in an inner-self model, it will help you understand some of those incomprehensible conflicts. It also explains those experiences when you feel genuinely happy and deeply fulfilled. The experience of being responded to in a way you always longed for can be ecstatic. It is worthwhile to think about "who" is relating to "who" in these wonderful experiences. Likewise, the next time you get into a tangle with your partner, see if you can reflect on your two inner-self systems. Many of my couples have

---

[5] I am aware that the proper wording here is who is interacting with whom, but have chosen to stay with the less formal wording.

done this and gained tremendous insight into their relationships, interrupting distressing dynamics that plagued them for years and boosting their happiness quotient.

One important note about naming your inner selves. Never use "inner cast" references in a critical or condescending or diagnostic way—"you're acting crazy because your abandoned, Angry Child is out of control right now." This makes the work very unsafe. Avoid telling your partner who their problem inner characters are, particularly when that partner is in a state of reactivity. Anyone who uses the work in this way is most assuredly stuck in a complex!

If you want to do more explorations of your "inner cast of characters," my book *Negotiating the Inner Peace Treaty*[59] will help with this. Look inward and name some of your inner characters. Then take some time to think about their formative histories, how they developed their perspectives, needs and concerns, strategies, and where they show up in your life. You can flesh them out and let them "speak," by writing about them in a journal. If you are in a relationship, you can talk to each other about these inner selves and work out ways to help each other when you get "hijacked" by the vulnerable ones and their protectors.

INNER EXPLORATIONS

Press Pause and Do Some Personal Inquiry

Imagine a recent disagreement with your partner. You are having a conversation, and suddenly something starts to happen. Your heart starts to beat faster, your breathing gets quicker, and you can feel a growing sense of pressure in your head and your upper body. This is what it feels like when you are being captured by a complex, with its cascade of associations from embedded memories that activate the nervous system and create a bodily response.

If you have the presence of mind to pause and take a few deep breaths with long, slow exhales, you might be able to slow down this activation, but this takes practice. Most people just get swept away by their upsets. They are not accustomed to tuning in and wondering what has just been set off. Once you have been hijacked by the stress neurochemicals that begin to pump into your bloodstream, you will not be able to get your thinking brain back online. You will be operating entirely out of the parts of the brain that will propel you into fight, flight, or freeze. People cannot resolve problems from this state. They are too activated in a sense of threat. The best thing to do at this point is ask for a time out. Nothing is ever resolved well when you are flooded with adrenalin and cortisol. You need to step back, calm down, and figure out what just happened.

When you get upset, it is an invitation to step back and spend some time discovering what the upset is really about. This is particularly true of repetitive upsets. The heavy lifting of this kind of inner work is in the beginning. Doing it over time will help you to stay calmer in situations that previously annoyed, distressed you, or sent you over the edge. Doing this work, you will eventually be able to manage yourself in the moment. Journaling helps a lot with this process because we tend to forget gradual improvements. In recording our thoughts and feelings we can see the upward trend over time.

Suspend Conclusions

When we get triggered, we immediately start spinning stories. We want to get an explanation for what is happening and what we should do. We spin stories about others and then we project them out. We become convinced about what others think and feel—particularly if we have lived with them a long time! We forget to ask questions where that person can help us to grasp something we don't understand. The next time you get upset, see if you can step back and suspend the narrative running in your head. Consider that you are spinning a story and telling yourself things about what is going on. Even when you are convinced that you *know* what is going on, consider that there might be another possible interpretation. Begin with what this situation is touching into in *you*. "Who" in you is upset and why? When you are doing your own discovery work, see if you can rerun the experience as if it were a screenplay. What is the story here and who are you in this story? Think about it archetypally. How are you cast? How are you casting your partner? What is the underlying theme of this story? How does it end? What lens are you looking through? Which of your inner characters is activated right now and thoroughly convinced they know the capital T "truth?"

Protective Strategies

We all developed protective strategies when we were small, to stay safe and get our needs met. We did this when we had little power, voice, or choice. The thing is that all of this goes into the unconscious and begins to operate automatically, as part of our personality. We carry these strategies forward into our adult years, and they cause a lot of relationship problems. As an adult you have more power, voice, and choice. When you develop your adult capacities and relationship skills you can lay these weapons down.

Take some time to examine what kind of defense strategies your inner protector-defenders engage in:

- Do you feel compelled to rage against this person for unjust treatment, for violating your rights?
- Do you want to get away, run and hide, avoid contact?
- Do you just give in, giving up what you really want or need because you are afraid of being rejected, punished, or abandoned?
- Do you apologize a lot and take the blame for things when you're not even sure you did anything wrong?
- Do you have a punishing voice inside, tearing you down, telling you that you are stupid, that you are only getting what you deserve?
- Do you start to feel light-headed, unable to think clearly, or freeze up?

All of these are defensive responses and indications that your Adult Self is not sufficiently online to manage what is happening. These reactions can also be indication of unworked trauma. Your Vulnerable Children have taken over and are running the show and their Protector-Defenders are attempting to shield you.

SOMATIC TRACKING

If you want a fast track into your own history, bypass your thinking and track your sensations. The next time you are feeling upset, let the story inside your head go, and notice what you are feeling in your body. Follow those sensations and ask yourself, "When have I felt like this in the past?" This is called "somatic tracking," and it is a powerful way of discovering your understory. When you track sensations, they will lead you into a string of earlier, similar memories where you felt the same way. The body remembers things that the conscious mind has forgotten.[60] Even if the memory you come up with doesn't seem to have anything to do with the present situation, spend some time with it. There is some connection. Spend some time in those earlier memories and discover a younger "self." See what she or he has to tell you about your formation.

- How old are you in this memory?
- Imagine yourself at that age and spend a few minutes reflecting on your life back then. You are visiting one of your "nested inner selves."
- If you have located a specific memory, what is happening in the memory? What are you feeling and doing in the memory? If there are others around you, what are they doing? How are you making sense of what is happening?
- In reflecting on this scene of the past, what did you need back then that you didn't get? What did you get instead of what you needed?

- It might be a wonderful memory. In what ways was it happy and fulfilling?

- What did you decide about yourself back then? What did you decide about the people around you? What did you decide about how life works for people like you?

- What kinds of strategies did you develop back then to get your needs met and to protect yourself from hurt in the future?

Give this younger self a name and thank them for the gift of letting you get to know them. Do some journaling about your discoveries.

This exercise will lead you into a greater understanding of your early formation. How you came to define yourself, your "rules for living," and decisions about how life works for people like you. You will gain insight into early decisions that you made that have followed you all your life, often completely unchallenged. We make lots of early decisions that become our worldview, our contextual norm, like a fish in water. You are examining the understory of your life and how it has shaped your understanding and interpretations of your life.

Reparative Resourcing

If in this exploration you uncovered something deeply needed by that earlier self, you can put your hand over your heart, and imagine sending whatever it is back to that younger self. Examples of unmet needs in our early lives are the need for love, comfort, protection, support, validation, affirmation, celebration, nurturing, belonging, understanding, information, limits, structure, food, shelter, time to just be a child, and so on. You can also imagine someone entering the picture who might have provided that need. Close your eyes and imagine these resources coming in and changing the outcome of the memory. Resources can be brought in by a person, an animal, a force of nature, even a dream figure. You can even imagine a different outcome, a "resourced" ending to what happened. If this is comforting, sit for a while with that memory— feeling the sense of resolution in your body. See if you can deepen this feeling of healing or resolution and allow it to imprint your nervous system. Early decisions about ourselves and about life can be "re-decided" in these imaginings.[61] Reparative experiences with strong emotional impact, even if only in our imagination, can help to establish new neural tracks that mediate distress.[62] We can remap the brain and integrate resources, reshaping who we are and how we operate in our present life. Imagination is a powerful thing, and much healing can occur when we bring a needed remedy into a painful memory.

For those people who have never thought much about having their own needs, the process of finding words for them can take time. One of the great contributions of Marshall Rosenberg and his *Non-Violent Communication* approach is that he offers a long list of both feelings and needs which can be found on his website.[63] Marshal encourages us to look underneath feelings to discover the underlying needs. When we are overwhelmed by feelings, it becomes more difficult to identify underlying needs. Once we can identify a need, we can begin to explore how to fulfill it.

None of us had perfect childhoods, and there are basic needs that when unmet will continue to haunt us into adulthood. A really attuned, loving partner can heal those empty places, but we can't always count on a partner to be in their best form, perfectly attuned to us. This can be particularly difficult for people with troubled pasts who have such a need for an attuned response. When we spend time doing our own inner work, we can communicate needs and feelings more effectively and evoke more compassionate responses from partners who want to love us well.

Dreamwork[6]

If you are a dreamworker, or work with a therapist or analyst who can help you examine your dreams, pay attention to the characters, settings, the feelings and the themes that present themselves in this theater of the night. Our dreams send us "postcards" from the psyche, giving us information about what is moving through us at a deeper level, below our conscious awareness or domineering Ego identities. What are your associations with the contents of your dreams? How might they be commenting on your waking life? While many people think of dreams as unintelligible phantoms of the night, once you begin to attend to them, they become a wonderful resource that provide insight and feedback on how we are operating in our waking lives and what we may not be seeing. They frequently provide "out of the box" solutions for life challenges. They suggest changes in perspective and shifts in our archetypal stances that could lead to different outcomes. Many people experience inspiration or profound healings in spending time with dream images and the archetypal energies the psyche brings to us in dreams, which can be integrated for the expansion of our creative potential.

Go with an Experienced Guide

While most people can manage this kind of inner work, some people have had difficult or traumatic experiences that remain out of memory until they begin inner explorations. The surfacing and possible re-experiencing of one of these memories can be over-whelming. If you find yourself remembering something very distressing or find it difficult to get back into present time, pause this process, and seek out some professional therapeutic help. Find an experienced guide to walk with you to unpack these things. Therapists are trained in a variety of modalities. Find someone who

---

[6] If you have never really thought about dreams as a creative, guiding, or healing resource, visit my website for a list of books that will help you get started on the dream working path. My favorite "first book" is *Inner Work* by Robert Johnson.

understands something about complexes, inner selves, schemas and life narratives, and how the body holds trauma.[7] Invest in your life to clear away impediments that have been interfering with your capacity for love and joy in this life. The healing work you do will open the door to the love you deserve.

Why Would I Ever Want to Revisit Painful Memories?

Sometimes people ask me why they would ever want to revisit painful memories. What possible purpose does it serve? My response is that we are not revisiting past experiences just to re-experience pain. The point is consciousness and healing. If you think you are not operating out of your history, you are mistaken, because the brain is an association machine, and you will never be free of the past as long as there are experiences in the present that remind you of it. When those old association "files" open, we instantly get a download of stress chemicals that flood the body. We are highly influenced by previous associations. When we re-process the way old memories are held, our life experiences take us down a different path, and we move through life differently.

All of us have foundational stories that need to be examined, and "re-storied." We need to strengthen our orientation around our resources and deepen our focus on what is good and beautiful in our lives. In this way we begin to strengthen the neural pathways that lead to our inner resources. Rick Hanson writes about how to do this in his books, *Hardwiring Happiness*,[64] and *Resilient*.[65] When you engage the process of re-mapping reactions, you are literally changing your brain. You can build the capacity to hold steady when you are in stressful interactions with a partner. This will open more doors for love and fulfillment.

---

[7] Therapists differ greatly in their approaches. Try to find someone who understands Jungian work or is trained in Voice Dialogue, Schema Therapy, or Internal Family Systems. Somatic psychotherapies are also powerful modalities that work to heal trauma—EMDR, Somatic Experiencing, and Brain-spotting are some examples.

What If I'm The Only One Doing Any Inner Work?

You may have a partner who is not that interested in doing inner work. You can still engage them in a learning conversation if you do your own work first and engage them with grounded humility and sincere curiosity. Do your own work first. When you have both calmed down, try engaging in a learning conversation with the following inquiries:

- "I've noticed that this is a pattern for us. This is what I figured out about me _____. (Avoid diagnosing or telling your partner anything about them. This is their work to do, and it evokes defensiveness when you do it.)

- "What do you think would help us move out of this difficult pattern we are in?"

- "What is upsetting about how I am approaching you about this?" You are likely to encounter projections here. Don't get caught in arguing with their projections. We will talk a lot more about how to deal with these in the next chapter on communication. For now, *listen for the needs* underlying their projections and feelings. Validate the needs, even if you don't agree with their projections or perspective. We will talk more about these dicey conversations in the chapter on Communication. The key is to stay with curiosity, in a "learning conversation."

When you make it safe for your partner to reveal their vulnerability to you, you will learn a lot. We tend to argue with partners when they are projecting on us, telling them they are wrong, or that they shouldn't feel that way. This does not calm the Vulnerable Children in them, who we are inevitably interacting with. Speaking "on high" or as a "more conscious person" is experienced as contemptuous. When your partner feels that you honestly want to understand, this is where you are most likely to learn something and to heal wounds that may have been there a long time.

By staying in a sincere, open curiosity, you will also learn about your partner's areas of sensitivity and their signature complexes. Over time, you will begin to understand each other's Inner Children and their Protector-Defenders. When people feel "gotten" instead of judged, they begin to relax. One of our greatest acts of love is creating an environment where your partner can move beyond their defenses. You can hold open this space in compassionate presence when you do your own work first.

Fragile or Unwilling Partners

Some partners can be very challenging. Their Inner Children and their Defenders get activated a lot. People can be so fragile that they cannot tolerate even gentle feedback or requests for change—even when delivered with clarity and kindness. It activates too much insecurity, fear, sense of failure, or shame in them. This makes interacting very difficult because we need to be able to exchange information to build a loving, cooperative relationship. If you are a person who feels demolished by partner feedback, do some early life work, and get your foundation of self in place. Our reactivity burdens a relationship and can wear out even the most loving of partners. If you are partnered with someone who struggles with this, it requires a lot of patience and compassion. If you do your own work and don't react to your partners reactions, sometimes your steadiness can help them to calm down. When both partners have difficult histories, there is a lot of work to do here—but two people committed to a process of growth and healing can make their way forward. The important factor is willingness and the commitment to growth.

GROWING BEYOND VERSUS SOLVING PROBLEMS

It is fascinating to see how when we do enough inner work, things that used to bother us so much cease to be such a big deal. This happens in life and it happens with partners as well. It's how we move beyond some of those irreconcilable differences. Of course, it is okay to ask a partner for some sort of change in the relationship, but when you do your own work first, you often discover that your complaints are not really about what you thought they were about. When you do your own work first, you will inevitably approach your partner from a different stance. This will be more likely to elicit cooperation and a compassionate response versus defensiveness or counter-complaining.

Einstein once said that you cannot solve a problem from the same mindset that created it. We exit many of life's difficulties by shifting to a different state of being and seeing. Solving the "unsolvable problems" of personality difference involves viewing these problems through a different lens and holding them in a different way. Many of a couple's difficulties will never be resolved at the developmental level they are relating from. They will have to grow beyond the domination of their Inner Children and employ the help of a clear-thinking Inner Adult who can view things differently, solve problems, and contain or comfort the distressed children inside. We never completely eliminate ancient vulnerable feelings, but we can manage them differently. We don't let our Inner Children run our lives or dominate our relationship. They become looked-after passengers on the bus of our lives, with calmer, wiser selves at the wheel.

IN SUMMARY

Activation is Invitation – We learn about ourselves when we react to others. Every upset is an invitation to understand yourself more. If you want to develop an amazing relationship—begin within.

Begin within – Do your own work first *before* telling someone else that they should be different. Do this so that you are not burdening the relationship with your own reactive complexes, defenses, and projections.

Engage the other – Once you understand your own reactivity, talk to your partner, so that they can understand you better. Make sure you engage a sincere curiosity about what they were experiencing. In the next chapter, we will discuss how best to communicate.

Continue doing your inner work – The more we reduce our reactivity, the less we burden a relationship. By doing our own inner work, we can "remap" our reactions, reduce our projections, and interact with our partners from a better place. These shifts in stance can evoke quite different responses.

Discover your interlocking complexes – Every couple has them, the places where you trigger each other. Partners who are seeking to become more self-aware can interrupt these difficult dynamics—create "exit ramps" off the conflict highway. You can make progress even if your partner is less willing to engage in this kind of work. Look at the places where the two of you get tangled up in reactivity. Think "inner cast of characters." Who is interacting with who? What would happen if you shifted from the "inner self" who is reacting to a different "inner self," from a different space inside? Get creative and see if the two of you can interrupt the cycle of reactivity with self-awareness, teamwork and pre-emptive planning.

CHAPTER 11

COMMUNICATION

"The single biggest problem in communication
is the illusion that it has taken place."
George Bernard Shaw

"Our state of mind can turn even neutral comments into
fighting words, distorting what we hear to fit what we fear."
Daniel Siegel

"It's not what you say, it's who says it."
Hal and Sidra Stone

"Words are mere symbols, chasing concepts they
will never catch."
Pittman McGehee

"We can't seem to communicate." It's what I hear all the time from couples in trouble. The many ways we try to get through to a partner when we don't feel listened to or understood only serve to make matters worse. Soon enough, John Gottman's "Four Horseman of the Apocalypse" begin to ride through the relationship—criticism, contempt, defensiveness, and stonewalling (stoic withdrawal). Some people use intensity to try to get through, they get louder and more insistent and while they may evoke a begrudging response, there is no heart in it. Psychologically minded people assign labels and theories that explain why the other person is so dysfunctional. Those who are not so verbally nimble resort to silence. Sheer exhaustion can take a person into a resigned withdrawal from which they cannot be stirred. Circular arguments that go nowhere are exasperating, but periods of prolonged silence can be even more disturbing. Many couples reach the unspoken agreement where they just don't talk about anything that would lead to conflict. The creation of these "no-fly zones" inevitably expands. Conflict is challenging, but silence is deafening.

When people can't communicate, their understanding of each other is riddled with distortion. Each new misunderstanding contains the echoes of previous hurts cascading into the present moment like falling dominoes. Unresolved hurt compounds with each new misunderstanding. As the lofty expectations of love's fulfillment fades, hope for the future goes with it and a fear of having made a terrible mistake begins to haunt the relationship. This begins the dangerous drift towards the rocky shoals of demise.

The countless books written about communication indicate its importance and how difficult it can be for two people to convey what they want to get across and for the listener to grasp what they actually mean. The process gets even more difficult when matters of the heart are at stake. Multiple priorities compete as love gets mixed up with the practicalities of life and all of our bewildering personality differences. In this chapter, I'd like to offer some of my own insights, and offer a collection of gems that I have gathered from others. Let me begin in the classic journalist's framework.

WHO, WHAT, WHEN, WHY, WHERE, AND HOW

Who

Most people don't think about this aspect of communication, but if you can grasp just this one idea, it will change your life.

Let's return to the model of having an "inner cast of characters"—all those sub-personalities and dimensions of self. When you are having difficulty communicating with your partner, stop and wonder *who* (in your inner cast) is speaking and *who* is listening and responding (in your partner's inner cast). Notice that different selves will come to the fore throughout the conversation (or argument). Who is speaking and what do they want? What do they fear? What is the underlying need?

Consider the archetypal stance that you are speaking from. Archetypes are systems of energy generated from the psyche. At the core of every complex is an archetypal energy and it can be felt in the body. Archetypes motivate behavior and shape our perceptions regarding what we are encountering, and thus our reactions. Our archetypal stances evoke things from a partner. For example, when you get frustrated and move into the archetype of the Critical Mother, you might evoke a Rebel from your partner and get a lot of push-back; or you might evoke your partner's inner Placater, who is seeking to calm you down, and get a compliant response. Another partner might become a Stonewaller and just silently ignore you— it all depends on your partner's inner cast.

If you are feeling vulnerable and insecure, what if you partner dismisses you and says, "I don't have time for your insecurities today!" What does your vulnerable, insecure Inner Child do with that? When it's a beautiful Saturday and you move into your responsible Get-It-Done self who wants to get that list of house projects completed, what happens if your partner moves into her Playful Nature Girl and says, "Forget the list, let's pack a picnic and go hiking!" How do you react? Can you shift states? Or does your Parental Get-It-Done inner-self lecture your partner about responsibility? Can the two of you find some inner flexibility and work out a balance between your Playful and Responsible selves? Or do you just tangle and get into a power struggle?

What about those arguments about money? If you have an inner Saver (born of your history of scarcity), and your partner has an inner live-for-the-moment Spender (based on living in deprivation), do these two inner selves get into heated arguments over how to manage money? This kind of power struggle is generated from complexes carried by your Inner Children and will always be unresolvable if you don't understand this. Rational arguments won't solve these dilemmas. You have to understand each person's history, the complexes that get stirred up, and the needs, fears, and demands of the Inner Children.

Does your partner's Needy Puppy Dog turn you off when he begs for sex or pleads for attention? When you call your lover at work, does that phone call elicit the attentive Poet Lover, or do you meet the Busy Businessperson who doesn't have time for your call? Who is calling? Who is answering? What is the archetypal energy each of you is operating out of and what is this evoking in the other? What story are you in and how are you being cast? How are you casting your partner? What might happen if you wrote a different story and were operating from a different archetypal stance? Would it evoke a different response? Think about it.

What

Some people don't think at all before they speak. They are just bubbling, expressing, or venting. What are you after when you are talking? Do words fly out of your mouth without ever considering how they are going to land in your partner's world, or do you overthink everything, because you are trying to manage the other person's reactions? Some people stir up so much anxiety about what they are about to say that when they finally speak, all the partner can hear is the anxiety. Our emotions travel with our words, and it is often the emotions rather than the words that evoke reactions in a listener.

If you want something from your partner, get clear on *what* you want before you begin. If you have a complaint, what do you want in terms of change? Try pairing complaints with requests as the starting point of a solution-oriented conversation. Present what I call "plate-size portions" of talk or a topic and then let your partner respond. Listening at length to multiple topics and issues is discouraging and overwhelming for many people. They don't know where to begin and they can't remember half of what you said. Try not to get pulled off into side discussions or arguments that have nothing to do with the goal in mind. If your partner "baits" you, learn not to bite the hook. Partners learn how to trigger each other and can become skillful at pulling each other off track. Consider the archetypal stance you are communicating from (the "who") and how your interactions might improve if you shifted to a different stance. Can you keep your Adult Self online, while managing your reactive Vulnerable Children? Can you locate a Wise or Compassionate Self instead of moving into defense? Can you activate curiosity and stay in a learning conversation? I constantly find myself telling couples, "Ask more questions!"

Demands.

Check for these. No one likes to be on the receiving end of a demand. A demand can masquerade under a "nice" request. How does a person know when something is being demanded? You know it when there is a consequence for not doing what the Demander wants. If there is a punishment involved for saying no, it is a demand. People who demand a lot may get the other person to go along, especially if that person has an Inner Pleaser, but this is not the same thing as full engagement, or buy-in. Sulking, withdrawing affection or sex, becoming passive-aggressive, or attacking and bullying is punishment and will never evoke wholehearted participation. If you wonder where the tenderness and cooperation went in your relationship, check for demands and punishment. Eventually these will extinguish both love and trust, and all you will have left is withdrawal or resentful compliance. Nowhere is this truer than in the realm of sex. Sex therapist and relationship philosopher Esther Perel tells us that when sex becomes an act of duty, or an act of pure caregiving, your partner may comply with your needs, but they will never "want" you.

If you are on the receiving end of a hurtful communication, it is important to wonder about the other person's intention. Many people confuse intention and impact.[66] Just because something your partner said (or did) landed poorly in your world, doesn't mean they intended it that way. Some people struggle to find words, have difficulty expressing feelings, and don't know how to ask for things clearly. Might this be you? How about your partner? When you are hurt or offended, can you move to curiosity? Sometimes your partner will have no idea why something upset you. Look within and figure out what got stirred up in you. How are you interpreting what just happened? When your partner is hurt or offended, same thing, begin with curiosity. When your recollection or interpretation of what happened is different, don't get pulled off into an argument over that. Keep in mind that we all have different subjective worlds, and in those differing worlds, things work differently. In coming to understand your partner's inner world, misunderstandings are inevitable. This is normal—don't catastrophize. If you are trying to get something across to your partner, do your inner work first, so that you can communicate with more clarity. What do you need or want in this situation, and "who" in you is wanting it?

Watch out for the tendency to mind read—we do this all the time, and it involves projection. Even if you think you already know what your partner is going to think, feel, or say, check things out. There is always more to learn here. Try not to fall into the romantic myth of, "If you loved me, you would just know what to do."

Partners are not mind readers or magical creatures. They need our help to understand who you are.

In the early stages of a serious relationship, you will begin to learn about your partner's areas of sensitivity. If they become upset about something that mystifies you, it's time to wonder, "What has just gotten activated?" How are their Inner Kids involved? This is your opportunity to learn something about your partner's formative history. It is a chance to understand their areas of sensitivity and demonstrate some compassion. I encourage you to also watch for things that light your partner up. When you pay attention to this, you learn how to delight them.

When and Where

There are better times and places to discuss matters. My husband used to complain that I often brought up important topics of conversation right as he was heading out the door for work. I didn't realize that I was doing this until he pointed it out. I was just listing things I wanted to talk about at some point, but my husband likes to address things as they come up (I like that about him). I considered this and made an adjustment, making lists and bringing things up when we had time to discuss them fully.

When I work with people who are having difficulty with their sex lives, I sometimes hear that one of them will bring up a household tasks or concern about the children in the midst of a sensual engagement. Talk about derailing the sensual flow! Mindful presence and a pleasure orientation are required for good sex. This is not the time or place to activate the energies of a Responsible Self.

When you have something to address with your partner, *ask if this is a good time.* There are days when people don't have the energy, time, or patience to engage in a fruitful conversation. Also keep in mind that you don't have to resolve everything in one sitting! People who are more anxious are likely to do this. Trust me, you can talk about things a piece at a time. You can resolve part of a problem, try something out, and revisit it at a later date. If you get too activated to be productive, you can table a topic. Do some personal work, calm your nervous system down, and come back to it later. If you are in a relationship with someone who gets easily overwhelmed, pay attention to this. You can see when someone has reached their window of tolerance; their eyes may become dull looking, their face might get flushed, or perhaps their foot will begin to bob up and down. People have "tells." When you see this, pause and ask how they are doing. You partner may have taken in as much as they can for now. This is a nervous system set, but often gets interpreted as "unwillingness." It is also why it is so hard to resolve things with some people. Once a person's nervous system starts to download stress chemicals, you can be sure that their thinking brain is offline. Pay attention to this—pressing forward when no one is home will escalate distress and lead some partners to avoid conversations in the future. Take a time out and come back to the subject later. If you are the one who gets overwhelmed, you have to let your partner know when you have reached your limit. When you can't process any more, ask for a chance to think about what has been said, but make sure that you come back to the issue later after you have figured some things out and settled down. This will reassure an anxious partner that you are not just avoiding issues or refusing to resolve things.

Don't Fight into the Night

There is an old adage about how partners should not go to bed angry. Yes, the sooner you resolve things, the better, but please do not fight into the night. If you fight when you drink, it may be time to examine your drinking patterns. When you are emotionally exhausted (or drunk) you will not be able to resolve things—go to bed and get some rest. By morning, you will be in a different state of mind and heart. You may even find that you have moved out of the whirlpool and what you were arguing about is no longer an issue. Much time and love are wasted when two people are engaged in fights where your Inner Children are frightened and angry, and no Adult is online. The comfort or reassurance being sought in these states cannot be extended by the partner because they are too activated to extend it! These scenes can get particularly ugly, and the harsh words spoken in angry moments are often remembered long after things calm down. When you are operating out of historical wounding and trapped in a cycle of interlocking complexes, get some rest, do some inner work, and then come back when your Inner Adults are onboard.

Why

Consider why are you talking and how you want your partner to respond. Partners don't always know and so they blunder. Help them out. Frame the conversation so that they can respond in a meaningful way, and check in to make sure they are in a space to provide this.

"I'm just venting."

A common complaint I hear from many women is that they don't want the Fixer to show up, they just want their partner to listen. Men love to be Heroes and Problem Solvers, so they will frequently provide suggestions. If you are seeking an audience to whom you can express your feelings—let the listener know that.

"Please provide comfort and support."

Sometimes you are seeking a presence we might call the archetype of the Comforting Friend. While similar to wanting a venting audience, this adds the need for someone to be on your side, perhaps with a dash of validation, empathy, encouragement, maybe a hug or a bit of "cooing." If you want this from a partner, check in and make sure your partner has the time and is in the space to do this. An impatient listener will only make you feel worse.

Do keep in mind that if all you do after parenting or working all day is complain about your day, your awful boss, or your difficult mother, you will start to exhaust your partner's listening ear. Having a committed life partner, doesn't obligate them to listen to a constant stream of life complaints. Eventually they will tune you out or start suggesting solutions, and you will feel "unheard." Don't relegate your partner to the archetype of Sounding Board. You can barrage a partner with so much negativity that they don't look forward to seeing you. Take some action for change. Get yourself a therapist who will help you resolve these areas of your life so that you are not stuck in a negativity trance.

"Let's make a decision about something."

Sometimes you really do want a solution about something—these are intentional "fix-it" talks. You may want something to change in your relationship, or you have a proposition to make—"Let's buy a different house," "Let's have another baby," "I want to quit my job and go back to school," and so on. Do your inner work first, sorting out your own inner conflicts and questions. If you think this will be a difficult discussion for your partner, find a good time and give them a heads up that it might be unsettling. If you are conflict-avoidant or have a strong Inner Pleaser, get in touch with (or develop) your Inner Boat Rocker. The Boat Rocker can hold steady while your partner's boat rocks, allowing your partner to steady themselves without you back-pedaling, and saying things like, "Oh forget it, it's not that important." Remember that all conversations begin with explorations and if your partner hits the brakes, ask them, "Is there any part of this you can get onboard with?" Stay curious if they get a bit reactive: "Tell me more about your concerns. What is this touching into?"

When two people want two different things, it is an invitation into discovery, not power struggle. Many times, if you let a reactive partner percolate on something, they have a chance to sort themselves out, and the follow-up conversation will be far more productive. Some people need to think about things a while, and they may not know how they feel or why they are upset right off the bat. Keep in mind that you can have multiple conversations about big decisions. These discussions will grow you as a couple if you practice the six capacities. Remember that the stance you communicate from makes a big difference in what it evokes!

The "you did something to hurt or upset me" conversation

When you feel hurt or offended, do your inner work first. Sort yourself out. What did this touch in *your* inner world and *your* history? Once you know, you will communicate from a different stance. You can disclose something of your inner world, rather than attack, plead, blame, or shame. This will evoke less defensiveness and encourage cooperation (an outcome of deepening the six capacities). Help this other person understand why something matters to you. If you are asking for change, offer a suggestion, but realize that this is the beginning of a discovery and solution-oriented conversation, not a demand (unless this really is a deal-breaker). Your partner may or may not be willing or able to do what you want. Keep in mind that if they understand you, they will be more likely to try to accommodate you. If what you are wanting from them is something they are willing or able to do, great. If not, keep exploring. What is in the way? What can they offer instead? If they cannot provide you with the change you want, can you view the situation differently—look through a different lens? Check the meanings you are attaching to what is happening. Might you hold this situation differently, in which case you react differently?

Serious conversations about "deal-breakers"

In a recent conversation with a couple, I was explaining the difference between an ultimatum and giving information about a deal-breaking situation. They were discussing his active addiction, and I supported the wife in conveying that if certain behaviors continued, she could not continue in the relationship. He turned to me and said, "Isn't that a demand? You're not supposed to demand … right?" I explained that the communication his wife was giving him was not a demand. It was information—a compassionate heads-up about her decision. It was delivered kindly and without contempt. The husband needed to decide what he wanted to do. He was free to choose to get into treatment or continue drinking. She was simply informing him of her plans. She had done a lot of inner work to resolve her inner conflicts about this. If you are living with an active addiction, abusive behavior, untreated mental illness, chronic unemployment, or repeated and unremorseful infidelity, you need to do your own work, and then have courage and engage in some serious decisions about the future of your relationship. When you do your individuation work, some things become clear that weren't clear before. When you get clear about who you are, and the kind of relationship you want to build with someone, you can speak without defense or rancor about what you can and cannot live with. It is an honorable, courageous, and compassionate thing to tell someone in advance that if something continues, you will need to leave the relationship.

The "I want to understand you more deeply" conversation

These are important conversations, and they build intimacy. If you have laid the groundwork by demonstrating deep, attentive, non-reactive listening in previous conversations, your partner will have more confidence that it is safe to reveal themselves. They will be more willing to disclose their inner world to you—their thoughts, feelings, vulnerabilities, and history.

As we grow closer, and our projections start to fall away, we will learn that there is more to know about this person we are building a life with. We really didn't understand them at the start. This is normal, but it can also be disconcerting. When we do our own inner work, we can see more clearly and love more dearly. As we mature, we don't need a partner to be our "ideal." We can handle who they actually are versus who we would wish them to be. A great deal of relationship growth has to do with allowing for differences, while remaining connected, compassionate, and cooperative. No two people will ever share the same thoughts, feelings, beliefs, conclusions, perspectives, preferences, needs, wants, and desires in every area of life. Difference does not mean that we can't make a life together. It invites us into a process of discovery, growth, and creativity.

How

In the next section I'm going to offer two communication protocols that I have found particularly helpful for couples. What I want to emphasize is that the structure of these protocols makes something deeper possible, so don't get over preoccupied with the protocols themselves. I like these two formats for communication because they promote two essential but seemingly opposing dimensions in a relationship—*differentiation* (knowing who you are, and being able to communicate about it) and *safe connection* (the sense of security that even when the two of you are different, the relationship—the "we"—contains that difference). What you are looking for is what begins to take place as you engage this other person more deeply. What is happening in the space between the two of you, as understanding develops. This is something beyond the words. It happens as people relax and begin to open to each other. It happens as they "cross the bridge"[67] into the other person's world and engage in what Martin Buber called "true meeting."

REAL DIALOGUE

Polly Young-Eisendrath is a Jungian analyst and psychotherapist. She and her late husband, Ed Epstein, created a process that they call "Real Dialogue."[8] In the Real Dialogue process there

---

[8] For those of you familiar with the technique of "reflective listening" or the Imago Dialogue, this process will be familiar. As you study it, it has some distinct differences as well.

is an emphasis on noting the shift that occurs in the space between the two people as they move beyond projecting or identifying with (or resisting) the projections of the other person. We pick up an enormous amount of "stuff" from the interpersonal space between us—more than we ever realize. Polly emphasizes that we each live in our own snow globe and when we get shaken up, it becomes difficult to see another person clearly, let alone understand them. Real Dialogues help parties navigate out of places of assumptions, patterned interactions, and identification or resistance against what is being projected onto us. As we sort things out and listen more deeply, safety increases. We can voice needs, concerns, and vulnerabilities that could not be voiced before. Real Dialogue is designed to be a process between two equals where there will be a growing allowance and curiosity regarding two separate subjective worlds. The process will not work if there is a significant power differential—where one person is beholden to (or employed by) the other, or where an abusive dynamic is actively going on.

In a dialogue, even when the two parties don't resolve their differences, both will have shifted in their way of relating to each other as they understand each other better, feel more "gotten," and consider both sides of what is being presented. The shift will be *in the space between them*. Much of our difficulties come from aspects of self that are outside of our conscious awareness—projections, reactions to projections, and how we identify with or resist those projections. Moving beyond a relationship impasse requires an internal shift rather than finding a "solution." You can learn more about Polly's approach to relationships and communication in her recent book *Love Between Equals*.[68] Here is a summary of the principles and process.

Speak for Yourself

Be aware that each of you has your own subjective basis for impressions, memories of what happened, interpretations, and projections of meaning and intention. Because of this it is important to stay away from inferring that you have the one true and objective memory or interpretation. Avoid speaking for the other person or even making "we" statements, which infers that you are speaking for both of you. Just speak about your own experience, impressions, thoughts, and feelings.

Listen Mindfully

Attend and attune. Do this for the purpose of paraphrasing and reflecting back what you heard. Try to suspend your own ideas and understandings and step into the other person's shoes. See if you can grasp what that person is experiencing from *their* perspective. What are they trying to get across to you? It is important to understand that you do not have to *agree* with what the other person is saying, thinking, feeling, or concluding! Resist the urge to interrupt, explain, or counter what is being said. This part of the dialogue is about understanding what *the other person* is experiencing. It helps if the speaker does not go on too long, so that the listener can stay mindful, rather than trying to remember the points being made.

After the other person has spoken for a time, reflect back your understanding of what they are trying to get across. Avoid beginning with, "I heard you say…" This phrase has been overused by people who are just parroting and not really seeking to understand the other person's experience. Many people find this phrase irritating. When you reflect back, it allows the partner to clarify things you didn't really understand. This may be because you did not hear what your partner intended or perhaps because they didn't communicate clearly enough. Ask them, "Did I get it?" They may want to add something more or state an aspect that you missed. After they do this, reflect that piece back. Keep going back and forth until the speaker feels satisfied that you have fully grasped what they are trying to convey.

Once your partner feels "gotten," it is your turn to speak. Now is your chance to respond to anything that was said. You can clarify a misunderstanding, or you might ask a question. Be mindful to speak about your experience only (use "I" language), rather than talking about what you think the other person is thinking, feelings, or intending (back to projection). Even using the word "we" implies that you believe that you know what the other person is thinking and feeling, and it is the same as you. Of course, sometimes you need to use the word "you" as in, "when you _____, then I _____." Just make sure you return to describing your own experience, not labelling or assigning responsibility to the other. It takes a lot of mindfulness and practice to shift into consistently speaking for yourself and avoiding our tendency to talk about what we believe the other person is thinking, feeling, or intending.

Mutual Witnessing

As the conversation develops, notice, and remain interested in what is emerging *between the two of you*. Feeling really listened to in our culture is a rare and wonderful thing. True presence is powerful. As we listen deeply, it gives us a chance to examine where we might have been projecting something that is actually originating in our own psyche. With a life partner, if you continue communicating in this way you will begin to experience a deepening intimate connection forming.

You may not reach any solution during this kind of a dialogue, but that is not really the goal. Although solutions and resolutions may occur, this is not a problem-solving exercise. The point is a deepening sense of understanding, which will automatically shift the relationship. A softening will occur, and in this increased openness, possibilities will emerge that were not possible when the two of you were in protective projection mode.

BADER and PEARSON'S INITIATOR-INQUIRER PROCESS

Ellyn Bader and Pete Pearson are a husband-and-wife team who founded The Couples Institute, which offers exceptional training in couples work. Utilizing a mostly online format, they have trained therapists all over the world. I have been particularly impressed by Ellyn Bader's open-hearted appreciation of other teachers' contribution to the field. She values wisdom from many sources and understands that different teachers bring different pieces of the puzzle to the many-faceted realm of relationships. Bader and Pearson emphasize that intimate relationships go through developmental stages, and it is our personal growth that moves a relationship forward.

One of the tools they have developed is called the "Initiator-Inquirer" exercise—referred to as the "I-I." Over the years, as I have given the "I-I" sheets out to my clients, they have told me that when they get into a conflict, they pull out their "I-I papers" to keep their discussion in a structured format, which helps them stay curious and engaged.

You will see some similarities in this protocol to Real Dialogue. In my work, I integrate the two methods to teach couples some powerful communication skills. The aspect that I particularly appreciate in the Initiator-Inquirer process is the emphasis on differentiation. The process allows the speaker (the Initiator) to learn more about themselves as they are revealing themselves and this requires the activation of a new level of personal courage. I also think of the Initiator and the Inquirer as archetypes that live within each of us that can be developed with intention. I have included the Initiator-Inquirer sheets in the Appendix of this book.

The Initiator

The Initiator is the person who is going to self-reveal. You must self-define and figure out what you want to convey, then have the courage and willingness to reveal yourself to your partner—to *initiate.* This can be difficult for people who have a fear of displeasing, hurting, alienating, or being punished by a partner. It is also difficult, if you have never really looked inward, to discover who you are, or if you have an underlying belief that you are unworthy or unlovable. For many people, opening up and talking about what is going on inside is terrifying, especially if you grew up in an abusive or authoritarian household where you were punished for speaking your truth. You may also have been in a previous relationship where speaking your mind and heart was not well received. In those environments, there was wisdom in not disclosing, but this can become habitual, leading to a long-standing belief that nothing good comes from talking about who you are or what is going on inside of you. In a relationship where two people are trying to establish intimacy, trust, and understanding, it is essential for partners to self-reveal. This protocol will make it safer, and over time, a couple will gain increasing capacity to do it with honesty, courage, and grounded presence. I invite you to consider that you might be projecting your past fears onto your current partner. Take a chance and see if this person can be trusted.

If you find that your partner cannot be safe enough to disclose yourself to, it limits what is possible for the two of you. If one or both of you cannot listen without becoming highly reactive, or if either of you use disclosures against the other in the future, this requires a lot of growth, and you probably need some professional help to get there. In some cases, you will need to consider whether you are living with someone who is sufficiently committed to the *process* of building a relationship—which includes the development of the six love capacities.

The Inquirer

In this protocol the listener is called the Inquirer. The work of the Inquirer is to maintain enough inner calm to truly listen, to avoid defending, arguing, or cross-complaining. Cross-complaining is something that partners do a lot when they feel defensive. One person will say something like, "Why didn't you transfer the laundry from the washer to the dryer like you said you would?" The other person will respond defensively by cross-complaining: "If I wasn't so busy picking up your wet towels off the floor, I might have remembered it!" Explaining in great detail, is another common defense. While you may have good reasons for what you did and why, this doesn't address or resolve the underlying feelings of the partner. Often these defenses will just escalate the other person's distress because they don't feel "gotten."

The Inquirer (listener) simply needs to hear and understand. They do not need to own the feelings, memories, projections, or conclusions that are being spoken by the speaker (the Initiator). Of course, the listener can be sensitive and responsive to what the other person wants, but they are not *responsible* for the other person's feelings. This is a hard truth to grasp and is sometimes used by people who want to be dismissive: "I am not responsible for your feelings." We are not talking about being dismissive here; that is not listening or inquiring. However, the speaker (the Initiator) should realize that whatever they are expressing is *their* issue. Discussing it does not mean that the listener is required to respond in any particular way. If the Inquirer wants to respond to something expressed by the Initiator, that's fine, however, it needs to be from a place of love and empathy, not begrudging duty or fearful capitulation.

When you are addressing something with a partner, it is important to *focus on one topic or issue at a time*. This can be hard to do for some people, especially for grievance collectors and highly anxious partners. Try to stay with one thing at a time to avoid overcomplicating the conversation. If you have more items to address, consider holding the rest for a later time… and quit on a win.

The Initiator-Inquirer exercise is about listening to learn—for both people. While the listener may be learning things, it is important for the speaker (Initiator) to be open to their own discoveries. It is not unusual for the speaker to begin to recognize things not in their awareness when they began to talk. In the space of a good listener, the speaker may realize feelings, associations with the past, early decisions that could be reworked, misconceptions, projections, deeper needs, and longings—all underneath the original topic of discussion.

It is important to note that most of us harbor mixed feelings about lots of things, and it is okay to change one's mind in the middle of this exercise if something becomes clearer. Being with a deep listener allows us to learn about ourselves, and this is an incredible gift of love.

NON-VIOLENT COMMUNICATION

Marshall Rosenberg developed another protocol for communication called Non-violent Communication.[69] He emphasizes that when we are addressing an issue, it is important to open it up with a description of what happened in the most neutral, objective way possible, avoiding labels, interpretation, or the assignment of motivation or meaning. We can then describe how it impacted us (feelings) and what we wanted and *needed* underneath those feelings. He points out that much of what we represent as "feelings" are actually our thoughts! He points out that when we can get down to the *basic human needs underneath the feelings*, we are really getting somewhere. Needs can be met in a variety of ways. Try this out next time you get in a tangle with someone. Listen beneath the words—especially if they are accusatory or shaming. Try to discern the need underneath what is being expressed and it will help with feelings of defensiveness. The other person might be afraid, outraged, hurt, frustrated, sad, and so on. Ask yourself, "What is the need? Is it reassurance, appreciation, safety, connection, acceptance, respect, consideration, accountability, empathy, or something else?"[70] When you think you might have discerned the need under the feelings being expressed, or the inflammatory words, reflect the need back to the person. When you "get" a person, they will start to calm down. You can then move into a more solution-oriented discussion.

It is important for us to remember that identifying what someone else wants and needs in a situation is the starting point in a conversation. We are not obligated to automatically comply. The first step is to understand, the next step is to move into an exploration of what would help to resolve things.

Marshal offers a powerful question that is a really nice one for couples to ask each other: "How can I make your life more wonderful?" Now, that's a question that will open a lover's heart.

ADDITIONAL THOUGHTS ON COMMUNICATION

How to be Dismissive

While we are not responsible for other people's feelings, some people are clueless or insensitive, and some are outright cruel. When you raise an issue with someone and they respond, "I am not responsible for your feelings," it acts as a dismissal and a mis-application of the truth that our feelings really are about our own histories, values, wants, needs, sensitivities, and complexes. While this is true, a person who responds in this way is lacking curiosity and compassion, and is being defensive rather than relational. Sometimes this response is used by someone with an avoidant attachment orientation who feels overwhelmed by another person's needs and feelings. It is also a gambit used when someone doesn't want to be in a learning conversation or admit that they have done something that has damaged the bond.

You Shouldn't Feel That Way

This is another way to be dismissive. There is nothing more frustrating, alienating, and possibly shame inducing than to hear your partner say, "You shouldn't feel that way." The point is that you do! Perhaps the listener just can't grasp *why* you would feel a certain way. That's not the point. The point is to try to see things from the *other* person's point of view—to inquire! The listener does not have to agree with the feelings, thoughts, conclusions, or projections being expressed by the other—they just have to get it, and hopefully take some time to explore what led to those thoughts, feelings, and conclusions. This works both ways. Just because someone believes that you were doing something intentionally hurtful doesn't mean that you were. You can validate another person's distress or fears without agreeing with their thinking. When you understand *how* they were interpreting your actions, you have a place to begin resolving things.

If you want to be intimate and feel connected with your partner, you will need to cross the bridge over into that other person's world so you can see things from the other person's perspective and imagine why they might be feeling the way they do. When either partner becomes upset, it indicates that something has gotten stirred up. There is something to learn here.

Think in Terms of "Weather Reports"

When people are upset, they express things with great intensity. Often the listening partner will come out of these conversations believing that what was expressed was the bottom-line truth. Not necessarily, but harsh words spoken in anger can stay with the listener a long time. I often find myself telling couples that emotions are like the weather. The weather changes. An intense "blow up" is sometimes like a "summer storm." Some compartment of feeling that has been under pressure for a while is thundering out. Once these feelings are expressed, the pressure system is relieved, and the stormy person settles back down into a sunnier state of being. Unfortunately, some people say some hateful things during their storming. Saying, "I hate you!" or "I'm leaving!" needs to be repaired as soon as possible. The weather changes, our feelings about the relationship can move from intense joy and gratitude to moments of anger and resentment across the course of one day. What we need to be really concerned about is "climate change"—when the feelings become stable over time. Chronic resentment or feelings of detachment are dangerous climates in a relationship.

I'm Just Expressing My Feelings

When I am working with couples, I sometimes need to interrupt a diatribe by one partner where they are ripping the other person to shreds with an assault of blame, shame, criticism, and contempt. Most of these sentences begin with "You _____." When I interrupt someone who is aggressively attacking their partner, the interrupted person sometimes looks confused. The response may be, "I'm just expressing my feelings! People are supposed to express their feelings, aren't they?" I then point out that there is a significant difference between expressing feelings (speaking about your own needs and experience) and tearing another person apart. You are not expressing feelings when you are denigrating someone's character, listing offenses, mind-reading, projecting intent, diagnosing deficiencies, criticizing, complaining, and making a case for how the other person is a villain, insensitive dolt, or a stupid idiot. This may indeed be someone you no longer want to be in relationship with, but judging, condemning, and assigning negative labels is not expressing feelings.

Think About the Inner Cast of Characters

Remember to think in terms of the "inner cast of characters." "Who" is speaking and "who" is listening? Certain thoughts and feelings held by one inner self, may not be held by others. Recall that we often have "mixed feelings." What we want to consider are aspects of self that have not been welcomed in the relationship. These can become "shadow selves" that remain in the "basement of the relationship" and can seek entry at difficult times, destroying the security of the bond and disrupting the life. The more you know your partner deeply, the safer you are and the less likely you are to be sideswiped by some shadow dimension of their personality.

Lying

Dishonesty is a real problem in a relationship. However, there are varying degrees of dishonesty. Some people are dishonest with themselves. They don't know themselves well enough to speak truthfully. They may promise things that they can't follow up on, which is very distressing for the partner. Some people "lie" because their Inner Pleasers want to tell you what you want to hear, without really checking in to see if "the full cast" inside can really back up the "yes." This is a function of being unconscious. Others know they won't follow up, but they are afraid of displeasing or disappointing you. Some people don't speak truthfully because they fear that they will be punished in some way. They are trying to manage your reactions. These are all problems, but they can be outgrown.

When a partner engages in lying to your face about significant foundations of the relationship, it becomes more serious. Gas-lighting is a form of lying where you sense that something is going on (or you may actually have evidence that something is going on) and the partner lies to your face denying it and trying to convince you that you are crazy, misreading the signs, or that someone else has lied to you. This often happens when an affair is discovered, and the more lying that takes place after the discovery, the more difficult it is for trust to be re-established. A large part of the lingering difficulty that betrayed partners have in getting beyond an affair is not as much about the sexuality infidelity as about the hurt of being lied to.

The Lie Invitee

Bader and Pearson wrote an important book about degrees of lying and point out that there is such a thing as a "lie invitee."[71] This is the person who is so reactive that he or she begins to evoke "truth avoidance" in the partner. I see this sometimes in couples where one of them is highly reactive to minor things. The conflict-avoidant partner would rather lie than go through another emotional upheaval. Of course, conflict-avoidant partners have their own work to do, but if your partner avoids telling you the truth because "you can't handle it," or you are a punisher, you might want to look at how *you* have contributed to this dynamic. Have you become a Lie Invitee? The more able we are to hear the truth and face everything about our partner (shadow and light) the safer and freer that person will feel to reveal themselves.

Pathological Liars

Let's be real. There are people in the world who lie regularly to manipulate or exploit others for their advantage. Some of them are quite practiced and so good at it that good people are taken in by them. These folks don't have easy "tells." Lying may be so engrained in their personality structure and may have worked so well for them over time, that they have no interest in breaking this pattern. We are talking about a serious character disorder here, where there is little regret, and no empathy about the impact of their exploitations. If you begin to sense that you are partnered with such a person, seek professional help, because there is no future with such a person if you want to be loved and cared for, and if you value trust and intimacy.

Love Languages

I want to close this section on a bright note. There is a little gem of a book written by Gary Chapman—*The Five Love Languages*.[72] Chapman has created five categories of "ways to love"—words of affirmation, quality time, gifts, acts of service, and physical touch. The important point of this book is that we tend to love our partners the way we would like to be loved. We give them what we would like to receive. The problem with this is that *our* love language is not necessarily our partner's. We need to learn our partner's love language in order for them to experience being loved well by us.

In my relationship workshops I always have partners ask each other, "When do you feel most loved by me?" People are often surprised by what their partner shares. They may have assumed that they knew this already, but they often learn something new when they ask this question.

CHAPTER 12

COMPASSION

"If you want to be happy, practice compassion."
The Dalai Lama

"We must learn to regard people less in the light of what they do or omit to do, and more in the light of what they suffer."
Dietrich Bonhoeffer

"Compassion is by definition relational."
Kristin Neff

Commitment is essential to the process of becoming a couple. Courage is necessary for staying on the path with an open heart. Courage mixed with curiosity means that we truly want to understand ourselves and the inner world of the other. Those who engage in personal inquiry and sincere learning conversations, stay out of the danger zone of defenses and protective disconnection. Learning conversations will move these lovers beyond projections and misunderstandings. They will learn how to love in a more meaningful way because they understand the unique particulars of their beloved—the history that formed them, "who" lives in their inner cast of characters, where they find meaning in this life, and where their heart needs healing. In the co-created safety of that mutual space, the unique quality of their shared life will grow; the bond will deepen, and the heart can remain open. It is a miracle of life that as we begin to understand another person more deeply, our compassion naturally flows.

What is Compassion?

Compassion is not pity. Pity involves looking down on someone less fortunate. In an intimate relationship pity is a close cousin to contempt. Compassion is not sympathy, which involves feeling for someone, but at arm's length. Sympathy is not sufficient in an intimate relationship, where we would hope that this person would be there for us in a meaningful way. In compassion, we are feeling with, sharing in the other person's joys and sorrows. We don't hold them at arm's length, we walk with them. Compassion carries us in difficult times. It is a soulful quality that springs from the deep Self. The traditional marriage vow states that we will remain, "for better or worse, in sickness and in health." True lovers have this commitment because of the value of the bond and their love of the unique particulars in each other. Commitment, courage, and compassion carry people beyond difficult losses and the unforeseen vagaries of life. Over time, loving couples build something akin to an emotional bank account. Their roots go deep, and when they hit a difficult time, they draw on this bank account. Committed couples, who have built a meaningful shared life don't cut and run when the going gets tough.

Compassion is a sibling of empathy, impossible to experience without it. Empathy is the capacity to put ourselves in another person's experience. It equates to what we talked about in the communication chapter—that until we "cross the bridge"[73] into the other person's world, we will not understand them deeply. We have to look out of the eyes of their history and experience and understand how life works over there.

Compassion differs slightly from empathy in that it involves a desire to act in response to another person's suffering. "What do you need right now? Is there anything I can do?" These are the questions that spring naturally from people with compassion. In an intimate relationship, we put our own personal concerns on hold to respond to and support the other.

Those who have not worked through their own emotional wounding can find it difficult to draw close to another person who is suffering. The resonance of a partner's suffering activates too much pain in their own history. People with limited emotional resources can't afford to spend their meager allotment on others. The result is that they cannot provide meaningful comfort or assistance to a partner in distress. This injures the sense of trust and security. When a partner is left to struggle alone it is experienced as abandonment or rejection. It conveys the message, "I cannot tolerate your vulnerability," even "You are only okay with me when you are strong." The one thing we want most from an intimate partner is to know that they will be there when we need someone, to help and to comfort.

SELF-COMPASSION

Compassion Flows Two Ways

Kristin Neff has built her academic career on the study of self-compassion. Neff and fellow psychologist Chris Germer are on a campaign to teach about the great benefits of self-compassion and to clear up its misconceptions.[74] They have developed a program to help people deepen this capacity, and Germer emphasizes that compassion is an omnidirectional capacity—it travels outward, but it also travels inward.[75] The inward flow of compassion is self-compassion.

Misconceptions About Self-Compassion Include:
– Having self-compassion encourages wallowing in self-pity.
– It will make you lazy and self-indulgent.
– It will lead people to become selfish and self-absorbed—we
  need to think of others before ourselves.
– It equates with weakness—a person needs to be tough and
  strong to get through life.
– High standards and harsh self-criticism are the only way to
  drive people to achieve.

Neff's research on self-compassion demonstrates that these ideas couldn't be further from the truth. People who are more self-compassionate ruminate less and are more resilient in life. They are better able to cope with tough situations. Because they do not engage in harsh self-criticism or punish themselves for setbacks, they take more risks and reach for higher goals. They are self-encouraging and persist more when they encounter difficulties. They are also less likely to make excuses and are more likely to take responsibility for their actions, which means they will apologize when they have hurt or offended someone. In their romantic relationships they are more caring, forgiving, and supportive.

Neff differentiates self-compassion from the construct of self-esteem and shows how self-compassion is more predictive of relationship success. While it is a good thing to have "self-esteem," it is important to note that self-esteem if often based on our Ego identity—thus it is an unstable aspect of our well-being. The sense of worth I am talking about in this book is sourced from the deep Self.

The self-esteem movement was set into motion in the late 1960s by psychologist Nathaniel Brandon. Later on, therapist Pia Melody[76] outlined what "healthy" self-esteem looks like. Unfortunately, an unhealthy "self-esteem movement" has become a part of our culture, with too much emphasis on external recognition, measuring oneself against others in an effort to be "the best," becoming driven, aggressively competitive, self-absorbed, and perfectionistic. I am certain this is not what Nathanial Brandon or Pia Melody ever intended. Garrison Keeler, in the show "Prairie Home Companion," joked about the self-esteem movement when he told us about the mythical land of Lake Wobegon and how, "all the children are above-average."

There are many people today who profess to have high self-esteem, but they are actually just self-important and entitled. Their fragile underlying egos can be easily deflated if they do not come out "on top" or receive a steady stream of outside validation. You can see how this would make their intimate relationships very difficult. When their Egos are threatened, these people get defensive and aggressive. Sadly, when inflated entitlement, self-importance, and a lack of empathy for others are major personality factors, we see a demonstration of one of our most noxious personality disorders—narcissism.[77]

Countering all of this is self-compassion. People with the capacity of self-compassion are more willing to look at themselves and engage in the inner work necessary to become good partners. Self-compassion is an antidote to shame and allows people to engage in "shadow work"—facing the unconscious and hidden things about ourselves that are hard to look at.

The Three Components of Self-Compassion:

Let's take a closer look at the three components of self-compassion outlined by Neff and Germer.[78]

<u>Self-kindness versus self-judgement</u>: Judging oneself is different than being accountable. Neff found that self-judgment and judgment from others tends to send people into shame, at which point they are less likely to take responsibility for something which requires repair or attention.

<u>Shared humanity versus alienation and isolation</u>: The next component of self-compassion has to do with how we are all

imperfect human beings. When we share a sense of common humanity, it links us with others rather than leading us into shame and the subsequent tendency to isolate ourselves. Neff reminds us that self-compassion is a significant antidote to shame.

Mindfulness versus over-identification is the third component of self-compassion. This speaks to our capacity to step out of the stories we tell ourselves and our tendency to over-identify with aspects of ourselves that are partial, and don't represent the larger picture of who we are. We are more than our roles, histories, or even our personality qualities. In mindfulness, we are encouraged to step back and observe ourselves, to reflect on our thoughts, feelings, actions, and reactions—to become more self-aware. Rather than remaining stuck in our stories, defined by our roles, at the mercy of our embedded complexes, we notice them but don't become over-identified with them. We come to understand that we are more than all of this.

Self-compassion mediates shame, and shame is the most corrosive emotion humans can feel.

People with self-compassion are gentler with themselves, and with less self-criticism and self-punishment, they are better at self-soothing. In being compassionate with ourselves, we grant our partners more latitude for their human weaknesses, recognizing that we all have fallen short in life. People with good compassion skills develop the capacity to communicate concerns, needs, and desires, in ways that are honest and direct, but kinder and more compassionate, allowing for the struggles and processes of the other. People with self-compassion are less reactive in difficult exchanges because their self-esteem is not grounded in a need for a partner to continually affirm and approve of them. This softens our defensive tendencies and invites a more open heart, leading to more loving responses and a more secure bond.

Compassion and Accountability

We all bring history into a relationship and that history contributes to the formation of our personal complexes. When we look through the lens of a complex, we interpret what happens to us in a particular way. We come into relationships with preconceived notions about who we are, who others are, and how life works for people like us. All of this can contribute to misunderstandings in love. Our unresolved attachment issues get stirred up and we project all of this out onto our unassuming partners. Becoming more aware of what we project onto a partner and how we assign intentions and motivations is part of being accountable. We do our personal work so that we are less likely to burden a relationship with all this confusion. People who do not labor under a burden of shame find it easier to be accountable. Self-compassion as an antidote to shame allows us to take more responsibility for our part in a relationship difficulty. That accountability is foundational to the building of trust in a relationship.

Shadow Work Versus Shame

The amazing thing about walking the path of life with another person is that we will continue to discover things about ourselves that were previously hidden from our awareness. In extending compassion to a partner, we open a no-shame space for our partner to engage in their own deep inquiry. There are so many ways in this life where we can feel like we are failing. The shadow companion of the sense of failure is shame, and one of the most terrible experiences of shame is the sense that we have become a disappointment to a partner. When we can develop self-compassion, we can find the capacity to be kind to ourselves, and extend this kindness to an imperfect partner, aware that we are all members of an imperfect humanity.

Loving people can listen deeply, without agenda or defense, and provide the space for a partner to connect the dots of their experience and move into deeper self-understanding. As insights are gained on both sides, compassion will spontaneously emerge. Defenses will begin to drop, and cooperation begin. In the loving light of a partner's compassionate presence, we begin to face things about ourselves that were previously avoided or utterly unconscious. Our intimate relationships are the most significant place in life in which we can do our personal shadow work—looking at disowned aspects of self, facing the hard things inside. The self-discoveries we can make in the field of love are profound.

The Toxicity of Shame

Shame is one of the most toxic emotions that a human being can feel. Researcher Brené Brown, tells us that shame involves the painful feeling that we are fundamentally flawed and therefore unworthy of love or belonging.[79] When we feel ashamed, we want to hide away and not be seen. We avoid people, numb out with substances, and engage in self-destructive behaviors. Shame will take your voice away and cause you to keep toxic secrets. Shame makes people aggressive and angry.

Men are particularly vulnerable to shame. In *Daring Greatly*,[80] Brené Brown tells the story of a man who came to see her after one of her talks on vulnerability. He wanted to convey how difficult it is for men to be vulnerable without significant shame. He believed that his wife and daughters would rather see him die on top of his white horse than watch him fall off. Many men, who are trained by our culture not to reveal vulnerability or weakness, feel a deep sense of shame when they come in contact with their own humanity. Men are expected be strong, heroic, steady, and brave. However, Brené reminds us that vulnerability is essential to intimacy, and while so many women long for men to draw close and self-reveal, it is no wonder that men have so much difficult with intimacy in love.

Anger is the one emotion that is truly sanctioned for men and they will often move into anger rather than feel vulnerable feelings like fear, anxiety, pain, longing, or sadness. In my work, I see men who are seeking to tolerate their more vulnerable emotions and as that capacity expands, they have significantly more fulfilling intimate relationships.

Brené tells us that we develop "shame resilience" when we can voice things of which we dare not speak to a trustworthy other. The experience of being known deeply and loved completely, in all one's shadow and light, creates a profound bond between the two people and it is one of the healing aspects of a really good relationship.

Sexual Compassion

We encounter many opportunities for shame in our love relationships, where the failures to be an Ideal Lover is inevitable. Part of my work with couples includes my certification as a sex therapist, and nowhere do I witness such a depth of vulnerability as when a couple is struggling to establish and sustain a meaningful sexual connection. Many couples power struggle or disengage over sex. They are reticent to reveal themselves openly, paralyzed by fears of rejection, at the same time filled with longing—the longing to be wanted, embraced, and affirmed as acceptable sexual beings. Sexual confidence and a willingness to explore are certainly sexual aphrodisiacs, but in the real world, so many people are overcome by shame, anxiety, and self-protection, that all manner of sexual dysfunction and avoidance prevail. Our need for compassion and self-compassion in the sexual realm is imperative and may be the true key to unlocking sexual doors. More on that in Chapter 14.

COMPASSION AND FORGIVENESS

The Dangers of Forced Forgiveness

In thinking about where to discuss the important topic of forgiveness, I chose this chapter because I believe that forgiveness requires compassion. This is a crucial component of relationship, but there are many misconceptions about forgiveness, often conveyed by religious teachings. The dark side of forgiveness is the pressure to re-embrace an offender who has done great damage, without any acknowledgement of harm, remorse, or accountability on that other person's part. In these cases, there is no reassurance that this person will not repeat the same damaging actions in the future. If there has been no acknowledgement for the hurt caused, no amends, no personal work done or real accountability, welcoming such a person back into your life opens the door for future hurt and transgression. When people do this, their vulnerable Inner Children move into perpetual vigilance or go into hiding. Our Inner Children know who is dangerous and who is not.

Repair Skills

Relationships require good repair skills, something that researcher John Gottman found in all successful long-term relationships—the capacity to repair[81] when the bond is damaged. Relationship expert, Stan Tatkin, emphasizes the importance of repairing an injury to the attachment bond swiftly and thoroughly,[82] but repair is an area of relationship that few people have skills in.

Repair begins with understanding what the injury was about, without defending and justifying one's innocence. *A repair does not require that someone admits they have done something "wrong," it is about repairing damage to the bond,* and restoring a sense of trust and security in the relationship. When we do this, it keeps the heart open; when we do not, the heart begins to protect itself. A good repair requires deep listening and attending to why something mattered—the meaning and interpretation attached, the history. If an apology is required, it needs to be offered—without shame. Even if no harm was intended and no agreements were broken, a hurt acknowledged is healing.

In *Why Won't You Apologize,*[83] psychologist Harriet Lerner has written an excellent book on forgiveness and the importance of a sincere and adequate apology. A real apology requires an acknowledgment of the hurt done and the impact that one's action had on the other person, *even if hurt was not intended*. That's the hard part. "I'm sorry you feel that way," is not an apology—and it contains an inference that the other person is making too much of something. An apology needs to be specific and without the addition of a "but" … anything beyond the "but" is a justification and a negation of the apology. When an understanding of the hurt experienced has been reached and an acknowledgement, along with any necessary reparations, has taken place, people can move more easily to forgiveness.

Sometimes, the possibility of repair is there, but it falls just beyond a wall of defense. In the movie, *The Divine Secrets of the Ya-Ya Sisterhood*,[84] we witness a poignant scene where the parents have been sleeping in separate bedrooms for years. This started a long time ago, after a particularly ugly fight. What was the fight about? They can't remember, but the standoff has been going on a long time. In the movie we watch each of them walk to the closed door of the other person's bedroom, raise their hand to knock, and then lose their courage, lower their hand, and return to their lonely room. Each longs for a reconciliation, but their vulnerable egos won't risk it.

BETRAYAL AND COMPASSION

I've written an entire chapter on fidelity, but I want to say a few words here because we require immense compassion and self-compassion when there have been breaches of sexual fidelity—which often feel like ultimate betrayals. Having compassion for oneself and one's partner doesn't come easily here. Those who keep their partners in their hearts and imagine the impact of their actions on that partner tend to be more faithful. Infidelity shatters not only the bond, but the betrayed partner's worldview. The discovery of infidelity evokes big relational questions and even existential questions, "Who are you ... did I ever know you? Was anything that I believed true? What can I count on in life, when the foundation of my life has just crumbled—can I trust anything?"

While the discovery of infidelity is like a bomb blast to the core of a relationship, there are times when long-standing and entrenched patterns need to be blown up. In the wake of discovery, unmet needs, mass confusions, resentments, and longings that have languished in the shadows are voiced. Everything becomes destabilized and all of this is on the table. In the crisis of discovery, partners are shaken awake, cracked open, and begin to re-evaluate their entire lives. They wonder if the relationship is worth re-building or re-investing in.

When I am sitting with a couple in the wake of the discovery of infidelity, I feel immense compassion for a couple's suffering, while holding the possibility that this experience may invite some deep inquiry and the potential for growth. The old relationship is dead, and a new marriage will need to be created. The question remains—will these two people choose to birth something new, to rebuild something from the wreckage? If there is too much unresolved hurt, and a strong reactivation of abandonment, mistrust, and defectiveness complexes, it may not be possible to move forward. Some people are broken and permanently embittered by this kind of heartbreak. Others find compassion for themselves and for the partner and activate the energy to recommit and create a relationship worth having. Whether you are the betrayer or the betrayed, infidelity invites us into some serious personal work.

We hurt each other in love. Sometimes it is intentional, most often it is unintentional. Sometimes it is out of pure selfishness, sometimes out of pure foolishness. We need a lot of compassion when we recognize the depth of our human vulnerability and how imperfect we all are. Every person on earth has suffered something that has led to personal areas of struggle. We don't always see these in the early part of a relationship, where our idealized view obscures our ability to see the shadow dimensions of our lover. In the bright light of our hopes and dreams we are elevated in that lofty realm—enchanted by the wonder of love. We will encounter the shadow dimensions of a partner eventually—the interdependency of a shared life will evoke it. When we do, we may wonder if we have made a horrible mistake. The question of whether to cut our losses and run, or to stay with our commitment and summon courage and compassion will hover heavily at this point. The answer is never easy, however we can reference something that Jung told us— "*When you are up against a wall, put down roots like a tree, until clarity comes from deeper sources to see over that wall and grow.*"

CHAPTER 13

CREATIVITY

*"It's my conviction that slight shifts in imagination
have more impact on living than major efforts at change."*
Thomas Moore

*"There's no such thing as creative people and non-creative
people. There are only people who use their creativity and
people who don't.... The only unique contribution that we
will ever make in this world will be born of our creativity.
As long as we're creating, we're cultivating meaning."*
Brené Brown

Most of the couples who come to work with me are wandering
in the swamplands of love—struggling with attachment wounds,
unfulfilled longings and expectations, small and large betrayals,
and the entanglement of their interlocking complexes. They are
embroiled in solutions that only make things worse. I do a lot of
repair work, but as trust returns and hope dawns there is a tipping
point where I will invite the couple into a larger context for their

relationship. It is the context of growing together and co-creating a relationship worth having. I point out that this will require a commitment to the development of capacities they may not have even thought about in their efforts to get their personal needs met. Jungian analyst James Hollis emphasizes that if we are to reach the promise of what love can offer in a conscious relationship, we must move beyond the search for a "magical other," and develop a certain "amplitude of soul."[85] When a couple enters this level of insight, they will begin to define and design a relationship that both of them want to inhabit, nurture, and protect.

Creativity is a core capacity of love. It is the dance of love, the play of love, the story of love and the re-storying of that story. In many ways, love is an art form—and two people will need to bring their creativity to it. It is my belief that creativity is ultimately sourced from the deep Self, that inner resource and guide that Carl Jung spoke of. The Self is referred to by many names, depending on your religious, philosophical, or psychological perspective. Whatever you call this inner compass and resource, when you get your taproot into it, paths open and things become possible that were never possible before.

Creativity helps us to transcend the boxes we put ourselves in, and as humans, we put ourselves in a lot of boxes. One of them comes from how we over-identify with all sorts of things that do not represent the totality of who we are—our roles, achievements (or lack of), beliefs, group affiliations, histories, the wounds we carry, even our personality characteristics. We internalize the labels, projections, and the expectations that others place upon us, and then we say this is "who we are." While all of these are aspects of our identity, they do not fully define us and over-identification with any of them will cut us off from the creative resources of the deep Self. The statement, "this is just how I am," is mistaken because all of us are in a process of growth and we can gain new insights and ways of being each day if we are open to those invitations. The Self is always seeking to grow us and invite us to transcend our boxes.

When we begin to dis-identify with some of these previous identities, it can be a bit destabilizing, and so we must learn to find our quiet center and reflect on our lives. As we begin to observe our inner workings and examine our "inner cast of characters," we will recognize the reactive complexes that contribute to our difficulties in life and relationship. The goal is to develop a Healthy Adult who can "drive the bus" of our lives, with our Inner Children as passengers. The "kids" inside of us need our care and compassion, but they should not be in charge of our relationships. Likewise, we need to contain the Inner Critics and Punitive Parents within, who would drive us into despair and shame.[86]

The shift from "need meeting" to "relationship as a path of growth" is a significant one. Earlier in our relationship our interests were most likely focused on our needs and finding someone who would fit our love-script and suit our Ego identity. Hopefully, in the process of moving beyond those initial projections, we begin to realize that this other person exists in his or her own right. What is difficult about this period is that it can send us into a period of frustration, even despair.

If it happens in midlife, it may correspond with disillusionment about everything—our sense of accomplishments or the level of our material accumulation. This is the Midlife Marriage Malaise, where people either end relationships and go in search of something to fill the void inside, or they begin some serious re-evaluation of their lives. There are no perfect partners—but this should not be an invitation to cynicism. Making a life with someone is not about finding someone "perfect." While the search for a perfect Soul Mate leads many people into a dead end, I can assure you that the potential of developing a meaningful, soulful relationship is completely possible—when two ordinary human beings set out on the journey of Individuation in Connection. Soulful relationships are not found, they are developed and sustained by two people devoted to an individuation process and creating a shared life together.

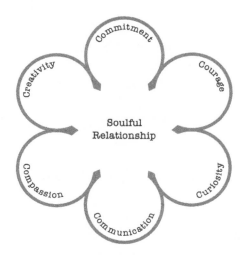

RELATIONSHIP CREATION

When a couple moves beyond operating at the levels of power-struggling and "need-meeting," They enter a process of creating a co-world that both of them will want to dwell in. Here are some questions that you can consider on your own, and together, that will help you to do that. It is not important that the answers match. We allow for differences. We are looking for the interplay and the value of what each person brings to the relationship.

INQUIRY QUESTIONS

- How well do we know and understand each other?
- Given the raw materials of who we are—what kind of relationship can we create together?
- What are our agreements and commitments to each other?
- What values and priorities will we uphold together?
- What experiences do we want to have together?
- Can we embrace our differences, acknowledge real limitations, while allowing for growth?
- How can our being together support our individual process of development, so that both of us can live more deeply into who we were born to be? Are we truly better together than apart?
- How do we need to grow—separately and together—to live into this vision?

Some of you are already living into this context intuitively. You have mastered the path of cooperative role-mates, have each other's backs, and support each other's process. I suggest that you ponder these questions individually and then make a periodic couple retreat in which you talk about the answers together. These questions need to be revisited again and again over the course of a lifetime, changing and adapting as life circumstances and the individuation process requires.

If you engage in this exercise (for yourself or with a partner) and the answers are too contradictory, you probably need the help of a couples therapist to sort this out. If you are facing the significant challenges of addiction, violence, abuse, or if you are living with someone who has a serious mental illness, or if you think your partner may have a pervasive, destructive personality disorder, I strongly suggest you seek professional help. Be courageous and do this. With all your good intentions and your willingness to commit, you need to sort out if creating and sustaining a life together is possible for the two of you. The suggestions I make here are for the garden variety difficulties that tend to crop up in most people's relationships where people can focus on personal development and co-creating with an engaged partner.

What's in The Way?

When you begin to define your relationship vision, you will see what's in the way. Keep the focus on yourself here, and make sure you don't cast your partner as the limiting problem. Even when there are obvious areas in which they need to grow, start with yourself and your contribution to the relationship difficulties. Your reactivity to your partner's annoying or troubling aspects is grist for *your* growth. When your partner hurts or aggravates you, what does it touch into in terms of your complexes, attitudes, and need to deepen your love capacities?

Take a look at your personal story and who you are in that story. How is this travelling forward into the present day? Perhaps return to the inquiry questions in the chapter on Curiosity. How are you casting the partner? How are your wounded Inner Children influencing or undermining your relationship? Are your reactions and sensitivities interfering with your capacity to communicate? This is where doing your inner work first can really pay off. Do your own work, *then* talk to your partner about ways in which you would like the relationship to change.

Do You Need to Update Your Relationship Story?

One of the problems I see in couples work is that people outgrow their reasons for being together and don't realize that they need to update their relationship story. Are you stuck in an old story? Many empty nest couples find themselves here. Do you need to update who you are to each other? Are you operating out of outdated conclusions about who your partner is? When was the last time you had an I-Thou encounter with them? Living in an outdated story and being cast in a particular way that no longer fits you can become intolerable.

Janice almost left her marriage because her husband refused to update his image of who she was. She wanted to be an equal partner and to be related to as if she was capable and intelligent. Joe could not grasp that she had grown up. When he met her, he was in the archetype of Hero Rescuer and she was the Damsel in Distress. The two of them entered into a mentor/protégé relationship, with Joseph in the role of protective, wise, advising guide (very fatherly) and Janice looking up to him for protection and guidance. Over time, she began to grow beyond the Damsel in Distress she had once been. By the time she reached the age of forty, she had raised two children, engaged in leadership roles in her volunteer work, and slowly earned an undergraduate degree. Janice wanted to be an equal partner and she wanted to pursue some serious career goals, and when they talked, she wanted to be taken seriously. Unfortunately, Joe felt threatened by her growing independence. He felt demoted. If Janice were no longer the Damsel in Distress, or Grateful Dependent, who would he be to her? They entered a period of conflict and struggle where Joe was unable to rescript himself or relate to her evolution. He had her frozen in time and she wanted out of the ice. They came to work with me, and I was able to help Joe see that his only option was to rewrite their story and update how he had cast her, or he would indeed lose her. These updates can be difficult for the person who wants the story to remain the same, but the truth is that people grow, and the foundation of a relationship needs to be flexible enough to adjust to this evolution. Joe and Janice slowly engaged the process of relationship re-creation and in updating their love story. They became more equal partners, invited in some playfulness, and deepened their love.

If you dare, explore how your partner is "casting" you in their world. This can be enlightening, but also disturbing. Remember not to take the answers personally—these are your partner's projections. We love our partner's positive projections but resent and resist the negative ones. Consider how you might be contributing to these characterizations. Consider how you would like to be cast instead and talk about this.

Consider the archetypal stances that you live from in your roles.

- Are there identities that you need to retire?
- Are you over-identified with some aspect of your life that is crowding out other possibilities?
- Do you need to evaluate priorities and perhaps shift some time, energy, and money so that the two of you are regularly nurturing the bond?
- Do you need to set some boundaries around where your time goes or the people who drain your life energy away?

- How much of your lives are involved in meeting obligations that are outdated in purpose and meaning?
- How much of your lives are you living to avoid disappointing or displeasing others?
- Are you living from a limited archetypal profile that indicates a lack of creativity?
- What new archetypal possibilities might you explore, integrate, cultivate that would open new possibilities?
- What would happen if you shifted states and lived out your roles from a different archetypal stance?
- How might that change the experience?

Shifting your archetypal stance can have powerful results in the quality of your relationship.

CREATIVE PATHS OUT OF CONFLICT

Creating "Exit-Ramps" Off the Conflict Highway

Every couple has their set of repetitive disagreements and places where they trigger each other and get entangled in their complexes. When a couple begins to work together as a team, they can identify these and create "exit ramps" off the conflict highway.

What should be abundantly clear by now is that we are not always operating from our "best selves." Remember that when we look through the eyes of our complexes it distorts what we are experiencing and concluding about what is happening. We attach meaning and motivation that may have nothing to do with what our partner is intending. Perhaps that other person is not being as critical or controlling as we are projecting. When we stop to really have an honest conversation, we come to realize that many of our feelings were generated by our own historical vulnerabilities. They may seem absolutely "true" when we are caught in a complex, but the more you become aware of your profile of complexes, the less likely you are to get caught in them, or when you do, you will exit them more quickly. Anytime you think you "know" what your partner is thinking, feeling, and doing, consider that you may be projecting. Ask some questions instead of jumping to conclusions. There is something to learn here. Become a team that works against the negative dynamics in your relationship. Make the dynamic the enemy instead of your partner. Put your heads together and find a way to "wake up" in the midst of all that unconsciousness. What can you say or do that might pull you back from the brink and interrupt the cycle? Each time you will gain more consciousness and eventually you may avoid these traps altogether.

The best time to do this is after a conflict has settled down. At that point, you can engage in your own inner work and explore why *you* get so activated. Then you can report back to your partner using conscious communication techniques. Take a look at the "shadow boxing" graphic below to see how your interlocking complexes go round and round, each activating the next reaction. Get creative and think about how you can interrupt this cycle. When each of you understands the meaning you are attaching to certain interactions and the projections that are flying back and forth between you, it becomes much easier to create those exit ramps.

Keep in mind that in our worst relationship conflicts, it is our Inner Children and their Defenders that are in trouble. You can list what you think is going on in your partner's world, but keep in mind that these are your projections. Your partner will most likely be defining him or herself in a different way. All of this invites learning and deep listening.

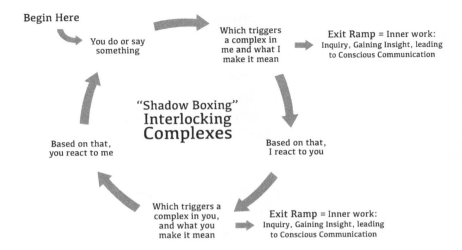

Begin Here

You do or say something

Which triggers a complex in me and what I make it mean

Exit Ramp = Inner work: Inquiry, Gaining Insight, leading to Conscious Communication

"Shadow Boxing" Interlocking Complexes

Based on that, you react to me

Based on that, I react to you

Which triggers a complex in you, and what you make it mean

Exit Ramp = Inner work: Inquiry, Gaining Insight, leading to Conscious Communication

Shifting States

Shifting states is a one of the most powerful capacities we possess in life. We can let go of things, and we can look at the situations of our lives in a different way, from a different stance. This requires personal insight. We have to become aware of the state we are currently in, then develop enough mindfulness to be able to step back, slow down, and disentangle from where we have been operating from—to find our calm core—to activate Observing Self. Once you have stepped out of the state you were in, you can consider what might happen if you related from a different state or archetypal stance in the situations of your life.

How do you achieve this shifting of states? Think archetypally and begin to notice the felt sense and perspectives of various states of being that you operate out of. Notice this at home as you parent, at work with your colleagues, notice your state of being and archetypal stance in your relationship and in your sexual life. How are you different in those different settings and situations? Consider that you move around and "shift states" in one situation to the next. Notice that you have this flexibility to access all these differing states and you don't have to be stuck in one. Become more aware of archetypal energies and the felt sense of those energies in the body. Notice the archetypal energies in the characters that populate your dream life and pull some of that energy into your waking life. Can you experiment with looking at a life situation through a different lens? Your "inner cast of characters" hold different agendas and ways of being and seeing. Can you experiment with operating from a different inner self who can perceive things differently, and relate from a different stance in a challenging situation?

Notice how situations change when you can "shift states" and approach them from a different stance. Notice how relating from a different place inside can change a negative interaction with your partner. This is deep work, but it can be immensely enlightening, and it opens paths of possibility. What might the two of you create if you developed this capacity and began to "dial around" the inner characters you relate from?

Troublesome Inner Selves

Do you house a Scared Little Girl who limits your life because she is afraid of everything? Do you house a Hungry Ogre who shows up when you don't pay sufficient attention to your blood sugar? What about those ambitious Selves—the Mad Housekeeper, the Professional, or the Empire Builder who conquers and dominates but cannot access tenderness or compassion? Do you steamroll over your own more tender selves? Do you house a Martyr who doesn't ask for what she needs and then explodes in anger, or a Pouter who appears when you don't get what you want? What about that Taskmaster who never makes time for play? Or the Warrior Princess or Demanding Bully who are the defenders of a Frightened Child behind them, convinced he or she will never get their needs met? Think about forces of nature as well—are you sometimes an Immovable Mountain, a Shrinking Violet, or a Tornado? Think about animal characters—do you house a Bull in the China Shop, a Mama Lion, or a Social Butterfly? Where do they show up and what happens when they do? Take some time to name your parts of self and think about them in a variety of situations—work-life balance, keeping house, money, parenting, in-laws, vacations, and sexuality.

Our Inner Children

We have a whole range of Inner Children inside at various ages, and with a wide variety of qualities. We cannot abandon them by the side of the road, we have to bring them with us. They will always be rumbling around and influencing us from behind the curtain of our awareness if we don't attend to them. They also have things to offer us—playfulness, soulfulness, innocence, intuition, creativity. Our Inner Children need to be passengers, not drivers of the bus. What are the concerns or vulnerabilities that your Inner Children carry? What kind of inner work do you need to do to soothe, calm, and resource these "kids behind the curtain"? Do you have an angry, demanding or entitled child who stirs up trouble in your relationship? The more inner work you do, the less your Inner Children will undermine your happiness. Discover them, dialogue with them, get to know them, and then resource them from your inner capacities. Consider employing the services of a therapist and engage in healing work where necessary.

Don't Get Stuck in the Form

We often get fixated on "one way" to meet needs or solve problems. When this happens, we are caught in this mistaken approach, which limits our creativity. When you examine your needs, wants, dreams, and desires, you may have an idea about *exactly* how they should be fulfilled; but consider that you are after an *experience* that is not limited to one form of fulfillment. There are many possible ways of having certain experiences that are not limited to one form. If you look at the banquet of your life, do you refuse to take in the good because your "favorite food" is not on the table? Widen your imaginative vision and consider how you might fulfill certain dreams without getting stuck in the form. If you can't get to Paris, can you create the experience of "being a Parisian" in another way? Who would you become if you could get to Paris? Being Parisian is an archetypal energy. Use your imagination, and explore how you might integrate this energy into your daily life. Be flexible. Be bold. Activate your imagination and get creative.

VITALIZING THE DEVITALIZED RELATIONSHIP

If you are bored with your relationship, you are not living deeply enough, and it is very likely that you have not encountered each other recently. You may have fallen into a sleepy bonding pattern that needs awakening. Are you growing as a person? When was the last time you visited the questions on Relationship Creation together?

I-Thou encounters vitalize relationships, but they can also scare your Inner Children—some of whom like things predictable. You may need to activate an Inner Boat Rocker and explore the outer regions of each other's psyches. Who is that person over there? Have you checked in lately? Some people purposely don't do this because they'd just as soon not know what is going on in that other person's inner life. That's one way to "feel secure," but it is a guaranteed drift into dullness, and it is dangerous to not really know the person you are living with. Can you activate some courage and curiosity and open up some inquiry?

Also consider dimensions that are missing in your relationship. When was the last time your Responsible Selves had a break, and you were free to just go and play? Play is a tremendously bonding experience for lovers. If you used to play, but haven't for a long time, where did those selves go? Did they get buried under piles of life's burdens and responsibilities? Also consider the selves that you left by the side of the road as you became more "adult." Is there a Granola Girl, Rock-and-Roll Guitar Player, a Poet, Marathon

Runner, or Free Spirit in your past? What would happen if you made space in your life to re-integrate that dimension of self?

The Paradox of Growth

One of the paradoxes of love is that when people are on a path of individuation, doing their inner work, their needs evolve. Some are met and disappear altogether. That's why periodically revisiting the "creation questions" at the start of this chapter is important. You want to know who this beloved person is becoming and how they are evolving. What is being called forward from the deep Self? As the safety of a soulful relationship heals us, it also causes us to look less to our partners to stabilize and reinforce our fragile egos. While there are real limitations in life, particularly in the later part of our lives, those limitations matter less when our interior worlds continue to expand. Differences fade in the light of a context that is far more profound; and certain "problems" that previously plagued the relationship will be transcended rather than solved. This echoes what Einstein emphasized—that problems cannot be solved from the same level of thinking (or being) that they were created in. The secret sauce of creating a wonderful relationship lies in deepening one's love capacities.

Love is ultimately an art form, and creativity is crucial to the process of creating a relationship that will nourish and sustain the two people in it. We are each born with seeds of possibility that lie sleeping in the seedbed of our psyches. Love shakes us from our protective husks and calls us into new identities. Love calls forward the courage to enter into a profound growth process that will help us actualize our greatest potential—this is what Individuation in Connection is all about.

PART THREE

CHAPTER 14

THE LABYRINTH OF SEXUALITY

"Sex is not something you do; it is a place you go."
Esther Perel

"Great lovers are made, not born. If you're looking for extraordinary erotic intimacy,
you will have to devote time and energy to it."
Peggy Kleinplatz

A book on love and relationships would not be complete without a chapter on the labyrinth of sexuality. While the struggle for sexual fulfillment in a long-term relationship really requires an entire book, I do want to provide some insights into the sexual difficulties that plague committed relationships and how the six love capacities can be applied to those quandaries. Most importantly, I want to propose that inner work related to sexuality can become a path of individuation.

We live in an odd society, saturated with provocative sexual images, but very reticent to talk openly and easily about our sexual desires, expectations, and the actual experience of sex. I became a certified sex therapist because I was encountering so much sexual confusion and suffering in the couples I work with. We have abysmal sex education in this country. Most of the people I work with lack sufficient information about the basics of sex—how bodies work—let alone how two people would go about creating a meaningful sexual connection. As with life, our sexuality has a history and a formation. In that formation, we internalize messages about sex and develop scripts and expectations that create a lot of problems when we try to relate to another person sexually. These confusing differences escalate anxiety, which interferes with arousal and pleasure. This leads to disappointment, invites power struggles, and creates a lot of insecurity.

The terms sexual function and dysfunction are in and of themselves problematic. Body parts function, but people relate. Sex is also imbued with an enormous amount of meaning, and has a lot do to with our sense of worth, well-being, identity, and how connected and wanted we feel with a partner. We are told that sex is a natural process, but the truth is that there are aspects of sexuality that are quite complicated, especially when you consider the differences in two person's subjective experience, expectations, and their limited capacity to communicate when overwhelmed by anxiety and embarrassment.

Since the advent of television commercials about Viagra, the world, all the way down to young children, has learned about ED. While most of us understand that ED refers to erectile dysfunction, in my view it should really stand for Eros Dysfunction—our inability to connect and relate in the sexual realm. In working with couples who are having sexual difficulties, I find that the problem is rooted in the vulnerability and defensiveness found in their interlocking complexes. A true Eros connection will take a couple beyond the intermingling of two bodies into an experience that is far more fulfilling than simply increasing frequency or having body parts that "function." While many couples use the word "intimacy" as a pseudonym for sex, I find that most couples have never really encountered their partner deeply, let alone had the courage to explore their sexual psyches. Sex means many things to people and can be experienced and expressed in a variety of ways. However, if a person has a difficult time tolerating powerful emotional states, they will most assuredly have difficulty with sex, because sex elicits a wide range of emotions. A couple will need to be able to move through embarrassment, feeling exposed, anxiety, hunger, fulfillment, insecurity, discovery, shock, despair, disgust, tenderness, delight, care, patience, passion, revelation, ecstasy, vulnerability, playfulness, sweetness, adventure, frustration, disappointment, awkwardness, and hopefully a good amount of pleasure as they share this special experience together. One of the foundations of a deepening sex life is the capacity to feel all of it, and to stay present and embodied, experiencing the sensations and the full spectrum of emotions that sex evokes. A couple must co-create their sexual experience over the course of a lifetime, as they grow as people, as they transcend their sexual complexes, adapting as they age, and as life circumstances challenge them. Sexuality requires the six love capacities—commitment, courage, curiosity, communication, compassion, and creativity.

Sex therapist Barry McCarthy[87] researched the correlation between sex and relationship satisfaction. He found that sexually contented spouses view sexuality as 15-20% of their relationship, with sexual satisfaction being just one aspect of their lives. When a couple is unhappy about their sex life, it begins to overshadow other satisfactions in the relationship. One or both of them may become preoccupied with how unfulfilling their sex-life is until it expands into 50-70% of their relationship dissatisfaction.

Sexual problems can be seen as the "canary in the coalmine," indicating trouble in other areas of a couple's life as well. Sex is one of the first things to go in a couple that has become emotionally disconnected. But many other things interfere with our sexual interest and energy. Caregiving and the responsibilities of life can take so much time and energy that it drains away our libido. While women tend to be stereotyped as the ones who become disinterested in sex, many men lose sexual desire under the stress and strain of work, or conflict in the relationship. This is not talked about openly, and the men I have worked with who experience this are embarrassed and dismayed when they don't fit the stereotype of the man who is always ready for sex. Once the rhythm of a regular sexual connection falls out of a couple's life, it is difficult to start it up again.

One of the most frequently asked questions in sex therapy is, "How often should we be having sex?" This question indicates that the couple is counting the behavior rather than thinking about the quality of their shared experience. "What is normal?" they ask me, and I have to tell them that "normal" must be defined by each couple, not by the articles they read in newspapers or what their friends tell them. A preoccupation with frequency, insecurities about appearance, rigid sexual scripts, fears of being seen as inappropriate or perverted, sexual expectations based on pornography, fears of being rejected and humiliated, an inability to become aroused, discomfort or pain during intercourse, and a desperate longing to feel wanted—all of these haunt couples in the bedroom.

In Chapter 6, we talked about the creation of "no-fly zones," and sex is one of the primary areas that couples find themselves unable to talk about. It becomes a topic that is so charged that they can't seem to enter it, and it begins to feel impossible to resolve anything, let alone initiate. People begin to harbor feelings that something is wrong with them, with the relationship. One partner feels hounded, the other feels cheated, and resentful about something that they expected to be an ongoing part of a long-term relationship. These are feelings that can become justification for seeking sexual satisfaction elsewhere.

People in sexual trouble want magic formulas for solving their problems. Often, they are seeking an ally to get their partner to be the person they want them to be. While most people want to know what to do, *the answer to their predicament lies in the realm of being, not doing.* What blocks people in the bedroom also blocks them in other areas of their lives. Yes, there are things to learn, and certainly most couples can improve their sexual communication, but if a couple wants to create a truly meaningful sexual connection, they must engage in a growth process and come to understand themselves and each other in new ways. They must hold their sexual problems in a new context. When people grasp how powerfully their interior stance impacts sex, *they begin to understand that a shift in their state of being can change everything.* The focus needs to shift away from preoccupation with performance, desire, frequency, and new behaviors. There is inner work to do here, and I suggest that each person begin within. Sex is a language, and it is important to understand our sexual formation, and to know "who" is showing up in bed. I suggest that instead of exploring new sexual positions that a couple explore a new archetypal position. Sex therapists Esther Perel and Tammy Nelson emphasize that sex is more than something we do; sex is a place we go. Our interior stance about sex is the foundation. Everything builds and flows from that.

Let's view sexuality through the lens of the six love capacities.

COMMITMENT, COURAGE, and CURIOSITY

In Chapter 8, we talked about commitment being to a *person*, a *process* and to *presence*. In order to create a sex life of rich interplay that both people want to engage in, a couple must commit special time and attention to it. Creating a sexual partnership is a *process*, and while sex involves skills, it is more than a behavior—sex is a language, an art form, a relational dance. Without courage and curiosity, we cannot move forward. Both partners need to explore and define themselves as sexual beings and then seek to understand the other.

Presence

When I stand in the grocery checkout line, I see headlines on popular magazines like, "How to spice up your sex life," or "How to drive that lover wild." Rediscovering that early passion is something many couples talk to me about wistfully. They are bewildered that their sex lives have fizzled, particularly as they became parents.

Peggy Kleinplatz[88] is one of our great sexology researchers, and the author of many excellent clinical works in modern sex therapy. She interviewed a group of successful long-term lovers who painted a surprising portrait of what "extraordinary sex" looks like. The number one component named by these lovers was "*being present, focused, embodied, and utterly immersed in the experience.*" This was followed by having a sense of "*connection and being in synch.*" Next was "*deep sexual and erotic intimacy, characterized by mutual respect and caring, and genuine acceptance.*" These couples had also developed a capacity for "*extraordinary communication,*" and "*heightened empathy.*" They approached sexuality as "*an adventure, a journey, an ongoing exploration.*" Being "*authentic, uninhibited, transparent, vulnerable, reveling in sensation, and surrendering to a partner,*" all of these were spoken of as important. While having an orgasm was valued, it was not the primary focus of the sexual experience, and participants seemed unconcerned about aging or physical appearance. Any couple capable of engaging at this level will inevitably experience what was also described as "*timelessness, a sense of awe, bliss, and peace.*"

Sex therapist, Maci Daye, asserts that mindful presence, moment by moment, is the key to erotic bliss. She emphasizes that sex is ultimately "*not about getting off. It is about getting here.*" Her book entitled, *Passion and Presence,* takes couples into the transformative path she developed in the workshop of the same name—which I highly recommend.

Sex is Never Just about Sex

We get a lot of underlying needs met through sex that have little to do with sexual release. When those underlying needs remain unfulfilled, no amount of sex will suffice. While we think of sex as a set of behaviors, we attach enormous meaning to sex and what we do in sex becomes highly symbolic. We seek sex for connection, comfort, nurture, reassurance. We want to be validated as attractive, and to experience the power of our ability to captivate or feel potent. While stress can inhibit sexual interest, some engage in sex as a stress reducer and a distraction from other worries. Some people use sex to discharge or resolve feelings of anger and for them, "make-up sex" is a heightened experience. Sex can soothe and reassure, but it will never permanently resolve deep feelings of emptiness, unworthiness, insecurity, or fears of abandonment. Sex can deepen a bond and connect us in a special way, but if it becomes an act of dutiful obligation, partners can feel even more lonely after sex than before.

Becoming a Sexual Adult

Becoming a sexual adult requires us to look at our sexual formation. We need to examine the scripts and expectations we bring into a relationship as well as the early messages and experiences that have shaped our formation. It is rare to find a person with a sex-positive history. The histories we live through are often filled with warnings, awkwardness, self-protection, shame, and for some, trauma. Many men come into a sexual relationship with a sense of entitlement, not understanding that a sexual relationship requires interacting with the psyche of their partner, lots of communication, and a process of co-creation. Power-struggles ensue, name-calling and shaming, pressure and demands, passive abdication, avoidance, loss of desire, and despair.

For Women—The Process of Defining and Revealing Your Sexual Self

I rarely meet a woman whose budding sexuality was supported in a wise, but sex positive way. Most girls are raised on cautionary tales with distinct division between "good girls" and "bad girls." They are urged to become "gatekeepers of their virtue," and the "voices of warning" they develop echo forward into their adult relationships. Their sexuality is shaped around a practiced "no" and they find it difficult to generate a genuine "yes," even after they are in a context where consensual sexuality is deemed to be acceptable—marriage.

What does it mean to be a sexual woman? Many women have no idea, other than trying to please a partner. When Sam asks Naomi what she wants in bed, she has no idea. She asks me, "What are my options?" Naomi has never read a book on sex, and Sam has been her only partner. Most women lack the education or the curiosity which would lead them to seek out information about sex or to self-define in a way that could be communicated to another person. You cannot discover your sexual voice when you don't know what to say. The script for many women is to be what the partner wants her to be. This is quite different from discovering oneself as a sexual being and communicating that to an interested partner. Being pleasing and accommodating is not a formula for kindling desire.

When I wrote *In Search of Aphrodite*,[89] I mentioned the archetype of Sleeping Beauty. This is the woman waiting to be awakened by a partner. Unfortunately, many women are partnered with someone who may also be inadequately informed about sex. If she is not with an "awakener," she may sleep forever.

Most men are raised on sexual scripts about how to "get sex," not how to engage a partner. Testosterone creates a powerful sex drive, but having a focus on personal satisfaction, mixed with a limited repertoire of skills and stances is not sufficient for creating a mutually enjoyable sexual partnership—especially if we are talking about the long term. In recent years, another problem has emerged. I encounter a lot of young men who have received almost all of their sex education by viewing Internet pornography. This leads to significant confusion about what women want, and how "real life" sex actually works. The pervasiveness of pornography has contributed to a chronic sense of sexual insecurity in women of all ages—the sense that they can never compete with the bodies or behaviors of porn stars.[90]

There are women on the other side of the spectrum, who are more sexually experienced. They may well have explored their sexual psyches, understand their turn-on templates, and can communicate what they want. This creates other problems for them. This can be intimidating for a partner who wants to be the more experienced person or someone who is expecting responsiveness versus assertiveness. Fears of comparison crop up. Sexually experienced women are often "slut-shamed" by insecure partners and told that their level of desire or sexual interest is perverted, or that they are too sexually demanding. I recall a couple I worked with where both were virgins on their wedding night. During their honeymoon she exhibited a great enthusiasm for sex. Apparently, this overwhelmed him. He commented that, "a good Christian woman would not be so interested in sex." That was the end of her interest. Twelve years later they were in my office trying to sort out *her* lack of desire. The Madonna-Whore split continues to be a challenge for women trying to find their way.

Both women and men have sexual experiences that are confusing, shaming, or invalidating, and these experiences can inhibit an exploration of their sexual potential or push them into a trauma-driven hypersexuality. Traumatic sexual experiences haunt the lives of both women and men and the lingering impact of trauma will continue to limit a person's sexual joy, freedom, and wisdom, until healing experiences or therapeutic treatment help them to remap the brain's trauma pathways.

THE COURAGE TO COMMUNICATE

The Five Love Languages defined by Gary Chapman's best-selling book are: words of affirmation, acts of service, gifts, special time, and touch.[91] All of these apply to our sexuality. When we think of sex as a language that we speak to each other, it changes the way we hold sex. Sex involves touch, words of affirmation, special time, acts of service (think mutual generosity here), and gifting oneself to another.

I find that many couples get entangled in the difference between affection and sex. Melody draws back whenever her husband tries to hug her, because she thinks he is seeking sex. Manuel is a highly affectionate man, and he is often just wanting the connection of a hug. He tries to hug her a lot, but because she feels her own internal conflict about not having enough sex, she avoids affection as well. They have never talked about this and Melody's sexual avoidance has led them to seek my professional help. It is not uncommon for a sexually avoidant partner to stop all forms of touch because they are concerned that any form of touch might arouse desires that they do not want to deal with. For a person who loves pure affection, the disappearing of all touch leads to a sensual and emotional deprivation that is hard to endure. Many men have told me that it is hard for them to ask to be held or caressed, and so they initiate genital sex. Sex is a way to get the need for comfort met without feeling embarrassed or less manly. Looking at the differing underlying needs that touch, affection, and sex meet is one of the things I help couples to explore openly, so that affection can re-enter their relationship without automatically being seen as pressure for genital sex.

Courage and Compassion—Finding Your Sexual Voice

We all have projections and assumptions when it comes to sex. Talking about and clarifying these requires that a person finds their "sexual voice." Entering a learning conversation about sex can be terrifying for some people. There are things that once spoken, cannot be taken back. I encourage you to revisit Chapter 11, particularly the idea around "who" is speaking and "who" is listening. If you are especially timid, and if talking about sex feels like you are rocking the boat to the point of capsizing it, you will need to develop your Inner Boat Rocker. The key to not capsizing a rocking boat is to avoid over-correction. Hold steady. Give your partner some time to absorb what you are saying and manage their own emotional rocking. What helps with sexual conversations is to be clear, compassionate, and to have done your own inner work first. You will recall that compassion has a two-way flow, towards self and other.[92] Compassion involves being kind, accepting that we are members of the human race, and being mindful about our words and actions. Clear communication about sexual needs and desires can be difficult because people are extremely sensitive about sex, but sexual communication never has to be unkind or threateningly demanding. In the midst of a request for something different, it helps to mention what you appreciate about your partner and their current efforts to please. Our inner Vulnerable Children are quite active in our sexual insecurities. We want to do the healing work necessary so that we can allow the Playful Children inside of us to romp, be silly or sweet. The capacity for play is a definite strength in this realm of life that can become deadly serious.

Sexual communication can include the non-verbal cues a couple develops in the invitation and the flow of sex, cues for certain behaviors or transitions. The actual words you use around sex is more important than people realize. Talk about what words appeal or repel in initiating, and throughout each stage of a sexual experience. How we refer to behaviors and body parts matters, and words can make or break the sexual flow. Sexual communication can also include sounds, facial expressions, and kinds of touch that encompass entire paragraphs of meaning.

Arousal Templates and Sexual Identity

Defining one's sexual identity is a process of learning, growing, and unburdening oneself from early messages and experiences that negatively impacted one's sexual formation. Sexual identity is not just about the gender one identifies with, or the gender of the persons you are sexually attracted to. Sexual identity is about what you would like to experience and express as a sexual being within yourself and with another.

People are aroused by different things, and the formation of an individual arousal template is part of our sexual history. Learning about your partner's inner world is what it takes to be intimate. This requires that you have a solid enough sense of your own personhood to hear revelations that may surprise, perhaps even shock you. Entering your partner's sexual psyche means that you are "crossing the bridge" into a foreign country—their inner world. You are not required to fulfill every imaginative fancy that your partner has, but coming to understand the underlying themes, needs, and meaning of a person's internal imaginings can give you insight into that person that can be had no other way. Sex is about pleasure, but it is also very much about meaning, and sex can be had from a variety of archetypal stances—the ground from which we enter into an experience. The freedom to define oneself beyond categories has also become important in today's world, and individuals are increasingly wanting to define themselves beyond boxes or binary categories.

Being a compassionate witness for another person's history or inner experience deepens intimacy. Being heard in a non-judgmental way can also lead to a profound healing for someone who has carried painful secrets or lived with shame for most of their entire life. We carry a lot of shadow material in our sexuality and sorting out the noxious messages and wounding experiences helps us get free of those influences. The shift from a transactional, need-meeting sexuality, to deep encounter, opens the door to healing and discovery, what we could call I-Thou sexuality.[93]

CREATIVITY AND ARCHETYPAL STANCES

People who want to spice up their sex lives often think that it involves new sexual positions, new behaviors, and perhaps toys and lingerie, even kink. While some or all of these can expand the sexual fulfillment of a couple, when I am teaching about sexuality, I emphasize over and over that they need to consider the stance from which they are having sex. Most people have never considered this. It is interesting to note that the very same repertoire of behaviors, done from a different archetypal stance will feel entirely different and evoke something different from a partner. This can lead to fresh discoveries that open new expressions of behavior, all spontaneously arising from that new stance.

The first rule of creativity is to let go of the known and get out of the box of scripts, expectations, and prescribed norms. Recall that archetypes are systems of psychic energy that move through the body, shaping the way we think and feel, and forming the lens through which we interpret our experience. When we shift the archetypal stance from which we engage in sex, we are doing more than shifting out of a predictable routine; we are interacting in a new way.

Take some time to consider "who" in your "inner cast of characters" shows up around sex. How active are your sad, fearful, insecure, or angry, demanding Inner Children? Consider their Protector-Defenders. Do you have strong Gatekeepers or Voices of Warning that whisper to you as you are moving into a sexual experience? How do certain inner selves block your spontaneous desire or response to a partner? Do you house any playful, curious, mischievous, or happy children inside?[9] Where are your Inner

---

[9] If you would like a further listing of archetypes, with a copy of my Sexual Essence Wheels, contact me at www.chelseawakefield.com.

Explorers or Adventurers? What would make it safe enough to explore? What qualities of being do you want to explore or live into that have yet to be incorporated? Who do you want to be to each other in your sexual expression? Can you move out of your Responsible Selves? Where do your two inner casts intersect in the bedroom? How do you get entangled and "who" in your inner casts is getting entangled? What fears do you have about your partner's judgments or reactions? Think about interlocking complexes. "Who" is interacting with "who" and what would happen if you changed the mix and match of archetypal energies? Can the two of you examine the cycle and discover where you get stuck? Find your courage, your curiosity, your compassion, and your voice, and have a learning conversation with your partner. Can you create exit ramps off the conflict highway? How might you enrich your experience?

THE MYSTERY OF DESIRE

Perhaps it has occurred to you by now that sex is not simple. When people reduce sex to a set of behaviors, it diminishes its impact on us as whole beings and we experience a loss of desire. When I ask women about the kind of sex they are having for which they have "no desire," my frequent response is, "Who would want to have that kind of sex?" Many people—men and women—have a lack of interest in sex not worth having. One of the developments I have seen in the last twenty years is an increasing number of men who say, "I want to feel wanted. I don't want a partner who is having sex out of duty, just to pacify me. I want her to be engaged."

Desire for What?

In every relationship there will be a higher desire and a lower desire person, and these roles may switch over time. During her many years as a sex therapist and researcher, Gina Ogden, suggests that we ask, "desire for what?" A particularly important question, particularly for women, who tend not to think in those terms. The answer to desire discrepancies is not found in a math equation— halfway between what one wants and the other wants. Those who are counting frequency miss the point entirely. One of my favorite books on the inner sources of eroticism, is by Jack Morin,[94] who invites us to explore the elements of our "peak erotic experiences" and identify the "core erotic themes" that can infuse future experiences with interest, passion, and fulfillment.

When I ask people about the most erotic experiences of their lives, I am often reminded that many of them involve the tension of anticipation, when our bodies were alive with longing. Some of our most erotic experiences don't include genital contact at all. Think about Eros—the flow of life energy in your life. When and where do you experience it? In many cases, it involves a shared experience of a creative kind, or shared exploration of ideas, or the achievement of some difficult project or physical endeavor. Sometimes this involves a flirtation that was never consummated. Desire is a double-edged sword, involving longing and fulfillment, anticipation and blocks to fulfillment. Too much time without fulfillment, and we become disheartened. Too little longing and the fulfillment becomes ordinary. Particular archetypal energies are in the mix in our peak erotic experiences.

Ethan recounts a memory of "the waterfall in the woods." He and Alice were hiking, and no one was around, "There was a cave behind the waterfall. We stood kissing each other passionately with the curtain of water pounding down in front of us. Then we stripped off our clothes and jumped into the stream pool in front of us, laughing and screaming at the chill of the water." Ethan and Alice are thinking people, but the two of them can still feel the Tarzan and Jane energy when they recount that memory and access their playful, adventurous, sensual selves.

Archetypal Turn-ons and Turn-offs

If you think about archetypal stance in sex, you will begin to figure out that some energies evoke sexual interest and other energies repel it.

Loraine talks to Trevor about how to approach her in archetypal terms. "If you want me to be that Sensuous Sweetheart, don't treat me like the Maid or your Mother. Picking up after you makes me the Maid. Asking you for the umpteenth time to help around the house makes me into your Mother."

Noreen tells me that she feels the most sexually attracted to Paul when he tells her to relax a while as he reads a bedtime story to their six-year-old daughter. Watching Paul as a Nurturer warms her heart and opens her body. When he gives her time to wind down, she likes to take a bath and shift states. She quotes the old "Calgon take me away" commercial as she explains that this lets her shift out of the task driven Responsible Mother and access the Earthy Sensualist inside of her.

Pouters and Condescending "Sexperts" don't invite sexual interest. Women are not turned on by Sexual Beggars and Needy Boys, especially if they have other children to take care of. Esther Perel states that when a woman engages in sex as another item on her to do list, she may take care of you, but she will never *want* you. Some women will comply with needs and demands, in the archetype of Nurturing Mother and Dutiful Wife/Partner, but there will be little fire or presence. The shift from Beggar or Demanding Bully into Poet Lover, Artist, Sage, or Swashbuckling Hero will evoke something entirely different in a partner. That dash of Bad Boy or Rebel energy may be just the shift required to kindle a flame that has been banked down under too much responsibility. Making the shift out of the "doing" mode of Responsible Parent into the "being" mode of a Sensual Self is one of the most challenging shifts parents can learn to do.

Riva tells me that the reason she refuses to engage sexually with Drake is that he comes at her with those Puppy Dog eyes. Drake was unaware that this was the reason she was rejecting him. Riva wants a Sweet Seducer, not a begging Puppy Dog, and with some inner work and intention, Drake makes that shift and draws her in.

Beth has told Brandon countless times not to come up behind her and grab her breasts as if they belong to him. It leads to a guaranteed "no" later on in bed. "He reminds me too much of the grabby guys in high school. I don't like the inference that he can grab my body anytime he wants to, and I'm not interested in having sex with an Adolescent Boy."

On the other side of this spectrum are women who are seeking to sanitize sex so much that eroticism never enters the bedroom. Women can get captured by a vulnerability where the setting for sex has to be "neat and nice"—what one of my clients called "tea-party sex." The archetypes of Shrinking Violet, Dutiful Wife, Martyr, Armored Amazon, Victim, Servant, Disembodied Saint, Good Church Woman, even Yoga Babe sexuality can move sex so far away from the instinctual element of the animal body that sex becomes too tepid for a partner who longs for more intensity. There are also Poor Little Match Girls who believe their flame is not enough to light anyone's fire. Women with histories of trauma can become over-identified with the archetype of Damaged Goods. In an adult relationship we need to make sure that our Vulnerable Inner Children are not the only ones showing up in bed.

For people with histories of emotional deprivation, it can be easy to overburden sex with a deep need for attention, validation, comfort, and nurture, needs that can never be fully satisfied by sex. Fears of abandonment or the deep sense of unworthiness cannot be chased away by frequent sex. There is inner work to do here so that sex is not about filling up emptiness or dispelling insecurity. Some people suffer from "leaky bucket syndrome," where the reassurance they receive doesn't fill them up because it is constantly draining out of the holes in their underlying self-worth.

Shifting Your Archetypal Stance Can Improve Your Sex Life

Gayle Delaney is a dream expert who wrote a book about sexual dreams.[95] Here's one that illustrates how a man was helped by a dream to understand how he needed to shift his archetypal stance in order for his wife to respond sexually.

"Michael dreams of taking piano lessons in which he is instructed not to 'storm' the keys, but to caress them and to treat the piano as an exquisitely sensitive instrument that would then produce beautiful music. On waking, Michael is reminded that his wife had recently said she felt more like a strategic military site that he stormed during sex rather than the sensual but delicate sexual being she felt herself to be. Prior to the dream, Michael resisted this communication—now he was consider moving from the Conquering Soldier to Maestro."

The Archetype of the Initiator

One of the common complaints I hear in sex therapy is that one partner is always doing the initiating. "Why can't *she* initiate occasionally?" asks Terry about Theresa. "I get tired of always being the one." Theresa tells me that she thought that Terry liked being the Initiator, so she never bothered. Denice and Jade are in a relationship where neither of them houses an Initiator. They have drifted into a companionate, but sexless relationship. Women are often conflicted about initiating, or perhaps I should say it doesn't always occur to them, especially women who were raised to respond, and accommodate, not initiate. Learning how to invite and excite a partner is part of the sexual dance and deserves some deep consideration and conversations about what each person responds to.

As we become more aware of what constitutes consent, coercion, and assault, there is an increased sense of hesitancy around seduction, which can be one of the most enjoyable aspects of the sexual dance. Once a person has self-defined and found their sexual voice, a couple can define their yes, no, and "keep on coming and capture my interest" signals. While having a partner with a sexual abuse history requires sensitivity, this can evolve into being overly careful, and missing experiences that would provide healing. Many partners stuck in avoidance want to want but don't know how to get there. The Initiator is an archetype and seduction is an art form involving an evocation which draws forth inner responses from the other.

Rosemary Basson's Female Sexual Response Cycle

Earlier sexual response cycles used in sex therapy were all linear. The most frequently referenced one, originating with Helen Singer Kaplan[96], begins with desire, moves into arousal, and leads to orgasm. In recent years, gynecologist Rosemary Basson introduced a model of female sexual response that counters this stair-step model, which has come to be understood by many as a "male sexual response" cycle. Basson offers a circular model instead.[97]

When I show Basson's model to women, they see that the entry point is "receptivity." Basson notes that for many women, sexual desire appears *after* arousal, not before, which means that after they engage and warm up to a skillful lover, they become aroused, and are happy they said "yes" to this experience, wanting more, something we refer to as desire. When the cycle ends with satisfaction, it encourages her to engage in future experiences without needing to have desire as the originating factor. This is a model of "responsive desire," and I see many women breathe a sigh of relief when they see this model. "You mean I'm normal?!"

Part of responsive desire is related to women's sexual script conditioning, but it is also related to having lower levels of testosterone and the burdensome caregiving requirements in women's lives. Women love the emotional "spin offs" of sex—quiet time with a partner, the possibility of engaged presence, attention, affection, holding, being caressed, feeling cared for. Women also long to feel attractive and can feel empowered when they can cast a spell of interest, or be a source of pleasure, and satisfaction to a desired partner. There is nothing wrong with having an inner Sexual Nurturer, Healer, Pleaser, or Earth Mother as your archetypal homeland. The key is choice, versus a default into dutiful obligation. There are other dimensions of sexuality that a woman can explore once she becomes aware of them, and she can still choose to nurture and please.

Boredom

Sexual boredom plagues many couples. Unfortunately, while we want the bond to be secure, too much familiarity can lead a couple to become too companionate. Friendship is important between life partners, but it is possible to become too comfortable with each other. Feeling like siblings or any form of parent/child pairing will send the sizzle right out of your relationship. Esther Perel reminds us that feeling too familiar puts a couple at risk for losing their erotic edge. "Fire needs air" she emphasizes, and she cites research in which she asked people about when their partner seems most appealing. Many of them stated that it was in situations where they are viewing that person "across a crowded room." They were seeing their significant other through distant eyes, as a separate person, engaged in something that showed them in their best light. Kahlil Gibran suggests, "Let there be spaces in your togetherness, and let the winds of the heavens dance between you."[98] If you are bored with each other sexually, you have stopped growing and you are no longer encountering each other at an exploratory level.

One of the downfalls of having orgasm as the gold standard of a successful sexual experience is that a couple can find a sexual routine that "works," and then begin to repeat it over and over, until there is very little engaged presence and no surprise involved. It is interesting how doing something completely new together, outside of bed, can revitalize a couple's sex life. It opens the doors of the psyche and moves us out of the familiar. Reconnecting with a "self" that was left behind in order to become "responsible and mature" can be a ticket for getting archetypal juices flowing again. Go find your long-lost Granola Girl, that Rebel Rock-and-Roll Guitarist, Audacious Flirt, Painter, Rock Climber, or Salsa Dancer.

Men Who Lack Desire

The stereotype is that men are creatures who are constantly seeking sexual satisfaction, often to the aggravation of their sexually pursued partners. Loss of male sexual desire is something not talked about in our culture, but one out of every five couples that comes to see me has a man who is avoiding sex. Elaine longs for Kevin to seek her out sexually. She is concerned that he is no longer attracted to her. The real problem is that their relationship is riddled with conflict. Kevin tells me that when they fight, sex is the last thing he wants to engage in. In his family of origin everyone avoided conflict and the couple's seemingly unresolvable conflicts have caused him to retreat emotionally and sexually.

It is a little-known fact that it is generally the man who decides that an older adult sex-life is over. The experience of "not being able to perform" leads to this. It represents how little we grasp that sex is *not* about the ability to insert tab A into slot B. If we return to the work of Peggy Kleinplatz, we find that extraordinary long-term lovers are not preoccupied with performance or the beauty of a young body. They have discovered presence, connection, mutual caring, genuine acceptance, and compassion. They can communicate about vulnerable feelings and still enjoy the world of sensation. When a later-life couple can move out of an inflexible sexual script, they can begin to share pleasure in new ways. Being in one's seventies and beyond does not mean that the desire for touch and pleasure or the experience of an engaged intimacy goes away.

The Archetype of the Spectator

Masters and Johnson, the early pioneers of sex therapy, named an interfering aspect of sexuality that they encountered in many of their patients who had problems with arousal. They called it the Spectator.[99] The Spectator is a version of the Inner Critic, a culprit that keeps us from being present in the moment and interferes with tuning into sensation and arousal. The Spectator is always watching from the outside, judging, and evaluating how we are doing. This is the opposite of being fully immersed and in the flow of the experience. Masters and Johnson created a series of progressive exercises, which they called Sensate Focus. In today's world, these exercises could be thought of as mindfulness exercises, because they encourage focused presence and noticing sensate experiences while suspending "outcome goals."[100] In the beginning of Sensate Focus, there is to be no attempt at achieving what most people think of as "the real thing." This creates a less pressured context, and people begin to experience reduced performance anxiety. When they begin to relax and encounter each other and in this relaxed state, responsiveness begins to develop naturally.

Orgasm as the New Performance Anxiety

Back in the early feminist years, women fought for the right to their own sexual pleasure. It took us years to overcome the Freudian myth that women had "mature vaginal orgasms" and "immature clitoral orgasms." Research still shows that only 1 in 3 women will have an orgasm with vaginal penetration alone, and that most require direct clitoral stimulation. While women enjoy orgasms, having one every single time is not essential for the woman who enjoys the "spin-offs" of sex. Several modern sex therapists have noted that the insistence that a woman have an orgasm each time has become a new performance anxiety for both partners. If giving a woman an orgasm has become the gold standard of one's sexual prowess, then failing to get her there makes the partner feel like a failure. I've also heard women state that they would have more sex if their partners weren't turning every encounter into a Hollywood production.

SEX AND SOUL

Gina Ogden was one of the inspirational sex therapists of our time. She passed away in 2018, and I am grateful for having known her and having shared many animated conversations about how we might move sex therapy beyond behaviors, functioning body parts, and research focused on counting and measuring.[101]

Gina began to question the existing trend of sexology research back in the 1990s when the focus truly was on countering and measuring. She asked a series of different questions that became a survey that eventually included 3,810 people. They were mostly women, but the survey also included a few men. This original research now resides at the Kinsey Institute at Indiana University. Gina asked questions about how sex *feels* emotionally, and what it *means* in people's lives. Because the answers contained so many references to experiences that transcended time and space, the survey eventually became known as "Integrating Sexuality and Spirituality"— the ISIS survey. At a gathering of practitioners in 2016, a collective decision was made to abandon the mythological name ISIS because it had become too associated with terrorism. A decision was made to change the name to the 4-Dimensional Wheel of Sexual Experience—not as poetic, but less charged. More information about Gina's work and the group of practitioners who have incorporated her perspectives can be found at 4-Dnetwork.com.

Gina Ogden reminds us that the most profound and satisfying sexuality spans the dimensions of heart, mind, body, and spirit. She was one of the first research sexologists to talk about how sexuality is symbolic and imbued with immense meaning. Sexuality and spirituality are more intricately linked than most people think. They both originate from the core of our being and open doors into the innermost reaches of the psyche.

It is interesting to note that when we read the writings of the great religious mystics their writings are imbued with a passion that is usually reserved for one's erotic life. They express intense love, longing, and a burning desire for the divine. In their union with the divine, they express a form of religious ecstasy that sounds very much like sexual ecstasy. There is a statue by Bernini, which is found in the Italian church, Santa Maria della Vittoria. This amazing statue shows the medieval female mystic Teresa of Avila, her heart has been pierced by God's arrow. She is in the throes of religious ecstasy, looking to all who recognize it like a woman in orgasm. A soulful sexuality requires the level of encounter that Martin Buber spoke of. This is a sexuality beyond need meeting, beyond keeping score or demanding that the other person be our sexual ideal. Encounter has to do with meeting another person at their essence. It is not behavioral—it is essentially spiritual. I-Thou sexuality honors the essence of the other. It is a true sexual encounter.

CHAPTER 15

FAITHFULNESS AND FIDELITY

"Courage is not a virtue or value among other personal values like love or fidelity. It is the foundation that underlies and gives reality to all other virtues and personal values. Without courage our love pales into mere dependency. Without courage our fidelity becomes conformism."

Rollo May

When we think of infidelity, we often think of sexual betrayal, but couples betray each other in a variety of ways.

Carl was fifty-five and started looking at his savings for retirement. It was woefully deficient, so he decided to invest the couple's life savings in a "sure thing" that was bound to accelerate their nest egg. He did not discuss this plan with his wife, Madeline … until it went belly up.

Eddie wanted to put off having children until he and Joyce paid off their hefty student loans. They talked about it and Joyce agreed, but a year later, she decided she didn't want to wait and stopped taking her birth control. Eddie is angry at this discovery and overwhelmed by the news that Joyce is now pregnant. She is devastated that her announcement was not greeted with joy.

George is married to Nancy, a Devoted Nurturer. They finally got their children off to college and Nancy is excited about the newfound space in her life. She is planning to take some classes of her own. George is concerned about his mother's declining health, particularly her declining memory. In a recent conversation with his siblings, they all agreed that mom would move in with George. He did not discuss this with Nancy; he just assumes that Nurturing Nancy would be willing to help with his mom's escalating care needs.

All of these are betrayals that involve rogue decisions that impact the partner significantly. They are decisions made unilaterally, without consideration of agreements made, or the potential negative impact that they will have on the partner. They are indications of not being "in" relationship. They damage the bond, or they might indicate that the bond is broken. Perhaps that sense of "we" was never established in the first place.

I've seen all of these instances in my work with couples, however, for most people, the discovery of a sexual affair feels like the ultimate betrayal. A sexual affair in a relationship that was understood to be monogamous destroys the narrative of being the special person with whom this very vulnerable, personal, symbolic aspect of life is shared. An affair disrupts a person's sense of reality—it creates an existential crisis. In the wake of discovery people wonder, "Did I ever know you? What else don't I know? Is there anything else in life that I am trusting that is not what it seems?" Betrayed partners have often forgone temptations or indulgences of their own, to protect the relationship and they are outraged at how their partner did not do the same. While there are many reasons why people break their promise to "forsake all others," almost all of these reasons fall into the category of a "misbegotten solution."

Looking More Deeply at Faithfulness

When we begin to delve deeper into what it means to be "faithful" or "unfaithful," my question is, "faithful to what?" Are you being faithful to a person, a commitment, a vow, a set of values? Or is it about duty and obligation, protecting your security, keeping the family together, or pleasing one's parents? Perhaps it is about maintaining a particular persona with the outside world, or not losing face with a religious community. Is the married man who is distant and cold, while maintaining a "virtuous" abstinence from extramarital affairs faithful? Is the Dutiful Wife who is completely checked out during sex with her husband, reviewing her to task list for the week, faithful? What about the person who has no commitment to the well-being or unfolding life of their life partner, and no investment in a process of co-creating or sustaining a relationship worth having? Where is the "faithfulness" in that?

I am always amazed at how most couples don't really define "fidelity," and how disturbed they become to discover how differently people understand what it means to be "faithful."

Where is the Line Between Friendship and an Emotional Affair?

Danielle has dragged Mario into couples therapy. They have been arguing about Mario's close friendship with a woman at work. She explains to me that this other woman, Misha, sends texts to Mario throughout the evening, and whenever Mario's phone dings, he goes running, and lights up if it is a text from her. This is what is bothering Danielle, who would like to spend undisturbed evenings with Mario focused on her. Recently Danielle read some of these texts and has accused Mario of cheating on her. Mario is quite defensive. "I've never touched the woman. We're just work friends who enjoy each other." He accuses Danielle of being unreasonably jealous and controlling. Then he tells her that she is not very attractive to him when she acts this way: "I can't be in a relationship where I'm not allowed to have friends!" Danielle is even more distressed now. Danielle turns to me. "He's having an emotional affair! Don't you see it?!" Danielle is hoping I can convince Mario to shut this "friendship" down. Is Misha a threat to Danielle—perhaps. Is Mario having an emotional affair—perhaps. But there is much more going on in the under-stream between these two than the argument over Misha.

In recent years, I am seeing an increasing number of couples who are upset because their partner has reconnected with an old flame on one of the social media platforms. Old friends and lovers can easily find each other today, and they can communicate through a variety of venues—often without the primary partner knowing. The discovery of these somewhat clandestine connections is often what brings a couple into my office. Connecting with strangers online carries a feeling of protected anonymity. You can be someone completely different than who you are in your other life. You can express suppressed dimensions of self—shadow dimensions, that would be too threatening to the equilibrium of the primary relationship. Is this just exploration and entertainment, or is it cheating? Who decides?

In today's world, the question about where someone is crossing the line has to be defined by every couple, because activities and involvements that would deeply threaten one couple, will not threaten another. As one of my colleagues recently said, "I would rather he would have slept with the next-door neighbor than have had to go through the betrayal of financial infidelity."[102]

What I observe is that when any outside involvement begins to undermine the connection with or the importance of the primary partner, it will be experienced as a threat. This can be a "friendship" that seems a bit too cozy, but it can also be a career, a hobby, or an involvement with a group. An over-devotion to the children can supplant the emotional and sexual connection with a spouse. Any outside involvement that draws a significant amount of energy away from the primary relationship will be a threat to the partner who loves connection. In talking to people, most of them do not understand that a relationship is a third entity that must be established, sustained and nurtured across the arch of a lifetime. Beyond attending to the partner, if a relationship does not receive any attention or energy, it will languish, even die. When a couple asks, "What happened to *us*?" they are referring to the loss of that third entity, the "we." The fraying of the attachment bond can either proceed or follow these outside involvements. When an intimate connection no longer provides nourishment, people will eventually turn elsewhere to find meaning and fulfillment. In an emotional desert, people will go in search of water.

Affairs pump dopamine, and dopamine will make you feel "high." Human beings long for experiences that will take them beyond themselves, and many affairs originate in this need. This is particularly true in the *Midlife Marriage Malaise*, when many people begin to evaluate how happy they are. They become aware that there is no longer an endless stretch of time left in which to fulfill their lives. An affair can cause the world to suddenly become filled with color and light, as if one has awakened from a long sleep. In midlife, many people want to know that they still have the power to attract, to excite, and to please. The limerence that is experienced in a profound infatuation, will cause a person to lose their moorings and be swept downstream by compelling feelings of exhilaration. The title song, *The Way He Makes Me Feel*, is from the movie *Yentl*,[103] sung by Barbra Streisand. It contains phrases like, "flowing through my body is a river of surprise," and "feelings are awakening I hardly recognize as mine," and "every time I close my eyes he's there." These describe the intensity and obsessional quality people feel when captured by limerence and its inevitable enchantment. Unfortunately, most people swept downstream by these shadow involvements are blind to the reality that they are under a spell and that strong idealized projections are operating that originate from their own psyches.

For couples who have a solid bond and are clear about their fidelity agreement, outside involvements do not become threats. We should all have outside involvements because they continue to make us interesting. Bringing the excitement of something we are learning or involved in back into our relationship vitalizes it! "Who are you becoming?" and "What lights you up?" are important questions in a relationship where two people are individuating in connection. But couples who have never established the "we," begin to over-invest in outside involvements out of the emptiness they feel in the relationship. Couples who have established a bond worth protecting, protect the bond because they value the relationship. They make U-turns out of danger zones.

Jealousy

Jealousy and insecurity are terrible feelings. There *is* such a thing as reasonable jealousy. However, controlling and policing a partner does not insure fidelity and certainly does not lead to a secure bond. If you feel that you need to constantly monitor your partner to ensure that they are not "straying," there is a significant problem in your relationship. This can indicate that the fidelity agreement was never really negotiated, or that the relationship is floundering. It can also mean that you are involved with someone who has a Rogue self inside.

There are people who are not really interested in or cut out for monogamy. When I engage in a Voice Dialogue session with people who are attempting to be monogamous, but find lots of reasons for straying, I discover an interesting set of Rogue Inner Selves. These Rogue Characters may not have attended the wedding, or they may have watched the Enchanted Lover at the altar with a jaundiced eye. They did not take vows of fidelity, or they had a lot of "qualifiers" around their promises, which make involvement with others understandable. You cannot *make* someone want to be sexually faithful, and trying to police, punish, or guilt someone into being such a person will only result in a world of hurt and drama.

If you are thinking of building a life with another person, it becomes important to understand their inner self system and "who" lives in there—not what you hope for or project in an enchanted limerence. It's best to look a bit deeper and see if your longing and idealization may have obscured your awareness of an Inner Frenchman, a Don Juan, a Social Climber, or an attention-seeking Seductress.

On the other side of this, if you are someone with a history of abandonment, unworthiness, and betrayal, you may have great difficulty with trust. If no amount of reassurance from a truly faithful partner will resolve these feelings of suspicion and jealousy, there is inner work to do. Unfounded jealousy will damage whatever bond you have with a good and loyal partner.

People who have affairs are rarely thinking about the under-lying reasons driving their behavior or the impact that the discovery will have on their partner. It is as if the Partnered Self goes offline and some Shadow Self has taken over. The Guilty Partner may kick in later. Many confessions occur in these moments of guilt and regret and the truthful answer to the betrayed partner's, "What were you thinking?!" is, "I wasn't."

One of the key questions I always want to unpack in working through the "what happened" stage is the unconscious drivers underneath the betrayal. Was this a disowned self that emerged from the shadow-land of the straying partner? "Who" was it in the inner self system of the straying partner that walked away from commitments of faithfulness? What were they seeking to experience or express and how did it become tied to the affair partner? Could this have been lived out in another context that would not have damaged the marriage so significantly?

The Individuation Affair

There are certain affairs that are a result of outgrowing the story of the original relationship. A person can begin to feel confined and want to live into a bigger story. One of the cruelest things we do is to put a partner in a box and not give them the opportunity to be seen as something more. Aspects of self that were previously sleeping in the seedbed of their psyche are coming online and seeking entry. The relationship, at this juncture needs to expand to encompass these new dimensions of self, but those negotiations are difficult for couples who do not understand Individuation in Connection. In a relationship that cannot grow in this way, this expansion of a person's life may get lived out with an affair partner. When something is coming online in a person's psyche, and they meet another person who is living that aspect more fully, there is always a draw. This is the nature of attraction, wanting to be closer to some aspect of personality and quality of being that another person carries. The conscious person realizes that this irresistible draw is an invitation to growth. When conscious people feel a sexual draw to another person, they take some time to look inward and to discover what is being stirred "in here" before wandering into the arms of someone "over there."

These stirrings may precipitate an important conversation with a partner to examine how their relationship needs to respond to this "wake-up" call.

Should I Stay or Should I Go?

Some relationships need to be over because the direction of the two partner's lives is so divergent that their continued attempt to stay together would inhibit living into who they were born to be. However, this deserves careful consideration and discussion with the partner. It is always best to alert a partner to a growing call to leave and have serious conversations about adjustments that would need to take place in order to stay. A relationship in which one partner has no interest in growing or resolving long-standing issues may need to end in its committed form. The story of "why we are together," may have run its purposeful course. However, such determinations are never easy, and a person considering ending a relationship needs to have done sufficient self-examination and discernment. It is my fondest wish that we lived in a world where a couple could have conversations about their disappointments and dissatisfactions, and where each person was practicing the level of listening outlined in this book. Most conversations about unhappiness get stuck at the gate of complaint and are met with counter-complaint or defensiveness. When a couple lacks the skills and the will to engage in a true dialogue, nothing is understood and little is resolved. It is not hard to understand how after multiple experiences of being unheard and not responded to, some people begin to look for happiness elsewhere.

Integrity

When I talk to people about integrity, I always emphasize that it is not just about "good behavior," or following a set of rules. Yes, integrity does involve honoring our commitments and "doing the right thing," but integrity also has to do with aligning the inner and outer life. Integrity is about a life structured on a foundation that is sourced from the deep Self. Take a moment and consider the integrity of your life. Is there an alignment between your inner and outer life? Do you know what I'm talking about when I mention an inner compass? Does your life partner understand this? When you think about fidelity or being faithful, what is it you are being faithful to? Who, in your Inner Cast of Characters is running the show? Fidelity and integrity should walk hand in hand. Integrity is developed by doing your shadow work, becoming more aware of what lives in you, clearing the clutter of limiting life complexes, and growing into the fullest expression of who we were born to be—the path of individuation.

CHAPTER 16

INTERPERSONAL DREAMING

*"Your visions will become clear only when you
can look into your own heart. Who looks outside, dreams;
who looks inside, awakes."*

Carl Jung

*"Dreamwork may be one of the best things available
for providing instant intimacy."*

Phyllis Koch-Sheras and Peter Sheras

Dream-sharing

It is important for a couple to create a shared dream of life together—who they want to become as a couple and what they want to experience together. In this section I want to talk about a different kind of communication and dreamwork—through sharing dreams of the night.

I have been interested in dreamwork since I was a teenager and began recording significant dreams in a journal at that time. What drew me to write them down was the powerful feeling tone of certain dreams. I sensed that they were helping to guide me in some way, encouraging me forward into a future that had yet to be defined. It is interesting to note that researchers are now looking more carefully into the function of REM dreaming and how it impacts our general well-being.[104]

In 1999, I became deeply engaged in the study of Jungian psychology and soon after I entered Jungian analysis. This immersed me in some serious dreamwork and deeper inquiry into what made me tick. I came to understanding that dreams speak to us about what is moving through the under-stream of our lives— elements that are out of awareness during our busy day but impacting us just the same.

Whether we recognize it or not, we are all invited into a journey of individuation—the process of becoming the unique individual we were born to be. We are far more than our histories or domineering Egos would lead us to believe. I have found my dreams to be a way of establishing a conversation with the guiding Self.

In my studies of Jungian psychology, I did not encounter any significant writing about dream-sharing in relationships, but I know that the couples who share their nighttime dreams have a deeper level of intimacy in their relationship. What is fascinating is that when couples begin to share their nighttime dreams, their psyches begin to speak to each other! Kahlil Gibran once spoke of love as a moving sea between the shores of two souls. This image speaks of that unconscious field that is created between two people who are deeply linked, and the invisible flow that begins to move between their two psyches.

Many of my significant teachers have been dream-sharing couples. My beloved teachers Hal and Sidra Stone, who wrote the book *Partnering*,[105] share how they employed dreams, shadow work, and the exploration of disowned selves to deepen their connection and work through the inevitable conflicts that arise when two people realize they are different. The last time I saw Hal Stone, we were standing in the kitchen of Hal and Sidra's wonderful Mendocino home, and I recall the luminous light in Hal's eyes. He was around ninety years old and there was a sense that he was already standing between this earthly realm and the great beyond. Hal shared a dream about receiving a "passport" to travel into other dimensions. In the days before he died, he had many dreams of crossing over that eliminated his fear of death and he died peacefully in his sleep a few days after sharing a lovely dream with Sidra in which a little girl took his hand and led him into the beyond.

My favorite guidebook for becoming a dream-sharing couple is *The Dream Sharing Sourcebook*,[106] written by psychologists Peter Sheras and Phyllis Koch-Sheras. It deals specifically with what dream-sharing might mean for a couple.

Teaching about dreamwork is beyond the scope of this book, but I encourage you to learn more about this source of inner wisdom, conveyed through visions of the night. While many people feel that dreams are unintelligible phantoms of the night, when we begin to attend to them, the themes, feelings, and images inform us about what is moving through us below the level of our conscious operation. When we attend to dreams, the psyche begins a conversation with the waking mind, sending guiding messages in the night. These messages from the deep Self offer us course corrections, compensate for things we need, and offer us new ways of seeing things. Dreams alert us to things we need to be paying attention to, they provide healing experiences, take us into new archetypal stances, and offer creative solutions for the problems of living. Even in the writing of this book, I have awakened with entire sections organized that were a mere jumble the day before.

When a couple begins to dream-share, their psyches will begin to speak to each other. It is not even necessary to "figure out" what the dream means. The mere telling of a dream will convey something to the psyche of the other. When you attend to the themes and images in the dream and notice your associations with them, you will begin to decipher their messages. I'll give you an example from my own life, where a dream-sharing experience helped me course correct something in my relationship with my husband.

The Wrecking Crew

Last year, I became frustrated with my husband because he had never unpacked a stack of boxes in his home office. They had been sitting there for three years after our last move (some of you will understand this frustration). I knew that they contained bits and pieces of his earlier life in corporate marketing—marketing campaigns he had designed, plaques and trophies received, files with old travel brochures, old magazines, and outdated newsletters, probably a lot of old junk mail as well. It was nothing he needed on a day-to-day basis, and that's why it sat. I wanted him to go through the boxes and clear the clutter! Still the boxes sat. I'm not an extreme neatnik, but this had gotten ridiculous. One day, my Critical Mother self got activated. I marched into the office, hands on hips, and announced, "Tom, I've asked you repeatedly to go through these boxes and unpack them. Here they sit, untouched. If something were to happen to you, I may just take them to the dump wholesale and get rid of them." Admittedly, I was in a complex, and this was not my finest moment as a Loving Wife.

That night my husband had the following dream. "*A big seaside festival has taken place and now it is over. The area is filled with buildings that were used to house the exhibits. The bulldozers are coming to plow them down. They are perfectly good buildings that could be repurposed for something, perhaps even to house the homeless. I am desperately looking for the mayor to stop the destruction.*"

He told me the dream in the morning as I was getting ready for work. As I was driving to work, his dream began to work on me. I realized that the dream was directly related to my pronouncement that I might take his unopened boxes to the dump. This is how it felt to his deeper psyche, treating the collected artifacts of his career life with such disregard. I returned home that evening, apologized and told him that I would take the time to go through the boxes with him. I realized that this is what he really wanted. I had previously considered this to be an unnecessary waste of time. We began to sort through the boxes and as we did this, he told me the stories of his life at work. There were years of wonderful creative ideas, memories of people who acknowledged his value, presented him with plaques and letters of appreciation, amazing corporate conferences he had organized all over the world, in a variety of interesting places. We kept some gems of remembrance and respectfully sent the remainder to its "place of rest." It was worth my time and patience. Mostly, it was worth the commitment of my presence. I never would have done this without that dream, which alerted me that I was in a mistaken "stance." I would have missed the opportunity to share in his inner life and learn more about the man who went off to work. The dream allowed me to shift my perspective and my archetypal stance.

Couples who share their nighttime dreams will discover that the dreams are inviting opportunities to discuss deeper feelings and concerns. They will take you to places in your partner's history and psyche that you have never heard about. As a result, information will be shared, and topics will be opened that would never have been opened before. Dreams often convey information that is below either person's waking awareness. Themes will present themselves; emotions will emerge; conversations will open to address what is happening at a deeper level—outside of our superficial daily operations. Dreams take us beyond daylight concerns and preoccupations, beyond the ego-identity and open doors into the deep Self.

CHAPTER 17

THE SOULFUL RELATIONSHIP

"As you go the way of life, you will see a great chasm.
Jump. It is not as wide as you think."
A Native American wise man (Quoted by Joseph Campbell)

"We waste time looking for the perfect lover,
instead of creating the perfect love."
Tom Robbins

"I love thee to the depth and breadth and height
my soul can reach."
Elizabeth Barrett Browning

Individuation and Awakening

I am recalling a conversation that I had one day with a young waiter. We were talking about the meaning of "individuation." He had not heard the term before. When I asked him what he thought the word meant, he said it probably had something to do with becoming an individual. I agreed, and then he told me a dream that illustrates the central theme of individuation. He said,

"In my dream, I thought I was awake. I thought my eyes were open. Then a second set of lids opened, and I could really see."

Individuation is about the ongoing process of awakening. As we start to wake up, we see all the ways in which we have been sleepwalking. As we gain the courage to look inward, we see the ways in which other people's definitions of who we are have limited our lives. We begin to rewrite old scripts and free ourselves from the oppressive influence of early life complexes. When our complexes activate, we pull out of them more quickly. We begin to recognize the pervasiveness of projection and to reconsider the conclusions we have reached about others, especially the intimate partner we live with. The mindful gap we develop between our triggers and our reactions increases, and with it a growing capacity to hold onto a calm core. All of this makes us safer partners and allows us to love more deeply and accept the love we long for in return.

The individuation journey continues until the last breath we breathe. As we deepen and grow, we realize that the stories we live in are too small for the size of our souls. As our lives become more aligned with the guidance from the Self, we discover a vast array of resources that come from this storehouse within. The inner work, which seemed so arduous at the start, becomes a part of the rhythm of life, increasingly rewarding as our eyes keep opening.

Individuation in Connection

While much individuation work is done in one's personal life, relationships are the place that really accelerate the process. I started using the term "individuation in connection" to counter the idea that the journey of individuation is a solo journey. Our consciousness affects everything and everyone around us. This journey of growth does not lift us *out* of life and relationship, it increases our capacity to engage them. The journey of individuation is particularly sweet when we can share it with an intimate other.

When two people engage in this journey together it takes the relationship into a completely new context which changes the feeling and interpretation of everything that occurs within that relationship. In this new context, problems that previously plagued the relationship will begin to vanish of their own accord because we are looking at life through a different lens and relating from a different internal place. The personal work we do helps us relax the complexes that hold us in their thrall. A second set of lids open, and we see through new eyes. In this newfound freedom, everything looks different. The more conscious we become of how our complexes and defenses limit us, the more we can separate out from these internal tangles. We grow in our capacity to step back and reflect on our experiences. Like five-year-olds who learn to "stop, look, and listen," before crossing the road—we learn to pause and reflect. The struggles we encounter become doorways into new insights and personal growth. As we do the work, possibilities emerge that were not even imagined in our previous state of being.

Tending the Inner Children

When we are operating purely out of a "need meeting" level of relationship, we are easily wounded in love. Two people cannot create a fulfilling relationship when they are entangled in interlocking complexes. Our Inner Children often pick our partners, and their needs, longings, and demands underlie most of the difficulties in our relationships. We cannot solve love's problems when our Inner Children are driving the process. We cannot let love in while our Inner Defenders have us armored up. Our most heated arguments take place when our Inner Children and their Defenders are fighting and struggling to get needs met. Inner Children want what they want, how they want it, when they want it. We have Wiser Selves within.

While compassion, attunement, and a sense of safety are essential elements in a secure attachment, we need to do our personal healing work, so as not to burden the relationship with wounds of the past. Yes, we want our partners to understand our areas of tender sensitivity, but if we demand that a partner be continually cautious of our tenderness or fragility, it will reduce the spontaneity and authenticity in the relationship. We need Adults on board to solve adult problems. That can only be achieved through inner work and the resources gained as we are increasingly guided by the deep Self instead of our fragile egos. The deepening dynamics of a soulful relationship require a more expansive inner self system. In healthy adult relationships, our older, wiser selves are leading. They are capable of soothing, reassuring, and sometimes containing our anxious Inner Children. As we do our own deep healing work, we reduce the need for a partner to be "ideal" all the time, a pressure that no one can live up to.

The Spiral Path

The journey of relationship is a spiral journey—just like the journey of individuation. We revisit dimensions of our lives from new states of being and understand ourselves in new ways. That shift will change our interactions in a relationship. That first cycle through a relationship is the most daunting and anxiety provoking—moving from enchantment to disenchantment. When we engage the process of personal growth, we avoid much suffering.

Does a focus on individuation end all future struggle? No, but avoiding struggle is not the point. Struggling is always worthwhile when the end point is a breakthrough into a deeper and more meaningful experience of life. What we want to avoid is the pointless struggle of the defended Ego, which will exhaust our spirit and cut us off from soul. To quote Jung, *"The meeting of two personalities is like the contact of two chemical substances. If there is a reaction, both are transformed."* Our intimate relationships can transform us in unexpected ways.

As we travel love's labyrinth path, we learn that letting go of the things that limit us has great reward. We relinquish old ways of being and seeing. Walking into unfamiliar places is anxiety provoking, but we gain courage as we walk the path and continue to awaken. Growth brings new inner freedom. It opens up new possibilities, but it is also destabilizing. In challenging times, we may fall back into old patterns—self-protective gambits that we adopted long ago—but once awakened, the path calls us forward. We recall the misery of the previous swamplands and navigate past them. Gibran's wise words ring true, love's work is to descend to our roots and shake us in our clinging to the earth—to free us from our husks.

The Person We Never Knew

Sometimes people ask me, "What do I do if it seems like I'm the only one doing any inner work here?" It's a good question, and it is difficult to remain in a relationship where you feel like you are the only person committed to growth. But be careful of the shadow tendency of spiritual condescension, where you believe that you have the one true path of growth. Do you have a fixed idea of what a "conscious person" looks like, what they do, and do not do, and what their spiritual practices should be? Keep in mind that when people feel judged and looked down upon, they tend to keep their inner life to themselves. Consider that it might be your own judgments that are blocking your partner's willingness to share their deeper Self.

I recall a couple I worked with some time ago. Phillip worked as a mid-level manager for a technology company. Sandra was a stay-at-home mom. They were recent empty nesters with their children scattered about the United States. Sandra was lonely. She explained that her husband never talked to her and he was an even worse listener. Sandra wanted me to teach Phillip how to communicate. What I came to understand was that when Phillip arrived home from work, he was met with a litany of complaints about everything that had gone wrong in Sandra's day—her elderly mother was difficult, the children never called and they seemed utterly ungrateful for all she had done for them; recently a friend slighted her by not nominating her to a church committee; and the lawn company had botched the pruning of the hedges once again. Phillip would retreat to his upstairs office or into a television program. During our third session I turned and looked at Phillip. I noticed he was listening to Sandra with great tenderness and sadness. He met my eyes. I paused and then I asked what he thought about as he drove to and from work every day. He was quiet for a moment and then he began. "I think about my life and the time I have left here on this earth. I'm grateful for my life and the many opportunities I have been given. I enjoy my work and I have wonderful children. Currently I am in a process of mentoring some of the younger men in my company, teaching them what I know about managing people. Since coming to couples therapy, I have been thinking a lot about the love capacities. I've been thinking about how I haven't been very present to Sandra. She's been trying to get my attention, but I haven't wanted to be around her. She complains a lot, and I often don't want the negativity, but I'm realizing that this is how she has been trying to connect with me. She does a lot of good work in the world, but I think she's lonely at home. Perhaps if I tried to listen more deeply, as you say, she would be less unhappy." Sandra turned to her husband in astonishment and responded, "Wow, Phillip, and I always thought you were shallow." This was the beginning of a turnaround for Phillip and Sandra.

Anytime you find yourself thinking, I know all about this person, stop yourself. It infers that there is nothing left to learn. We can live with someone for years but never really know them deeply.

There will be rooms of their inner house that you may have never visited. Consider dropping your picture of who you are living with and try encountering them freshly.

It is important that we continue to update our understanding of who we are living with, so we avoid the trap of relating to them as who they used to be. An I-Thou encounter can happen at any time, but you have to be present and create a space of safe inquiry for the soul to show itself. Here are some things to wonder about:

- Who have you become over the years since I last checked in with you?
- What matters the most? What lights you up and inspires you? Where are you finding meaning?
- What are you grappling with and how are you meeting the challenge?
- When you struggle where do you draw your strength from?
- What does your Soul long for that has yet to be experienced or expressed?
- What gifts of yourself would you still like to give to the world?
- How can I best support you in your own evolution—your journey of individuation?
- What do you suppose the deep Self is orchestrating in our relationship? What is being brought about by the two of us being together that would never happen if we had never joined our lives?

INDIVIDUATION IN CONNECTION

When Carl Jung wrote his prophetic essay on the possible marriage back in 1925, he was describing the kind of relationship that most people are seeking in the 21st century—where we are encountering each other and actually relating, rather than just being mere Role Mates. We have very few guidebooks to help us attain this depth of relationship. It is my hope that this book will move you beyond the search for that mythical "Soul Mate" into the inner work required to create a deeply meaningful, soulful relationship— a truly attainable goal in the world of us ordinary humans. Jung emphasized *"without an awareness of how projections and complexes obscure our vision and prevent us from actually encountering the other, there is no true relationship, only actors on a scripted stage."*

When we stop treating a life partner as an actor on our stage, the whole relationship changes. True relationship begins when we acknowledge that this other person has an inner life separate from our own. To really begin a relationship, we must have a true encounter and come to understand that other person's inner world. When both people do this, we have the foundation for an intimate, meaningful, conscious relationship. At this stage, we can begin to co-create a shared story, to develop a co-world where both people can flourish. Once engaged in this process, it will drive the evolution of both partners. Couples that begin to co-create instead of power struggle enter into the land of the open heart, gaining confidence in their capacity to navigate the terrain.

In his book *Resilient*, psychologist Rick Hanson wrote, "The more I work with people, the more I realize that if we are going to have soulful relationships that are deeply fulfilling, we must engage the soul in that work. Loving is not just the province of heart, mind, and body—it is most assuredly a spiritual journey—a journey of personal development around depth and meaning."[107]

Erik Erikson, the famous developmental psychologist, believed that the distress people feel is caused by their inability to garner the inner resources needed to master whatever developmental phase of life they are in. The success of loving and being loved ultimately depends on our growth as individuals. We need to do our personal work so that we are not burdening our relationships with our demanding projections and reactivity. In becoming more self-aware we will be able to focus more intentionally on the development of Love's Capacities.

Love's Capacities

– Commitment – to a chosen *person*, to the *process* of relationship, and to *presence*—showing up, and remaining engaged.
– Courage – to remain on the path, to face oneself and one's partner—shadow and light, to let go of old narratives and live into a larger story, to recognize and move beyond projections, and to reveal ourselves authentically in that mutual process of growth and discovery.
– Curiosity – the sincere and sustained effort to look inward, to learn about our formation and to engage in necessary personal work, in shadow work; then to engage in the ongoing process of seeking to encounter and understand the inner workings of our chosen beloved.
– Communication – staying in a lifelong learning conversation rather than assuming we "know" our partner; becoming more present and intentional about listening deeply; avoiding defensiveness, checking out projections, asking clarifying questions, listening beyond the words into the underlying needs, and attending to what is seeking to emerge from this other person's soul; speaking for ourselves and becoming more self-aware about what we truly want to convey, and "who" in us is speaking.
– Compassion – for our own innate, imperfect humanity and for the humanity of the other; treating each other with kindness and working toward consciousness and mindfulness in our interactions.
– Creativity – the ongoing work of the creation of a co-world, a world that is meaningful and worth inhabiting, a world that nourishes and supports the growth of both people—the journey of individuation in connection.

When two people are on the journey of Individuation in Connection with each other, we are not wandering lost. We are drawing from the resources of the Self, and the context of our lives together will take on the quality of a sacred journey. Open to the mystery, the entire relationship will be lifted to a new level, in which old preoccupations and entanglements fall away and everything is held in a new context—seen through a different lens of understanding. While we still experience complexes activating and find ourselves projecting our "stuff" onto our partners, we untangle from all of this much sooner, and don't fall into the same defenses and catastrophic narratives we found ourselves spinning in the past. Our life together becomes more courageous and compassionate. We become less reactive and more present. Commitment becomes deeper and easier as we realize that we are part of a larger story. We sense that something is being brought about by our being together that transcends the limitation of our Ego-based understanding. We are being resourced by the deep Self and we can trust in the unfolding of life.

The 21st century opens us to new possibilities for loving and being loved. Never before have we had such freedom to choose who we love and how we love, but with this opportunity comes the necessity to develop as individuals. We cannot live into the promise of what love can hold by operating at the same level of relationship that ruled previous centuries. If we want to create a soulful relationship, it requires our commitment to inner work, and the deepening of our capacities for loving and being loved. This is how we reach the flowering of what love can be. Individuation in connection is the pathway to the realization of that dream.

ACKNOWLEDGMENTS

I have had many wonderful teachers over the years and have absorbed untold gems of wisdom that are woven into my philosophy and practice. However, there are certain teachers who stand out and I'd like to give them special recognition.

Carl Jung lived in another era, but when I discovered his work, I found a homeland. What I most appreciate about Jung's work is his integration of psychology and spirituality, and his belief that we each possess an inner compass that exists beyond our Ego identity— the deep Self. Jung's analytic psychology became a philosophical foundation for my work, as well as a context for living. I have a deep appreciation for the many brilliant and wise women who gathered around Jung, and whom he lifted up and supported in their intellectual and soulful contributions to depth psychology. They have been my most treasured teachers. In addition, Jungian analyst Keith Parker walked with me through a decade of growth, deepening insight, and the healing of a father wound. While I have been in other forms of psychotherapy, it was a combination of the Jungian analytical work and subsequent somatic work that allowed me to transcend thorny complexes that had troubled me since childhood. This work is what has allowed me to align my outer life with my deepest essence, and to experience the full flowering of my life.

Bob Haden, the founder of the Haden Institute, and subsequent director, Alan Proctor provided me a platform to develop and teach my own synthesis of Jung's work with other clinical and transpersonal perspectives. Susan Sims Smith introduced me to Hal and Sidra Stone. Their teaching on the Psychology of the Selves and the Voice Dialogue method took my "inner cast of character" work off the pages of a journal into an understanding that our "selves" can be understood as energies in the body, made conscious, interviewed, and worked with creatively. The Stones also made it clear that we all tend to over-identify with certain set of selves, and taught a method of separating out from those limitations so that we can explore the gold of undeveloped, and disowned (shadow) selves.

I am grateful for the gentle soul and insightful teachings of Pam White, at the Asheville Center for Group and Family Therapy. She gathered a group of wonderful therapists together and we took a deep-dive into training in the psychodynamics world of Transactional Analysis and Re-decision Therapy, and added Al Pesso's Psycho-motor work. Pesso's teaching gave me a introductory awareness of how much the somatic dimension of experience impacts who we are and how we live and love. Daniel Siegel, Peter Levine, Stephen Porges, Diane Poole Heller, and Louis Cozolino have had a big impact on my thinking about attachment and interpersonal neurobiology – how much our nervous systems impact how we relate. Other teachers I have studied with who furthered my development as a couples therapist, are Ellyn Bader, Polly Young-Eisendrath, Stan Tatkin, Esther Perel, Terry Real, and Travis Atkinson. I am influenced by the writings and research of John Gottman, Susan Johnson, and I greatly appreciate the spiritual perspectives on relationship expressed by John Welwood.

In 2009, I met the wonderful sex therapist, writer, teacher, and friend, Gina Ogden. She passed from this life in 2018. Gina was an amazing encourager, and I treasure the hours of discussion we shared about transformative methods of sexual healing, and how sexuality can be a path of individuation. The inspiration for my book, *In Search of Aphrodite,* was born on a weekend visit to her home in Cambridge, talking at her kitchen table, swimming in Waldon Pond, and watching the waves on Singing Beach.

In recent years, I am indebted to Dr. Rick Smith and Susan Sims Smith, who convinced me to come to UAMS and begin the Couples Center, to provide relationship and sex therapy, and train clinicians in this important work. My position at UAMS has allowed me to train an ever-expanding audience of clinicians in methods and perspectives that help couples create meaningful, enduring relationships.

I have had many wonderful friends who have supported and encouraged me over the years. You are so very dear to me. Thank you to all of you, especially Layne and Ken Racht, Carmon McGee, Sara Nafziger-Shelly, Shirley Nicholson, Laura Chapman, Susan Schoenbohm, Jeremy Taylor, Tom Yeomans, Ellen Dionna, Kanji Ruhl, Ruthie Harper, the great guys of the Pam White group, Mary Jo Marchisello, Roseanne Eichenbaum, Sarah Hatcher, piano teacher Trudy Anshutz, and John "Gipsy" Bullard—the "big brother" of my twenties.

Many thanks to Dr. Steve Buser, Chiron publisher, who encouraged me to develop these ideas into a book, and patiently awaited its delivery.

Molly Rector provided editorial assistance when I was floundering with containment and mixed metaphors.

Finally, I am deeply grateful to my husband, Tom. You are my dearest love. The secure base of your continual encouragement and support of my unfolding journey has given me the freedom to evolve and expand my reach, confident in the constancy of your love, and the celebration of each new success. I have become a better person because of you. We have lived the journey in this book, found our way out of swamplands, deepened our capacities, and continue to write a wonderful love story as soulful partners.

ABOUT THE AUTHOR

Chelsea Wakefield, PhD, LCSW is a therapist, author, and internationally respected teacher who holds a lifelong interest in powerful processes that heal wounded hearts and bring more meaning, love, and connection to our lives. With her compelling perspectives on living and loving, Dr. Wakefield is a popular keynote speaker, inspirational workshop leader, and a sought-after clinician. She is an Associate Professor and Director of the Couples Center at the University of Arkansas for Medical Sciences, where she offers couples therapy, sex therapy, and trains clinicians in her innovative clinical work. Her work is undergirded by a belief that we all have an inner compass that we can reference, which will lead us toward wholeness. As a Jungian oriented practitioner, she has been on the faculty of the Haden Institute since 1990, where she teaches in the Dreamwork and Spiritual Direction programs.

In 2009, Chelsea created a powerful retreat experience for women called the Luminous Woman® Weekend. The experience invites women into a deep exploration of their unique beauty, and archetypal potential, opening vistas of new possibility in every area of their lives. The Luminous Woman® program has developed into an ongoing community of women who can stay connected online and meet in person to sustain their Luminous Living.

Her previous books are *Negotiating the Inner Peace Treaty: Becoming the Person You Were Born to Be*; and *In Search of Aphrodite: Women, Archetypes, and Sex Therapy.*

In her off hours, Chelsea alternates between quiet time contemplating life, treasured time in deep conversations with friends, and laughing with her talented and hysterical son Tommy. She loves to balance her inner life with the sensate world of culinary creativity, which her husband eagerly appreciates. Together, they enjoy quiet weeks on winter beaches, discussing the characters and plots of movies and television series, and walking arm in arm along the romantic streets of Paris.

If you would like to learn more about Chelsea's future events, attend a Luminous Woman® or Labyrinth of Love workshop, book her as a speaker, or train with her, you can contact her through her website: www.chelseawakefield.com

APPENDIX

The Initiator-Inquirer Process

Initiator *Revealing one's self*

Focus On One Issue Only
Before you begin, get clear on your main concern.
Check your partner's readiness.
Stay on track with this one issue.
Describe what you want.

Express Your Feeling & Thoughts
Feelings are often complex and can even be contradictory.
Are you sad, scared, angry, or happy?
Go beyond simply expressing one feeling.
Look for the vulnerability that may be underneath your initial feeling, e.g. sadness, fear, jealousy, hurt, guilt, etc.

Remind Yourself
This is my problem. It's an expression of who I am. It's about me revealing myself and being willing to express my own thoughts and feelings.

Avoid Blaming, Accusing or Name-calling.
Blaming stops you from knowing yourself.
You have a role to play in being heard.
You may wish to acknowledge some positive aspects of the situation.

Be Open to Self-Discovery
Explore your personal, inner experience.
Keep going deeper into how you feel.
What does this tell you about yourself?
How do you respond?
How do you think and feel?

Remind Yourself
This process is about my willingness to take a risk to speak or discover my truth, and about increasing my ability to tolerate the expression of our differences.

Inquirer *The Effective Listener*

Listen Calmly

Don't defend yourself, argue or cross complain.
Remind yourself that you don't have to take what's said so personally.
Hold on to "The Big Picture."

Ask Questions
Develop an interested and curious state of mind.
The questions you ask are designed to understand your partner's experience.
Can you come up with any examples on your own that will let your partner know you really understand?

Remind Yourself
Am I in a place to listen with openness?
I do not own this problem.
I do not need to get upset.
It's up to me to manage my reactions.

Recap
Repeat back to your partner, as accurately and completely as you are able, what you've understood.
Check it out with your partner to see if it's complete and accurate.

Empathize
Do your best to put yourself in your partner's shoes.
Respond with empathy.
Keep making empathetic statements until a soothing moment occurs.
You can hold onto yourself and still imagine what it's like for the other person.

Remind Yourself
My partner is a separate person with their own feelings, thoughts, personality and family history. I only need to listen, not look for solutions.

The Conscious Relationship Roadmap

ENCHANTMENT
Idealization Phase; "Limerence" - lots of interlocking projections. "You meet my needs! You are everything I had hoped for!"

DISENCHANTMENT
Surprises, differences, misunderstandings and disillusionments. Protests begins with attempts to return to Enchantment. "You are not who I thought you were!" Early attachment patterns surface. What felt safe now feels dangerous as partners begin to operate out of protective defenses.

STRUGGLE AND ANGUISH Phase –
Concern that this relationship is a terrible mistake. Power struggles ensue – withdrawal, blaming, punishing, criticism, anger, defensiveness, manipulation, lying, turning to others, distancing, breaking up, or the realization of a need for growth.

PERSONAL AND INTERPERSONAL WORK BEGINS.
Partners gain insight into themselves and each other & claim responsibility for their part in the creation and resolution of difficulties. Skills are learned; capacities are developed. Projections are withdrawn and interlocking complexes are untangled. Couple learns new ways of being and seeing each other.

CONSCIOUS RELATIONSHIP
Partners embrace the process of "Individuation in Connection" with all its challenges and rewards

Commitment to each other and the process of deepening love's capacities: courage, curiosity, communication, compassion, & creativity.

Relationship is increasingly sourced from the Deep Self & Soulful Connection beyond the Need-driven Ego.

INDEX

REFERENCES

Atkinson, Travis 260, 277, 279
Bader, Ellyn 36, 92, 127, 169, 177, 260, 276–279
Bader, Ellyn & Pearson, Pete 276, 277
Basson, Rosemary 227, 280
Bonhoeffer, Dietrich 179
Bowlby, John 43, 45, 46, 95, 276
Brandon, Nathaniel 182, 183, 225
Brown, Brené 43, 123, 128, 186, 193, 278, 279
Buber, Martin 105, 119–121, 165, 232, 278, 280
Carotenuto, Aldo 105
Chapman, Gary 177, 218, 261, 280
Coontz, Stephanie 110, 111, 278
Dalai Lama 179
Daye, Maci 214
Deikman, Arthur 61, 277
Delaney, Gayle 226, 280
Ecker, Ticic & Hulley 276, 278
Fisher, Helen 10, 275
Germer, Chris 181, 183, 279, 280
Gibran, Kahlil 45, 228, 244, 276, 278, 280
Gottman, John 87, 93, 188, 260, 276, 277, 279
Goulding, Bob & Mary McClure 278
Hanson, Rick 53, 148, 256, 276, 278, 281
Haule, John 275
Hollis, James 20, 194, 275, 279
Johnson, Robert 12, 147, 275
Johnson, Sue (Susan) 43, 132, 260, 277, 278
Jung, Carl (CG) 2, 3, 4, 20, 30–32, 34, 44, 61, 69, 71, 75, 85, 101, 106, 118, 120, 131, 191, 194, 243, 252, 255, 256, 259, 275, 277
Karpman, Stephen 91, 277
Kleinplatz, Peggy 209, 229, 280
Lee, S & Schwartz, N. 275
Lerner, Harriet 188, 279
Masters & Johnson 230, 280
May, Rollo 233
McCarthy, Barry 211, 280
McGehee, Pittman 153
Melody, Pia 183, 218, 279
Michaels, Mark & Patricia 275
Mitchell, Joni 119
Moore, Thomas 193
Morin, Jack 223, 280
Murray, W H 109
Neff, Kristin 179, 181–184, 279, 280
Ogden, Gina 222, 231, 260, 277, 280
Perel, Esther 15, 17, 112, 131, 158, 209, 213, 224, 228, 260, 275
Pinkola Estes, Clarissa 131
Plato 9, 13
Roosevelt, Eleanor 123
Rosenberg, Marshall 146, 172, 278, 279
Sagan, Carl 57
Scharff, David and Jill Savage 275
Schleifer, Hedy 120, 278, 279
Shore, Allan 276
Schwartz, Barry 16, 20, 114, 211, 275, 278, 280
Shaw, George Bernard 153

NOTES and REFERENCES

INTRODUCTION

[1] Carl Jung's essay on Marriage as a Psychological Relationship appears in the *Collected Works of C.G. Jung, Volume 17: Development of Personality* (1954) Princeton University Press, (1992) London: Routledge.

CHAPTER 1

[2] Fisher, Helen (2004) Why *We Love: The Nature and Chemistry of Romantic Love*. New York: Henry Holt and Co.

[3] Tennov, Dorothy (1979, 1999) *Love and Limerence: The Experience of Being in Love*. Lanham, Maryland: Scarborough House.

[4] Johnson, Robert (1987) Ecstasy: *Understanding the Psychology of Joy*. San Francisco: Harper and Row.

[5] Haule, John (1990) *Divine Madness: Archetypes of Romantic Love*. Boston: Shambhala.

[6] Hollis, James (1998) *The Eden Project: In Search of the Magical Other*. Toronto: Inner City Books.

[7] Crowe, Cameron (1996) *Jerry McGuire*. Gracie Films.

[8] Young-Eisendrath, Polly (2019) *Love Between Equals: Relationship as a Spiritual Path*. Boulder: Shambhala.

[9] Perel, Esther (2017) *The State of Affairs: Rethinking Infidelity*. New York: HarperCollins; (2013) TED Salon. https://www.ted.com/talks/esther_perel_the_secret_to_desire_in_a_long_term_relationship?language=en

[10] Michaels, Mark & Johnson, Patricia (2015) *Designer Relationships: A Guide to Happy Monogamy, Positive Polyamory, and Optimistic Open Relationships*. New York: Cleis Press.

[11] Schwartz, Barry (2005) *The Paradox of Choice: Why More is Less*. New York: Harper-Collins.

[12] Hollis, James (1993) *The Midlife Passage: From Misery to Meaning in Midlife*. Toronto: Inner City Books.

[13] Lee, S. W.S. & Schwarz, Norbert (2014) Framing Love: When It Hurts to Think We Were Made For Each Other. *Journal of Experimental Social Psychology*, 54, pp. 61-67.

CHAPTER 2

[14] David Scharff and Jill Savege Scharff (2011) *The Interpersonal Unconscious* Lanham, Maryland: Jason Aronson. The Scharffs write about this interpersonal "field," referencing the work of psychoanalysts Antonino Ferro and Madeline and Willy Barringer who wrote extensively about the "bi-personal field" that develops between two people engaged in deep work. While the Scharff's writing focusses primarily on the unconscious realm

between analyst and analysand, it also applies to any intimate relationship where unconscious worlds begin to intersect, which happens in every intimate relationship.

[15] Dream Lover is a term adopted from Polly Young-Eisendrath in her work *You're Not What I Expected* (1993) New York: Morrow and Co.

[16] Stone, H. & Stone, S. (2000) *Partnering: A New Kind of Relationship*. Novato, CA: New World Library; Young-Eisendrath, Polly (1983) Hags and Heroes: Jungian Psychotherapy with Couples. Toronto: Inner City Books.

[17] Gottman, John (1999) *The Seven Principles for Making Marriage Work*. New York: Three Rivers Press.

[18] Hollis, James (2015) *Hauntings: Dispelling the Ghosts Who Run Our Lives*. Asheville, NC: Chiron Publications.

[19] Bader, Ellyn & Pearson, Peter, Schwartz, Judith (2000) *Tell Me No Lies: How to Stop Lying to Your Partner and Yourself in the 4 Stages of Marriage*. New York: St. Martins Griffin.

CHAPTER 3

[20] Shore, Allan (2016) *Affect Regulation and Origin of the Self: The Neurobiology of Emotional Development*. New York: Routledge; Siegel, Daniel (2012) *Pocket Guide to Interpersonal Neurobiology: An Integrative Handbook of the Mind*. New York: Norton & Co.

[21] Gibran, Kahlil (1923) *The Prophet*. New York: Alfred Knopf.

[22] See Volumes 1, 2, and 3 of John Bowlby's original *Attachment series, the first of which was Attachment and Loss*. Attachment and Loss was republished as a 2nd edition in 1999 by New York: Basic Books; also see Bowlby, J. (1988) *A Secure Base: Parent-Child Attachment and Healthy Human Development*. London: Routledge.

[23] Cozolino, Louis (2014) *The Neuroscience of Human Relationship: Attachment and the Developing Social Brain*. New York: Norton & Co.; Siegel, Daniel (2012) *Pocket Guide to Interpersonal Neurobiology: An Integrative Handbook of the Mind*. New York: Norton & Co; (2011) *Mindsight: The New Science of Personal Transformation*. New York: Bantam Books.

[24] Shaver, P. & Hazan, C. (1987) Romantic Love Conceptualized as an Attachment Process. *Journal of Personality and Social Psychology, Vol. 52, No.3*, pp. 511-524.

[25] Siegel, Daniel (2012) *Pocket Guide to Interpersonal Neurobiology: An Integrate Handbook of the Mind*. New York: Norton & Co.

[26] Solomon, Marion & Tatkin, Stan (2011) *Love and War in Intimate Relationship: Connection, Disconnection and Mutual Regulation in Couple Therapy*. New York: Norton & Co.

[27] PLOS Biology (Vol. 3, No. 3, pp. 529-535), https://journals.plos.org/plosbiology/article?id=10.1371/journal.pbio.0030079, accessed 5/3/2020.

[28] Hanson, Rick with Hanson, Forrest (2018) *Resilient: How to Grow an Unshakable Core of Calm, Strength, and Happiness*. New York: Harmony Books; Hanson, Rick (2013) Hardwiring Happiness: The New Brain Science of Contentment, Calm, and Confidence. New York: Harmony Books.

[29] Ecker, B., Ticic, R., Hulley, L. (2012) *Unlocking the Emotional Brain: Eliminating Symptoms at Their Roots Using Memory Reconsolidation*. New York: Routledge.

[30] Tatkin, Stan (2011) *Wired for Love: How Understanding Your Partner's Brian and Attachment Style Can Help You Defuse Conflict and Build a Secure Relationship*. Oakland, CA: New Harbinger.

[31] Hanson, R. (2013) *Hardwiring Happiness: The New Brain Science of Contentment, Calm and Confidence*. New York: Harmony Books.

CHAPTER 4

[32] Van der Kolk, Bessel (2014) *The Body Keeps the Score: Brain, Mind, and Body in the Healing of Trauma*. New York: Penguin.

[33] Deikman, Arthur (1982) *The Observing Self: Mysticism and Psychotherapy*. Boston, MA: Beacon Press.

[34] Wakefield, Chelsea (2012) *Negotiating the Inner Peace Treaty: Becoming the Person You Were Born to Be*. Bloomington, IN: Balboa Press.

[35] Schema therapy holds that we have 18 underlying maladaptive schemas (which can be thought of as "complexes") these correspond with "modes" that we use to manage and cope with them (which can be understood as "inner characters"). For a basic introduction to the world of schemas, I refer you to *Reinventing Your Life* by Young, J. and Klosko, J. (1993). New York: Penguin Putnam. There are many other books published about Schema Therapy that have a more clinical perspective.

[36] Atkinson, Travis (2020) Schema Therapy for Couples: Interventions to Promote Secure Connections. In *Creative Methods in Schema Therapy; Advances and Innovation in Clinical Practice*. (Gillian Heath and Helen Startup editors) New York: Routledge.

CHAPTER 5

[37] Young-Eisendrath, Polly (1993) *You're Not What I Expected*. New York: William Morrow & Co. For a more clinical read see her 1983 book *Hags and Heroes: Jungian Psychotherapy with Couples*. Toronto: Inner City Books.

CHAPTER 6

[38] Gottman, John (1999) *The Seven Principles for Making Marriage Work*. New York: Three Rivers Press.

[39] Johnson, Sue (2008) *Hold Me Tight: Seven Conversations for a Lifetime of Love*. New York: Little, Brown and Co.

[40] Hollis, James (2015) *Hauntings: Dispelling the Ghosts Who Run Our Lives*. Asheville, NC: Chiron Publications.

[41] Karpman, Stephen (1968) Fairy tales and script drama analysis. *Transactional Analysis Bulletin*. 26 (7): pp. 39–43.

[42] Bader, Ellyn & Pearson, Peter - handout from *The Couples Institute*. Menlo Park, CA.

[43] Gottman, Julie S. & Gottman, John (2015) *Ten Principles for Doing Effective Couples Therapy*. New York: Norton.

CHAPTER 7

[44] In the Chartres labyrinth, this six-petalled center stands for the sacred rose, a symbol of the Virgin Mary and the blending of human and divine love. The rose in Christianity also parallels the lotus in Eastern spirituality, as a symbol of enlightenment.

[45] Carl Jung believed strongly that quaternities were representations of wholeness. Gina Ogden, designed a four-quadrant model to explore sexuality—heart, mind, body, and spirit. For more information on her 4-D (Dimensions) approach to sex therapy, see www.4-DNetwork.com.

CHAPTER 8

[46] Coontz, S. (1992) *The Way We Never Were: American Families and the Nostalgia Trap.* New York: Basic Books.

[47] I have worked with a number of couples who were in arranged or parent orchestrated marriages, the majority of them being from India and Pakistan.

[48] https://www.nytimes.com/2015/06/27/us/supreme-court-same-sex-marriage.html accessed on 4/4/2020.

[49] Schwartz, Barry (2004, 2016) *The Paradox of Choice: Why More Is Less.* New York: HarperCollins; https://www.ted.com/talks/barry_schwartz_the_paradox_of_choice?language=en.

[50] Young-Eisendrath, Polly (2020) *Love Between Equals.* Boulder, CO: Shambhala; & (1993) *You're Not What I Expected.* New York: William Morrow.

[51] Buber, Martin, translation by Walter Kaufmann (1970) *I and Thou.* New York: Charles Scribner's Sons.

[52] Schleifer, Hedy, in her TED Talk she uses the metaphor of "crossing the bridge." https://www.youtube.com/watch?v=q4H2NpBq7Es.

CHAPTER 9

[53] Gibran, Kahlil (1923) *The Prophet.* New York: Alfred Knopf.

[54] Stone, H. & Stone, S. (2000) *Partnering: A New Kind of Relationship.* Novato, CA: New World Library.

[55] Bader, E. & Pearson, P. & Schwartz, J. (2000) *Tell Me No Lies: How to Stop Lying to Your Partner and Yourself in the 4 Stages of Marriage.* New York: St. Martins Griffin.

[56] Brown, Brené (2012) *Daring Greatly: How the courage to be vulnerable transforms the way we live, love, parent, and lead.* New York: Avery Publishing.

CHAPTER 10

[57] Johnson, Sue (2008) *Hold Me Tight: Seven Conversations for a Lifetime of Love.* New York: Little Brown.

[58] Stone, D., Patton, B., & Heen, S. (1999) *Difficult Conversations: How to Discuss What Matters Most.* New York: Penguin Random House.

[59] Wakefield, Chelsea (2012) *Negotiating the Inner Peace Treaty: Becoming the Person You Were Born to Be.* Bloomington, IN: Balboa Press.

[60] Van der Kolk, Bessel (2015) *The Body Keeps the Score: Brain, Mind, and Body in the Healing of Trauma.* New York: Penguin Books.

[61] McClure Goulding, Mary & Goulding, Bob (1997) *Changing Lives Through Redecision Therapy.* New York: Grove Press.

[62] Ecker, B., Ticic, R., Hulley, L. (2012) *Unlocking the Emotional Brain: Eliminating Symptoms at Their Roots Using Memory Reconsolidation.* New York: Routledge.

[63] Rosenberg, Marshal (2015) *Nonviolent Communication: A Language of Life.* Encinitis, CA: PuddleDancer Press.

[64] Hanson, Rick. (2013) *Hardwiring Happiness: The New Science of Contentment, Calm and Confidence.* New York: Harmony.

[65] Hanson, Rick with Hanson, Forest (2018) *Resilient: How to Grow an Unshakeable Core of Calm, Strength, and Happiness.* New York: Harmony.

CHAPTER 11

[66] The idea of separating intention from impact is emphasized in the 1999 book *Difficult Conversations* by Stone, D., Patton, B. and Heen, S. New York: Penguin Books.

[67] See Hedy Schleifer's TED Talk. https://www.youtube.com/watch?v=HEaERAnIqsY.

[68] Young-Eisendrath, Polly (2019) *Love Between Equals*. Boulder, CO: Shambhala.

[69] Rosenberg, Marshal (2015) *Nonviolent Communication: A Language of Life*. Encinitis, CA: PuddleDancer Press.

[70] Needs and feelings inventories https://www.cnvc.org/sites/default/files/2018-10/CNVC-feelings-inventory.pdf https://www.cnvc.org/sites/default/files/2018-10/CNVC-needs-inventory.pdf.

[71] Bader, Ellyn, Pearson, Peter, w/Schwartz, Judith. (2000) *Tell Me No Lies*. New York: St. Martin's Press.

[72] Chapmen, G. (1992, 2015) *The Five Love Languages*. Chicago: Northfield Publishing.

CHAPTER 12

[73] Hedy Schleifer – Crossing the Bridge, TED Talk. https://www.youtube.com/watch?v=HEaERAnIqsY.

[74] Neff, K. & Germer, C. (2018) *The Mindful Self-Compassion Workbook: A Proven Way to Accept Yourself, Build Inner Strength, and Thrive*. New York: Guilford Press.

[75] Germer, C. (2009) *The Mindful Path to Self-Compassion: Freeing Yourself from Destructive Thoughts and Emotions*. New York: Guilford Press.

[76] Melody, Pia (1989, 2003) *Facing Co-Dependence*. New York: Harper Collins.

[77] Neff, Kristin and Beretvas, S. Natasha (2013) *The Role of Self-compassion in Romantic Relationships,* Journal of Self and Identity, 12:78-98.

[78] Neff, K. & Germer, C. (2018) *The Mindful Self-Compassion Workbook: A Proven Way to Accept Yourself, Build Inner Strength, and Thrive*. New York: Guilford Press.

[79] Brown, Brené (2012) *Daring Greatly: How the Courage to be Vulnerable Transforms the Way We Live, Love, and Parent*. New York: Avery/Penguin Random House.

[80] Brown, Brené – ibid.

[81] Gottman, John w/Silver, Nan (1999) *The Seven Principles for Making Marriage Work*. New York: Three Rivers Press.

[82] Solomon, Marion & Tatkin, Stan (2011) *Love and War in Intimate Relationships*. New York: Norton.

[83] Lerner, Harriet (2017) *Why Won't You Apologize? Healing Big Betrayals and Everyday Hurts*. New York: Gallery Books.

[84] 2002 American film based on the 1996 Rebecca Wells book of same name.

CHAPTER 13

[85] Hollis, James (1998) *The Eden Project: In Search of the Magical Other*. Toronto: Inner City Books.

[86] Atkinson, Travis (2020) Schema Therapy for Couples: Interventions to Promote Secure Connections. In *Creative Methods in Schema Therapy; Advances and Innovation in Clinical Practice*. (Gillian Heath and Helen Startup editors) New York: Routledge.

CHAPTER 14

[87] McCarthy, Barry (2015) *Sex Made Simple: Clinical Strategies for Sexual Issues in Therapy.* Eau Claire, WI: PESI.

[88] Kleinplatz, Peggy, et al (2009) The Components of optimal sexuality: A portrait of "great sex." In *The Canadian Journal of Human Sexuality,* Vol. 18 (1-2).

[89] Wakefield, Chelsea (2016) *In Search of Aphrodite: Women, Archetypes and Sex Therapy.* New York: Routledge.

[90] Please note that I am not on a rampage against all pornography – there are feminist porn producers who have created some very interesting productions. My concern is that the industry itself continues to be filled with exploitation; how early viewing of pornography has shaped the sexual arousal patterns of young men in ways that makes relational sexuality far more difficult; and how viewing it can become increasingly compulsive and has spawned an entire treatment industry for "porn/sexual addiction."

[91] Chapman, Gary (2015) *The Five Love Languages: The Secret to Love That Lasts.* Chicago: Northfield Pub.

[92] Neff, Kristin (2013) The Role of Self-compassion in Romantic Relationships. *Self & Identity,* 12: pp. 78-98; Germer, Christopher & Neff, Kristin (2019) *Teaching the Mindful Self-Compassion Program.* New York: Guilford Press.

[93] This is a reference to the soulful encounters spoken of by Martin Buber in *I and Thou* - English translation by Walter Kaufmann (1970) New York: Scribner & Sons.

[94] Morin, Jack (1995) *The Erotic Mind.* New York: Harper Collins.

[95] Delaney, Gayle (1994) *Sexual Dreams: Why We Have Them and What They Mean.* New York: Ballentine Books.

[96] Singer Kaplan, Helen (1983) The Evaluation of Sexual Disorders Levittown, PA: Bruner/Mazel.

[97] Basson, Rosemary (2002) Rethinking Low Sexual Desire in Women. *BJOG: International Journal of Obstetrics and Gynecology.* Vol. 109, pp. 357-363; (2019) Are Healthy Parental Attachments and Resilience to Societal Objectification Basic to Women's Sexual Health? *Archives of Sexual Behavior* 48: 1683-1687.

[98] Gibran, Kahlil (1923) *The Prophet.* New York: Alfred Knopf.

[99] Masters, William & Johnson, Virginia (1970) *Human Sexual Inadequacy.* Bronx, NY: Ishi Press.

[100] Brotto, Lori, et al. (2016) Mindfulness-Based Sex Therapy Improves Genital-Subjective Arousal Concordance in Women with Sexual Desire/Arousal Difficulties. *Arch. of Sexual Behavior* 45: 1907-1921.

[101] Ogden, Gina (2006) *The Heart and Soul of Sex.* Boston: Trumpeter; (2008) *The Return of Desire.* Boston: Trumpeter.

CHAPTER 15

[102] Look for Dr. Lin Jovanovic's upcoming programs on Financial Infidelity.

[103] 1983 film starring Barbra Streisand.

CHAPTER 16

[104] Naiman, Rubin (2014) *Hush: A Book of Bedtime Contemplations.* Tucson, AZ: New Moon Studio. https://www.youtube.com/watch?v=moUhiZryC7A.

[105] Stone, Hal and Sidra (2000) *Partnering: A New Kind of Relationship.* Novato, CA: Nataraj Publishing.

[106] Koch-Sheras, Phyllis & Sheras, Peter Sheras (1999) *The Dream Sharing Sourcebook.* Los Angeles: Lowell House.

CHAPTER 17

[107] Hanson, R. & Hanson, F. (2018) *Resilient: How to Grow an Unshakeable Core of Calm, Strength, and Happiness.* New York: Harmony Books.

CPSIA information can be obtained
at www.ICGtesting.com
Printed in the USA
LVHW031051021221
704908LV00004B/167/J